PARTICIPANT OBSERVATION

Participant Observation

Theory and practice

JÜRGEN FRIEDRICHS
HARMUT LÜDTKE

SAXON HOUSE | LEXINGTON BOOKS

Published by

SAXON HOUSE, D. C. Heath Ltd.
Westmead, Farnborough, Hants., England.

Jointly with

LEXINGTON BOOKS, D. C. Heath & Co.
Lexington, Mass., U.S.A.

ISBN 0 347 01049 0

Library of Congress Catalog Card Number 74-26355

Printed in England by Eyre & Spottiswoode Limited at Grosvenor Press, Portsmouth

Contents

APPENDICES

List of tables

List of figures

Preface

The textbooks concerning the methodology of social science are so numerous that one loses all perspective. It is not the purpose of this book to simply expand the set of more or less exact, more or less encyclopaedic-like complete works. It restricts itself to the presentation of a specific empirical method: participant observation. This restriction allows for a more extensive and refined study of the method. Besides its theoretical foundation, practical problems and the possibilities of its application are also analysed by referring to exemplary material, especially that of a recent field study.

Apart from the theoretical analysis of its classical, descriptive and exploratory application, there is no systematic and practically tested methodology for participant observation comparable to those of other sociological research methods. Participant observation will probably gain importance in the near future similar to that of other methods, e.g. interviewing. Therefore, the laying of its methodological foundation must be seen as a necessary attempt at developing social research in a direction combining strict empirical criteria together with broader dimensions of reality. This coincides with the aim of this book: the controlled, i.e. standardised participant observation of various objects in a field by several observers on the basis of a uniform observation schedule. Only this specific form of participant observation allows for the comparison of observed objects – that upon which the testing of empirical relationships in the field is based.

It is typical of a great number of standard works dealing with empirical social research that they present on the one hand single techniques of inquiry and procedures of data control as distinct one from the other, and on the other hand restrict themselves to formal, meta-empirical models of data from which the general standards of inquiry, data transformation and control are derived. In spite of, or because of, the high theoretical and methodological niveau of these works, many of them have one crucial shortcoming: the feedback between the methodological standards and the problematic reality of practical field research.

It is without doubt a result of the extreme but necessary division of labour and the lack of cooperation between methodologists and researchers. The consequences of these shortcomings for the practical availability of methodology are obvious: a widespread amateurism, ad hoc designs of instruments without the knowledge of already existing experiences; e.g. those usually published in methodological discussions in empirical studies, or in special articles in special methodology oriented periodicals which are not easy to get hold of. This in turn makes a comparison of single studies more difficult. It may also result in resignation or even attitudinal barriers erected against empirical strictness.

Only in what were lucky exceptions could an integration of pure method and practical research be reached. Such studies give rise to the claim that well-understood methodology[1] should learn from and be refined by the problems, mistakes and further developments of empirical studies.

This is what transpires in a later evaluation of the methods and instruments which were used in a study: i.e. one doesn't ask about the substantial results of a study alone, but also about its possible contribution to the improvement of the available methodology. One example of this procedure which proved important sociologically is the study by Stouffer et al.: *The American Soldier*, 1949, where, as a result of the empirical findings, a special volume was published about applied and, to an extent, newly developed methods.[2] Another classical social science study that initiated a very fruitful method-criticism and various follow-up studies[3] is the work done by Adorno et al.: *The Authoritarian Personality*.

With the presentation of this book, we have tried to make a contribution to producing a cumulative, research-oriented methodology. A new theoretical reception of the method of participant observation and of the standards of its research strategy is the starting point. It has been expanded by the above mentioned application possibilities and the critical comparison with the interview method (Part I).

Following Part I is the presentation of the data collection procedure used in a large empirical research project, in which for the first time, in 1966, a great number of research objects (73 Houses of Juvenile Leisure Activities, briefly: youth centres) were observed with the schedule simultaneously. In Part II the manner of application is demonstrated and at the same time structural antecedents, interference factors and other restrictions existing in the practical field are analysed. On the basis of these sources of error and selected material of study, and reflecting on the theoretical part, an attempt is made to present the optimal application and analysis methods of the instrument and its chances of working successfully.

The third part of the book deals with the problems of the research personnel. With the exception of questions dealing with interviewer training, this problem has been grossly neglected in most of the handbooks. In Part III, organisational and didactical questions concerning instruction and operation of observers are discussed. This aspect must be understood as being an integral component of the method itself; characteristic of this is the separation of observer and researcher, i.e. standardisation implies uniform observer behaviour.

In addition to a rich bibliography, the appendix contains a classification of different observation objects and situations for which specific standards and strategies of inquiry are suggested.

Finally, the examples of observation schedules of recent studies which are presented in the appendix, are to demonstrate even better the practical applicability of the method.

The authors feel bound to the basic principle that theory and empiricism are not opposites; that they should not represent two rational positions on which to base a scientific division of labour; and that empirical research is only acceptable when seen as a function of theory. It is the intention of this book to try to comply with this claim. It should serve basically as a textbook for students as well as a manual for social researchers, as it is not only based on theoretical work but also informs about 'research done on research' and offers practical assistance. It is also meant for sociologists, experimentally and research oriented education experts, and social workers who consider the empirical analysis of their professional fields as the basis of their educational praxis.

Those who are interested in micro-social processes in small groups under relatively easy manipulative, experimental and organisational conditions, may feel that an important area of observation method was neglected in this book: that of observing limited systems at relatively short time intervals and with the possibility of highly refined measurement and data analysis, at which the observer is only marginally participating in or standing outside the field.

This aspect would have obviously gone beyond the realm of the theme. Besides, work done in this area is the most advanced today. The complexity of social fields which are not subject to any experimental or quasi-experimental conditions (conditions which could perhaps hold true for the limited unit of a classroom group), and the need for appropriate methods for their observation have thus far felt the lack of an approved conception of field observation much more.

This book is based on the joint studies and discussions of both authors over a period of several years. For this reason a great number of mutual inspirations, criticisms and expansions have merged in their contributions. Friedrichs was mainly responsible for the first and Lüdtke for the second part of the book. The third part and the appendix were written by both. The translation is based on the German second, revised and enlarged, edition published in 1973.

We are indebted to the *Pädagogisches Zentrum in Berlin* and its former director, Professor C. L. Furck, who made the origin and publication of this book possible. We are grateful to Miss Nancy Derr and Mrs. Alice Gallasch who translated the book.

Jürgen Friedrichs, Harmut Lüdtke
Hamburg, Autumn 1974

Notes

1   Here we are not referring to the other, complementary level of philosophy of science – e.g. K. R. Popper, H. Albert – but the methodology of strategy and technique in social research, its theoretical assumptions and its practical application. Examples of general forms of these operational methods can be found among the works of Zetterberg (1954, 1967), Lazarsfeld and Rosenberg (1955), Cicourel (1964).

2   Samuel A. Stouffer et al., 1950.

3   An imminent critique of method which brought consequences for the validity and theoretical interpretation of results can be found among the works of Hyman and Sheatsley (1954) and Hyman (1955). Included in the second group of works is the study done by Roghmann (1966).

PART I

Theory and Methodology
of Participation Observation

1 Observation as a Method in Social Research

The methods of social research have evolved from a refining and systemising of the daily processes used to collect information from reality. The interview in its developed form, represents a standardised conversation between two persons, and the group discussion represents a conversation among several persons. In the same way, content analysis is based on a systematic reading and analysis of texts; the laboratory experiment contains planned and controlled sequences in specially produced situations; finally, participant observation registers perceptible actions in 'natural' situations on the basis of a preset scheme.

All of these methods have the following purpose in common: (a) to gather data, and (b) to do this in the easiest verifiable way, i.e. findings must be abstractable from author's subjective cognition. The criteria of scientific knowledge are the methods used to collect information whereas it is inter-subjectivity which is the criterion of a scientific method.

Contrary to other methods of social research, e.g. the interview and the experiment, observation does not fulfil to the same extent the demand for a strict method because the distortion of perception by the observing subject can only be reduced to an insufficient degree. Today, however, it seems possible to systemise the method of participant observation even more, and in this way, advance towards a strict research instrument.

Some time ago den Hollander (1965) called attention to 'social description as a problem' and he stressed the fact that not even the most objectively meant description of social events is free of selective prejudices or assumptions about the field. Bruyn (1963, 1966) went even further and tried to found the method of participant observation upon a theory of phenomenological knowledge alone. In view of the many problems of observation pointed out by both authors, it will be necessary to stress the quantification possibilities of the method. Here we cannot go out from *verstehen*, intuition or intro-spection as being the decisive constituents of observation, as did den Hollander (1965, p. 22 f) and, also, to an extent Denzin (1970). We have to start with a stronger separation between observer, observed and researcher, all of whose mutual relationships must be accessible for a systematic examination. It cannot be the duty of observation, through its statements, to present a part of reality (e.g. a school class) in such a way as to give the reader the feeling of reliving the situation, as den Hollander (1965, p. 223) assumes.

3

Instead observation should make statements which, levelled at a context of social science theory, prove true accordingly. While den Hollander and largely even Bruyn (1966) suggest intuitive, self-critical description as a way out of the numerous problems of observation, we will try to examine the scientific distance between the observer and the object as a way to improve technique. To do this, a theory of analytical-empirical knowledge will be used as a basis.[1]

If one shares Cicourel's (1964, p. 67) demand for a better participant observation theory, the main question will be how this technique can be methodologically refined, to give it the dignity of a social scientific procedure. Interviewing will be used in the following as a standard, because a higher degree of reliability and validity can be reached with it. (However, the experiment will remain the model of scientific exactness, in which the variables are strictly isolated and manipulated, and where the hypothesis is transferred into exact operational conditions.)

The minimal condition must be that participant observation satisfies the demands of inter and intrasubjectivity. In addition to this, the demand for an error theory for participant observation must also be satisfied (Atteslander, 1969, König, 1967).

The first question is what should be considered reality within the observation. This leads to considerable philosophical discussions which cannot be carried far enough here. For this reason a number of assumptions which make up the consistence of analytical thinking shall be formulated in summary form: reality is only reflected in language and in the image created by theories (assumption of isomorphy).

> The categories and types being abstracted from the world of phenomena cannot simply be found by us in itself, e.g. because of their catching each observer's eye. Contrary to this, the world presents itself in a kaleidoscopelike stream of impressions which must be organised by our minds, i.e. largely by the linguistic system in our minds. The way in which we divide nature, organise it by terms or ascribe meaning to it, is to a great extent determined by our taking part in an agreement to organise the world in such a manner. This agreement holds true throughout our community of language, and it is organised by the patterns of our language. (Whorf, 1963, p. 12).

It is through observation, during which a linguistic agreement is entered into, that those facts to be called reality in the scientific sense are first produced. Den Hollander stresses this also (1965, p. 206). The aim of observation is to describe a behaviour sequence in such a way that a maximum of convergence of reiterated observations of one observer as well as an agreement between different observers observing the same sequence is reached. The convergence of their information can be called reality; or better said, reality can be found in the categories of the researchers' language.

1.1 Types of observation

According to Scheuch (1958, p. 210) observation is

the recording of facts, perceptible to the senses and on the basis of a set plan in which the researcher maintains a receptive position in confrontation with the research object. This receptive position distinguishes observation from the interview and the experiment, in that one dispenses with evoking the desired reactions by verbal as well as other stimuli.

The types of observation can be described in a simplified form in the following way:

	Participant	Non-participant
Controlled, standardised	1	2
Uncontrolled, unstandardised	3	4

When arranged according to exactness the following order results: 2 > 1 > 3 > 4.

The *first* type corresponds with a study in which the observer takes part in the action sequence of the observed actors. The observer adopts a role within the sequence in which his activities are carried out in principle on the same level as those of the others (König, 1956, p. 36). That means that the observer has a good chance of taking part in the typical actions and groupings in his field, be it as an average group member or as an outsider who has made his role convincing to the other members (see 3.2). The observation itself is regulated by a predetermined observation schedule which defines what is to be observed. For this type of observation a dimensional analysis and a theoretical model of the object are prerequisites. That means there must be definitions of the observation units and hypotheses which will then be proved by the observation (Mayntz, Holm & Hübner, 1969, pp. 89, 100).

The *second* type corresponds generally with the experiment. There is also an observation schedule but the observer is not involved directly in the action sequence. He is to be found, e.g. behind a one-way window. This could also be the case in the observation of history, mentioned by König (1967, p. 124, f): the study of historical sources and statistics, etc. Contrary to König, however, the definition of observation should remain restricted to the simultaneousness of an event and the recording of it in order not to over-extend the terminology.

The *third* type corresponds to the observations done in cultural anthropology. Here the field was too big and often too unexplored to lay down a systematical plan of observation. On the other hand, however, the observer did take part in the lives of the groups to be studied as was the case in classical anthropological studies such as those by M. Mead, F. Kluckhohn, R. Firth, G. Bateson, O. Lewis.

The *fourth* type can be classified more or less as accidental daily observations: a passer-by observes a happening on the street; a journalist is travelling through a foreign country he wants to report about.

The following deals with observation type one alone, that is, with participant, structured and standardised observation. Because of the lack of standardisation of this method, which would have corresponded to a development of type three to one, participant observation has retained, to a great extent, the character of an exploratory technique, leading to the discovery of hypotheses and to the first description of the research object. This can be gathered from the relatively small amount of literature dealing with the methodology in participant observation. The consequence of this, of course, is a restricted use of the method in sociology. According to Scheuch (1967, p. 138) methodological contributions to the research interview begin to appear regularly in the 1920s. For participant observation, the beginning of such contributions might be placed at more than twenty years later.

Considering all the disadvantages which have been attributed to participant observation up till now, some of its advantages are:

1   It avoids the discrepancy between real and verbal behaviour. Interviews especially suffer this disadvantage. Often statements are made in interviews which are not in accordance with the factual behaviour of the interviewed persons (La Piere, 1934; Kutner, Wilkins & Yarrow, 1952; Linn, 1965).

2   It allows observation in situations when questions only meet with misunderstanding or try to evoke attitudes which are first created in the interview situation; often such facts (e.g. information about child rearing) are brought to light by means of natural settings only. The interviewee is not conscious of them and they are therefore not easy to get at by questioning (see Heyns & Lippitt, 1954, p. 371).

3   It allows the identification of processes which could otherwise only be brought out by an inconvenient chain of repeated interviews or content analyses (see Katz, 1953, p. 81; Denzin, 1970, p. 186, f).

4   The observation of behaviour does not depend on the verbal capabilities of the interviewed person. Just such class-related capabilities reduce the range of interviews, group discussions and possibly the content analysis.

6

1.2 Participant observation in cultural anthropology and sociology

Up to now, participant observation has been used as a method of social research mainly in the field of cultural anthropology. One may be able to trace it back to the fact that an exact study of a culture is only possible by taking part in this culture's daily life. In other words, the researcher was not able to inform himself through documents, but had to go into the field. Another reason may be that at least at the beginning of his participation in the field, communication via language was not possible. For the time being, the researcher was dependent on observation for his information.

The problems involved in the method of participant observation can be most clearly seen when studied within the fields of cultural or social anthropology because they are much more pronounced than in sociology. A constituent property of anthropological observation is the cultural distance between the observer and the foreign culture. Its negative sides include language difficulties and endless material. Its positive quality is the discovery of social routines; at the beginning the researcher must pay equal attention to everything.[2] While the ethnologist must reduce this cultural distance to understand, the sociologist has yet to create it (Strecker, 1969, p. 6). Further, the observation object of the cultural anthropologist is usually much more complex (one whole culture) than that of the sociologist who observes only a small part of a culture (as in the study of the youth clubs). A good example of cultural anthropology-related problems in field research is the study edited by Whiting (1963).

The fact that observation in cultural anthropology has hardly ever been conducted on the basis of an exact research plan is likely to be a consequence of the complexity of the object to be observed. Cicourel (1964, p. 53) writes: 'Anthropological field reports reveal very little of the initial experiences of the research or of the procedures used for deciding the meaning of a given event.' Becker (1958, p. 660) also criticises the unsatisfactory methodological reflection. In studies with participant observation, he demands that they should give the reader the opportunity to check the conclusions of the author on the basis of the material given. This can only be possible when the author presents the 'natural history' of his data collection as well as a redefinition of his concepts in the course of his investigation (see Jensen, 1937; Nadel, 1951, p. 149). 'The findings are presented as if the problems of access, maintaining contact, terminating contact, did not influence the finding and interpretation of data. The report, as Vidich notes, has a timeless quality' (Cicourel, 1964, p. 70).[3] Naroll (1962, especially p. 84) demonstrated just how great the changes are during observations in anthropological studies and what a big influence variables like length of stay or knowledge of the language of a foreign culture can have. An excellent example of such a 'natural history' of the participant observation is Whyte's (1961) appendix 'On the Evolution of Street Corner Society'.

Denzin (1970, p. 194, ff) demonstrates a procedure in participant observation that even allows a researcher who did not base his work on a previously explicated theoretical model, to introduce his material in causal explanations – in other words to generalise. At the same time, this procedure makes the analytical steps transparent for the reader. 'Analytical Induction' as the procedure is called, is based on the principle that when testing theory, examples are to be so chosen, that the chance of discovering a negative (falsifying) example is maximised. Generally several steps follow consecutively:

1   A rough definition of the phenomenon to be explained is formulated.
2   A hypothetical explanation of the phenomenon is formulated.
3   A case is examined in light of the hypothesis, with the object which decides if in this case the hypothesis coincides with the fact or not.
4   If the hypothesis does not coincide, either the hypothesis is reformulated or the phenomenon is redefined, so that the case is excluded.
5   After checking a small number of cases, a practical assurance can be reached, but the discovery of negative cases refutes the explanation and makes a reformulation necessary.
6   The procedure of checking cases, redefining the phenomenon and reformulation of the hypothesis is continued until a general relation is found, in the course of which every negative case brings about respective revisions.

An increasing tendency towards quantifying has also been ascertained among the cultural anthropologists by Lewis (1953, p. 454, ff). Recently, in Germany, Strecker (1969) has made a far-reaching contribution in the field of cultural anthropology, in the method of participant observation. It deals primarily with the role of the field researcher (see also section 3.2). In comparison with cultural anthropology, social research has seldom used the method of participant observation. The first observations made, reach back into the nineteenth century when LePlay (1855) studied European workers and Riehl (1851) travelled through Germany. The first studies, as such, originate from the Chicago School of North American sociology: from Anderson (1923), who made a study of hobos, and Cressey (1932) who arranged for the observation of interaction in a dance hall in which girls could be rented as 'dance ladies', analogous to rentable cars and thus called a Taxi Dance Hall. The expression 'participant observation' was coined by a sociologist from this school: Lindemann (1924, p. 183) differentiated between an 'objective observer', who approaches a culture from outside using interviewing as an instrument, and a 'participant observer', who researches a culture from within, using observation. Later, the Lynds and their co-workers (1929, 1937) made two elaborate studies of the North American small town 'Middletown' using interviews and participant observation.

The classical study using this method was done by Whyte (1961) and originates from the 1930s. Whyte spent more than three years (1937–40) living in a part of Boston he called 'Cornerville'. He analysed the relationships between two groups of Italian immigrants, the 'North Street Gang' and the 'Italian Community Club'. Because of the exact description of his problems, ranging from the role he assumed to the final recording of his findings, his work has been closely connected with the further development of the method up till today: his method was refined to a degree in a later study (Whyte, 1948).

In later works the method was used on limited research objects such as: industrial organisations (Roy, 1952, Roethlisberger & Dickson, 1956, Dalton, 1959, 1964); music bands (Becker, 1958), a mine (Jantke *et al.*, 1953), youth centres (Kluth, Lohmar and Pongratz, 1955); youth and tourist groups (Lessing, 1967, Kentler *et al.*, 1969); a restaurant (Whyte, 1948), as well as on relatively complex objects such as communities (Chapple & Arensberg, 1940, Warner & Lunt, 1941, Arensberg, 1954, Kluckhohn, 1956, Wurzbacher, Pflaum *et al.*, 1954). Recently, the method of participant observation has frequently been used in studies of areas such as deviant behaviour, as collected in the works of Douglas (1970) and Friedrichs (1973a).

In England during the Second World War, an attempt was made at gaining systematic observation data about the moods and reactions of the population using the institution 'Mass Observation' by single persons in factories and offices (Madge & Harrison, 1938; Mass Observation, 1940, 1943; Pearse & Crocker, 1943; Willcock, 1943; Ferraby, 1945; Turner and Mass Observation 1947). These experiences, however, were not continued after the war, one of the causes being the insufficient possibility of standardisation of such extensive observation.

A great number of studies on non-participant observation gave support to Bales' (1948, 1954) categorised scheme for observing discussions in small groups, a technique which can be used as an instrument in participant observation under certain circumstances (see section 4.3.3).

In order to give the reader a complete summary of the studies done up till now, the following list has been put together showing important studies arranged alphabetically according to observation fields.

List of important studies using participant observation

Field	Author(s)	Year of publication
Communities	Arensberg	1954
	Chapple & Arensberg	1940

Field	*Author(s)*	*Year of publication*
Communities	Kluckhohn	1956
	Lynd & Lynd	1929, 1937
	Turner	1947
	Vidich & Bensman	1958
	Warner & Lunt	1941
	Wylie	1969
Residential	Berger	1960
districts	Dore	1967
	Gans	1969
	Liebow	1966
	Polsky	1969
	Whyte	1943, 1956
Organisations	Atteslander	1959
and offices	Dalton	1959
Mine	Jantke *et al.*	1953
	Mass-Observation	1943
	Pearse & Crocker	1943
	Roethlisberger & Dickson	1956
	Roy	1952
	Schneider	1950
Military	Sullivan, Queen & Patrick	1958
	Treiber	1973
	Whyte	1948
Hospitals,	Caudill *et al.*	1952
psychiatric wards	Goffman	1961
	Lüdtke	unpublished
	Roth	1963
	Schwartz	1964
	Siegrist	1972
	Tausky & Piedmont	1968
School classes	Bandemer	1962
	Finckh	1962
	Lüdtke & Friedrichs	unpublished
	Roeder	1965
	Sommer	1963
Children's		
playgrounds	Friedrichs	unpublished

Field	Author(s)	Year of publication
Gangs	Jansyn	1966
	Polsky & Kohn	1959
	Short & Strodtbeck	1965
	Spergel	1964
	Suttles	1968
	Trasher	1927
	Yablonsky	1962
Police patrols	Bittner	1967
	Black	1970
	Feest & Lautmann	1971
	Feest	1973
	Reiss	1967, 1968a, 1968b
Court rooms	Lautmann	1973/1972
	Milewski	1971
	Peters	1970
	Schumann & Winter	1973
Prisons	Friedrichs et al.	1973
	Galtung	1958
	Harbordt	1967
	Hoppensack	1969
Special forms of deviant behaviour		
Hobos	Anderson	1923
Theft	Blankenburg	1973
Homosexuality	Hooker	1967
	Humphreys	1970, 1973
	Weinberg & Williams	1970
Nudist camp	Weinberg	1973
Youth centres	Bals	1962
	Grauer	1973
	Kluth, Lohmar, Pongratz et al.	1955
	Lüdtke	1972
	Lüdtke & Grauer	1973

Field	Author(s)	Year of publication
Tourism	Hallwachs	1969
	Kentler, Leithäuser & Lessing	1969
	Lessing	1967
Horse races	Scott	1968
Public places		
Dance musicians	Becker	1963
Taxi dance halls	Cressey	1932
Billiard rooms	Polsky	1969
Students of medicine	Becker et al.	1961
Youth groups	Sherif	1951
Religious sects	Festinger, Riecken & Schachter	1956

1.3 On the ethics of participant observation

Every research plan must be able to justify itself to the members of the scientific community as well as to those involved and the co-workers.

The leading interest of the researcher, i.e. understanding, cannot only be seen as a characteristic of his personality but rather as a part and product of the society of which he is a member. In spite of the individual responsibility of the researcher, in the end, those involved bear the direct and indirect consequences of his work; either because of the influences he has on the field or because of the effects caused by his findings about others. Both of these remain hidden from the researcher to a great extent, because his participation is limited and the named effects can be long term or cumulative.

This political function inherent in science was especially pointed out by Habermas and has continually led to reflections on the relationships of science as a social system and theory of cognition (Friedrichs, 1973b, Chapter 1). The question 'which research projects are relevant?' is not the only important one. Important, too, is the question 'which obligations should the researcher assume when *applying* the method?' The discussion about the duties of, especially, the social sciences to society has led to a politicising of the different professional groups in recent years. In this way, the American Psychological Association has made rules for carrying out experiments.

This politicising can also be seen in the numerous articles on professional ethics in the social sciences. It deals with standards of the autonomy of the researcher from higher authorities (the state being the most important), the publication of the findings and the maintenance of the interests of those involved; in short, the context of values of the researcher which are not dealt with in the discussions on the theory of science.

If science is part of a process of understanding and reduction of a historically superfluous power, not a part of the stabilisation of this power, and if it is valued in terms of the material and cultural level of development of a society, then it is logical that this cultural and material level should make up the major part of such professional ethics.

The close relationship between the researcher and the field in participant observation and the researcher's participation in the activities of others are not conceivable any more without a professional ethic. There are not, however, any universal rules which could be applied in the same way to a covert observation of the behaviour of a judge (Lautmann, 1973) or to an overt observation of working conditions in a factory or a partial deception when giving the aim of a research project on police patrols (Black, 1970).

On the one hand, the researcher can only see himself or be seen by those involved as a spy or a voyeur. Erikson (1967), Humphreys (1970) and Polsky (1973) have emphasised this danger: especially in studies of deviant or tabooed behaviour, the researcher is betraying those involved with his curiosity when he has no immediate political goal: namely to reduce the conditions and processes of discrimination. It is only then justifiable to probe into the private fields of action of others when the chance is given, *not* to use the results against those involved. Thus, it is completely justifiable to ask the question: does not additional stigmatisation against homosexuals automatically arise when their actions generally (Hooker, 1967) or specifically in public toilets become the objects of 'neutral' observations and scientific publications? (Humphreys, 1970, 1973).

Such things inevitably lead to certain shocked reactions in many people who, as a result, may look with a certain prejudice upon homosexuals.

This is the effect of generalising about persons on the basis of categorical characteristics, the behavioural correlates of which science has been trying to differentiate. Both above-mentioned authors are aware of this risk, of course. They undermine the potential voyeurism of the reader by allowing this attitude to appear as part of the discrimination of society as it appears in the field of observation. Because of the fact that these and similar studies can illustrate the mechanism of discrimination, the relationships between deviant and conformed behaviour, and the subtle as well as obvious forms of social control exerted upon these persons daily, the political consequences justify their scientific exactness.

On the other hand, in situations where the researcher studies persons or actions negatively sanctioned by society and/or explicitly stated laws, he himself comes in conflict with these laws. Haferkamp (1973) reports that as a participant observer he witnessed criminal actions executed by juveniles,

13

but refused to testify about them. The participant observation of Humphreys cost him an arrest. At present the legitimisation of research as a 'science' is not sufficient to insure institutional protection of scientists carrying out observation, like the protection given to a doctor or clergyman. 'The social researcher enjoys no other legal protection than that enjoyed by every citizen in his daily business' (Sommer, 1971, p. 166).

A third aspect of the ethics of the researcher stems from the advantage he has over the average actor in the field simply because of the information he has. Because he has more insight as to the antecedents of the field and the situation of those involved, he can perceive facts which should lead to coun-selling or clinical help. Examples of this might be: the identification of workers, during the observation of working conditions, who are being exploited in spite of regulated wage agreements or protective labour legislation, and are not informed of this; or the identification, during the study of housing conditions, of an isolated, potential suicide victim. Here begins the duty of the researcher to undertake direct or indirect action, perhaps, even when it can't be hidden from those who are not involved. Otherwise the researcher may be judged in terms of the help not given, even when there are no external sanctions. The unanticipated moral and political consequences and their conceivable prevention must be a part of the general strategic calculations of research for the participant observer in the same way that method and technical exactness are.

Notes

1   This improvement lies in the testability of direct experience of the observer by way of an external control from the researcher. The fact that we know more about social facts subjectively than we do about physical facts in that we 'understand' the reasons for an observed act, is the foundation for neither an independent scientific method (as being claimed by certain meta-critical or hermeneutical schools), nor does it replace the necessity of a hypothetical generalisation of such knowledge, according to Popper (1958, p. 413). *Verstehen* makes it easier to gain access to social facts. The hypotheses themselves must of course be intersubjectively controllable by means of an empirical method. The systemising and standardising of everyday 'methods' guarantee the necessary distance between observer and object. For more information on this problem, see Schütz (1953).

2   This, at least a scientific standard, does not, alone, however, guarantee objectivity. It can often happen that an inexperienced and more involved observer, lacking knowledge of the foreign culture, sees it through eyes affected by his own cultural presumptions. This leads to a reflection of his own prejudices in the results.

3 A more detailed account of Cicourel (1964, p. 58):

Field research could be even more beneficial for others engaging in participant observation if problems of access, interpretation, and the like could be inserted at the place of discussion in the text. On the one hand, many references to contact with subjects often use terms stated in vernacular not explained to the reader and report material without it being clear as to how the researchers discuss that their subjects think or mean something without providing the documentation for such statements. This kind of description at a distance makes difficult the comparison of the data of different researchers.

2 Prerequisites of Standardised Participant Observation

It should be plausible that the classical form of participant observation by an individual uncontrolled field researcher is objective only to a small degree, even when the researcher restricts himself to a more or less systematic collection of sociologic or ethnographic material, or to the exploratory development of hypotheses. But even in this stage of summary description and formulation of hypotheses based on selective facts, the methodological problems of a social description pointed out by den Hollander were neglected for a long time. The exploratory and unstandardised field research contains numerous possibilities for making method objective, e.g. by explicating the origin of its statements (compare part 1.2); however this technique of making method objective has never been fully developed.

The fact that cultural anthropology has made important contributions towards the formation of general concepts and theories in sociology, can be considered as significant for the status of this discipline. To a great degree the single studies done in cultural anthropology have the character of monographs based upon naïve observation. Because they deal entirely with cultures as a whole, numerous cultural and social anthropologists have been misled by their theoretical awareness and use selective observation material. Because of the lack of empirical criteria, the theoretical elements of this material were not able to be put to use. As a result of this, contradictory generalisations had to arise. This can be illustrated in the example of the idea of totemism as a global category for various observation data (Lévi-Strauss, 1965). Other examples of such controversies in cultural anthropology can be found in the criticism of M. Mead by Terman and later by Bernard (1945) as well as in the discussions on sociological functionalism.[1]

The deficiencies become very clear when one sees that the analysis of the observation material as a possibility for minimising mistakes, didn't even present itself as a problem of method at first. By means of extensive or typological description, the observer wanted to present a 'picture' of his object as true to nature as possible, to an uninformed audience, whereas he was usually dealing with a very complex field: a community, a 'culture' or a 'society'. The most important problems met were those of a physical nature, language and role problems. Even today, some cultural anthropologists resemble the 'travelling discoverers' of the nineteenth century, secure in the appreciation of their pioneer accomplishments in society (or only within their specific scientific community). In accordance with their idea of science at that time, most cultural anthropologists' empirical intentions were to make additive studies in sequences and of an exploratory nature. As a rule, the observations had nothing to do with an *a priori* intended testing of theories in a strict sense. The only criterion for data analysis was to make up an understandable, that is impressionistic, reproduction of the observations, and produce evidence or plausibility for the generalisations of the observer, whose phenomenological and intuitive skill at interpreting played an important role. Since the 'logic of data analysis' consisted primarily of an appeal to the audience to use its inductive capabilities to complete the generalisations of the observer (or the observers) by means of a number of examples or illustrations, one can hardly speak of sufficient intersubjectivity in this method. Therefore participant observation always ran the danger of not thoroughly checking ethnocentric prejudices held by observers as well as their respective audience (see also de Laguna, 1957, Fischer & Zanolli, 1968).

Wylie (1969) proceeded in this way in the analysis of his participant observation of a French village during 1950–51. Interpretations were based on conversations of the following kind:

> The old man Anselm never thought about anything else except his work; and with the exception of harvest time, he always worked alone. He never got involved with any other person, not even with a woman. The old man Marnes also always avoided having too much contact with another person. He didn't talk to anyone about anything but the weather and the condition of the harvest. Old Allibert never appears in public . . . It is without a doubt not just a coincidence that these . . . men are among the wealthiest in the community . . . (They) are admired for the way they never get involved with others . . . The others believe it is clever to keep the important things to oneself and to avoid conflict with others as much as possible. At the same time, however, contact with others is very important to them.

The author draws the general conclusion: 'Using this social conception, the people of Peyrane try to live a life on the one hand with the others, but on the other hand alone. They do this by being friendly to the others on the surface, but at the same time hiding what they consider to be their true selves' (Wylie 1969, p. 207, ff).

Kentler *et al.* (1969) analyse their observation material in the same way, except that to a certain extent, they use more detailed situation-related protocols, and base it on a theoretical frame of reference.

This model of data analysis remains basically at the level of naïve 'anecdotes in describing behaviour' which present results of observations which are not methodically controlled. . . . (and) are usually the recording of what the observer believes to have seen as characteristic of the behaviour of a person, and not that of objective facts in a situation. (. . .) Here we are dealing with the reproduction of feelings, values, prejudices and projections of the observer, but not with the impartial identification of the exact situation discovered (Hasemann, 1964, p. 816).

It is quite obvious that at this level, especially, observation faults based on selective perception (see 3.1) cannot be controlled in practical conditions, because the results are understood as being direct inductions from (mistaken) single observations (see section 4.5).

Typical of the classical form of participant observation is how inadequate results became the evaluation standard of the whole method. The reason why (e.g. when compared with the interview) participant observation has such an alleged restricted range of exactness is not logical but rather historical. For this reason, there is a great need for revision. An important question which must be systematically analysed is: To what degree can participant observation be applied on the basis of statements about relationships, i.e. on the basis of correlation or multivariate analysis, time sequences and comparative research? Can its application ultimately be based on that upon which the long-range tested and proved interview is based? These questions, however, cannot be decided on the basis of the material and results at hand. The greater the need for empirically relevant research in the realm of the 'known' industrial culture today, the more specific and at the same time more complex the problems to be examined become, and the more precise the instrumental preparations for such research projects become, the more timely is the demand to discuss these questions.

The division of labour which seems obvious: exploration = observation, examination = interview or experiment, must be considered as without foundation, mainly for the following reasons. Since the limits of the interview in field research have become clear (see section 5.1) especially in terms of validity of data concerning actual behaviour patterns, empirical social research is able to analyse the most diverse types of variables only according to the principle of optimal range and with different procedures complementing one another.

The opinion, which is still widespread, that participant observation is automatically less 'objective' than the procedures of an experimental, or non-participant observation nature (which are today classified as 'systematic observation') is based upon a conception of objectivity which is too narrow. The alternative participation/non-participation of the observer, structural simplicity/complexity of the object and strictness/looseness of the observation categories, which are· to a certain degree set by both of the observation classifications, do not in any way determine a measure of objectivity (see König, 1967). The objectivity of an observation procedure cannot be measured in terms of an *a priori* nature inherent in itself, but rather in terms of the relationship between an optimal method and the resulting relevant statements about the object, as well as the intersubjective plausibility of these statements. The data collected by different observation procedures may differ in terms of the dimensions of the objects (e.g. laboratory situations or natural settings), but not in terms of their *a priori* objectivity. The categories of a participant observation will become more complex accordingly; or one may say more holistic as interpreted by the Lewin school of thought. One may say, then, that a method of observation is 'objective' in so far as it exploits possibilities of intersubjectivity as rationally and effectively as possible.

If the instrument of participant observation is to be applied in a standardised form, certain conditions will have to be met, limiting its application which has been almost unbounded up till now:

1 *The principle of repeating the same observations by simultaneous or parallel observations.* This means there must be a plurality of observation objects (e.g. several communities rather than one) and/or plurality of observers. In the simplest case, several observers observe an object; either the same process with simultaneous participation or samples of situations or processes which are parallel to one another and comparable. One can measure the reliability of their observations by measuring the concordance of their results. This procedure was used by A. and R. Tausch and their collaborators (1960, 1962, 1965, 1966) in the non-participant observation of teacher/pupil interaction in classrooms.

2 *A result of this first condition is a separation between research director and observer.* The researcher (or research team) should no longer be the person (or persons) who do the observing. The researcher should train several observers (at least two) and send them into the field in his place. There is hardly any mention of this separation of roles in literature, despite the fact that this procedure is common in the interview. Katz (1953) is the first to emphasise a kind of field study in which researcher and observer are not identical. This brings with it important methodological consequences: the researcher is forced to make the formulations of the observation scheme more exact. He must be more exact when making his concepts and hypotheses operational. The same behaviour sequences can be observed by several observers, something which allows for the measurement of reliability. This distinction between researcher and observer also relieves the observers psychologically and spreads responsibility. In this way they are freed from a bias of the isolated researcher whose attitude in the field is often made up of

excited expectation of especially those results which confirm his hypotheses and bring subjective distortions into the observations. The observer to whom an assignment has been delegated does not have to comprehend completely the theoretical consequences of the data he has collected. On the contrary, this is not even desired, because he will be able to work more openly and be more relaxed. The only drawback is that he will be strictly bound to the observing scheme.

3 *The observation field as well as its dimensional analysis is limited.* It is hardly possible to observe a whole culture or community in exact detail. Because the participating persons and situations are so numerous, our knowledge as it stands today is not sufficient to allow us to identify and record the many relationships and interactions completely and exactly. For that reason it will be useful to choose research objects which are rather uncomplicated, i.e. (a) have few differing situations, (b) relatively few persons or persons whose actions are relatively similar, and (c) are relatively isolated from other situations (see section 4.2).

Condition 3 does not imply that a methodological approach to more complex objects like whole organisations or communities is generally impossible. It only means that the complex of observable categories represents perhaps a selective but possibly representative section of reality of the whole field. In this way, the *methodical* choice of variables and field categories becomes a prerequisite for a standardised participant observation. It is only possible when a minimum amount of information about the object is already to hand. This information can be obtained through explorative preliminary inquiries or through useful sources such as literature or documents about the object. The choice of relevant observation categories must, then, be based upon (a) a complete number of well-defined variables of the object within the framework of the research project (dimensional analysis). In addition to this, (b) a theoretical model of the object which allows for deducing empirical hypotheses about the relationships of the variables (constructing models)[2] should be to hand when observation is to be used to test hypotheses and as a result of this, a definite relationship of structure and meaning of the field has already been postulated (Mayntz, Holm, Hübner, 1969; see also Schütz, 1953, p. 27; Goffman, 1959, p. 249). This model provides the criteria for choosing the 'relevant' observation categories from the universe of possible categories, but it does not necessarily provide the criteria for choosing the empirical components (e.g. persons involved, physical objects, status symbols, length of interaction etc.) of these categories. In this way, quite a bit of margin is left for the collection of data in the observation which is more accidental than prestructured.

4 *An exact observation scheme must be formulated.* Each observer is given an exact plan telling him what and how long to observe. Important situations

are specified and indicators are provided (the observer is to compare these with the concrete situation); verbal formulations in the scheme are used to try to structure the perception of the observer (see Chapter 4, especially 4.3).

5 *Definition of observer's role.* Participant observation requires an initial stranger to take a role which is accepted by the members of the observation field. The better the strategic position of the observer's role, i.e. a role which provides the least limited entrée to relevant situations and which causes the fewest changes in the field, the easier it is to secure relevant information. In standardised participant observation, the observer plays an even more important role methodically. This is because the reliability, the validity and the comparability of the data are even more dependent on the observer. In order to avoid influences the observer might have on the behaviour of those to be observed, the possible role of the observer in the field should be tested before the research begins. In such cases where a fitting role does not already exist, pretests should be conducted to determine at least in a basic way, how and to what extent the observer will probably change the field (see section 3.2).

Notes

1   See the vivid presentation of Malinowski's and Radcliffe-Brown's contradictory magic theories by Homans (1960, p. 306, ff). The anthropologists rely on the observations of rituals in different segmental societies, all of them, of course, in different contexts. Malinowski refers to the magical rites performed by the Trobriand islanders to bring luck in harvesting and fishing. Here, the function of the magicmaking is to reduce fear and to increase the social support of confidence and resoluteness in continuing the productive work. Radcliffe-Brown refers to the ritual of childbirth among the Andamans, which, in his opinion, has the function of contributing to the survival of the group. This is accomplished by making all important events in life into festivities. Both interpretations of magic are incompatible when stated in this form. However, according to Homans, they can be made compatible at another theoretical level. If both observations were based on a theory of functional requirements of a segmental society and of magic rituals in relation with these requirements, and if there were some kind of instrument for classifying each observed event according to its (possible) effect upon these requirements within a specific situational context, then probably an empirical comparison of both observations as well as the formulation of more differentiated hypotheses with higher plausibility might have been possible. They probably would have stated that magic is not the same as magic.

22

2   Here it is methodically unimportant if the model is an ideal-type-like generalisation (i.e. the bureaucratic structure of a company), a somewhat empirically sturdy model (e.g. the origin and development of human contact among the neighbours in a quarter of a city) or a model based on specific norms (e.g. a liberal teaching system of a comprehensive school) just as long as they allow for the deduction of empirically testable hypotheses.

3 Two Basic Problems in Participant Observation

3.1 Selective perception

Extreme subjectivity is the basic obstacle in the way of making inter-subjectively valid observations. If one considers observation as being a 'kind of world experience' (König, 1967, p. 107), then every such experience is structured by the individual. We now know that individuals can agree about their experiences, but this agreement is merely an overlapping of their statements, whereas an often greater part has actually been perceived by only one individual.

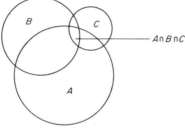

Fig. 3.1 The observation of an incident by three individuals

The statements of three witnesses A, B and C made about an automobile accident are almost never completely the same. The correct statements which are the same (verbally formulated observations) $A \cap B \cap C$ are fewer than the total set of statements made by A, B and C. A simple look at the theory of probability may clarify this fact: If the total number of correct statements made is 100 per cent, and if 60 per cent of A's answers are correct, 50 per cent of B's answers are correct and 30 per cent of C's answers are correct, then the portion of correct answers on which at least two individuals agreed is:

$$P(A \cap B \vee B \cap C \vee A \cap C \vee A \cap B \cap C) =$$
$$A \cdot B + B \cdot C + A \cdot C - 2ABC =$$
$$0 \cdot 6 \cdot 0 \cdot 5 + 0 \cdot 5 \cdot 0 \cdot 3 + 0 \cdot 6 \cdot 0 \cdot 3 - 2(0 \cdot 6 \cdot 0 \cdot 5 \cdot 0 \cdot 3) = 0 \cdot 45$$

The portion of correct answers on which all three individuals agreed is even smaller: $P(A \cap B \cap C) = A \cdot B \cdot C = 0 \cdot 09$.

According to this, all three individuals (observers) agree on only 9 per cent of the total number of correct answers, i.e. 9 per cent of the descriptions of the incident can be accepted, as long as one has not accredited one of the individuals with being a better observer or more objective right from the beginning (e.g. this is often the case with a policeman). If this has happened, then the statements themselves must be weighted by criteria of objectivity, and these criteria could be prejudiced. This formula would be: $P(xA \cap yB \cap zC)$, x, y and z being the weighting criteria. We constantly make this kind of weighting in our daily lives. We determine the importance of statements made by other people on the basis of an implicit and prejudiced scale of objectivity. We believe the statement of a good friend rather than one of a distant friend, and the statement of a respected person rather than one of a person of bad reputation.

One can derive from the above thoughts, what the aim of an exact participant observation, in the form of a scientific method must be:

1 One must increase the number of identical statements (in the example $A \cap B \cap C$) until its maximum equals the total number of true statements.
2 One must explain the criteria used for weighting, and if possible reduce them to one criterion. One must try to see that all individuals can be equally objective on the basis of this one criterion (mathematically the factors x, y and z would disappear).

Analytically speaking, problem 2 precedes problem 1; only after problem 2 is solved or at least errors of this kind are minimised, can problem 1 be approached. Both problems appear together in actual observations, i.e. one problem implies the other.

Where do these problems come from? One can assume that each observation is structurised by the observations which preceded it (see Madge, 1967, p. 122, f). The observer's general attitudes towards people and objects taking part in an event (sympathies, reputations, etc.) are some other criteria which cause the structurising of observations. Both perceptions are influenced by the goals (imaginations of a state to be realised) of the observer, who may not even be aware of this. In this way 'certain content is favoured, hindering the identification of other content' (Hasemann, 1964, p. 809; see Kaplan, 1964, p. 133). This becomes a vicious circle which Atteslander (1969, p. 125) describes as: 'We only believe what we see; unfortunately we only see what we want to believe.' When only certain incidents and persons draw the observer's attention, then his perception is selective; the criterion for selectivity has just been outlined. Selective perception is also a factor in choosing those people with whom the observer is in contact. This can perhaps be traced back to what Strecker (1969, p. 40, f) mentions as 'the egalitarian attitude of the researcher who shows the same scientific and human interest to all of the members of the society, but whose attitude is directly contrary to the principle of inequality which constitutes every hierarchical system'. Vidich & Shapiro (1965, p. 31) were able to prove that the participant observers were not able to judge a proportionately large group of people in a small town because these people did not belong to an upper prestige group; the observers had more contact with persons belonging to the middle and upper classes. On the other hand, the Lynds, in their field study of Middletown, overlooked a very rich millionaire family with four brothers, which had such a large political and social influence on this small town that when one of the brothers was buried, the whole town stopped working (Lynd & Lynd, 1937, p. 75).

Selectivity does not only affect the beginning of a series of observations, but can also have strong effects even during the process of observation. An event observed once, e.g. 'X initiates most of the interactions of group A', can lead the observer to assume that X always initiates the interaction in group A. As a result all further observations of group A will be made under this assumption, in spite of the fact that another time Z initiates the interaction, X initiating only certain interactions in certain situations. This sampling of observations was either too small and/or later observations were preformed on the basis of assumptions made from earlier observations. The observer always sees the same because he made a false assumption in the beginning and never corrected it.[1] He should have recognised such assumptions and turned them into hypotheses to be tested in following observations. The same is true for the elements of *verstehen* in observations: if Bain (1967, p. 123) writes that in participant observation one is learning by, among other things, ascribing to the actor the same feelings that one believes to have in the same situation, he overlooks the tentative character of such suppositions. They, too, can only be allowed as hypotheses which the observer should put into operation and test by making further observations.

Verstehen generally belongs to the context of discovery and not to the context of justification. That means, it doesn't qualify an observation or a description but rather designates that which is to be observed and described (see also Kaplan, 1964, p. 143). Generalising emotions or effects which are subjective is comparable to the questionable method of introspection in earlier psychology, especially that of the Würzburg School, which to a great extent was superseded by behaviourism.

Faults made in recording or reproducing results gained by an observer cannot usually be corrected. The real problem is that these faults can't even be identified, because the presentation of the results appears to be a plausible unit. Campbell (1958, p. 341) clearly pointed out the difficulties involved here in connection with work done, dealing with problems in human communication:

> Let us suppose that we communicate the content of a newspaper through an hypothetical randomly imperfect teletype system, on the one hand, and through an imperfect human being on the other. The product of such a teletype would appear, to a later human unit, as bizarre, imperfect,

randomly distorted, and, beyond a certain degree of information loss, unintelligible (. . .) . But the output of the human transmission and memory unit, no matter what degree of information loss, is apt to *appear* to a later human unit as intelligible and usable as a base of action. This appearance of plausibility and comprehensibility in the output can accompany a total loss of the input message.

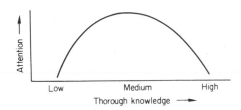

Fig. 3.2 Assumed relationship between attention and thorough knowledge

One of the reasons for this fact might be traced back to another effect of *Verstehen:* namely the tendency of the observer, in our case, to produce meaningful units already in the phase of reception of information. In this way he leaves out or changes incidents which are, according to *his* understanding, contradictory or impossible to interpret. We can see from this just how necessary an observation schedule really is (see section 4.3).

If one assumes generally that during the process of observation the following relationship (see Fig. 3.2) between the attention of the observer and his thorough knowledge of the incidents to be observed exists, then another error in observation is the *overlooking of the obvious*. These are the phenomena one is, so to say, already too familiar with. An example: during a three-day training course for participant observers in the study on youth centres, not one of the participants came late to the sessions, something that could have easily happened. This most probably would have been overlooked by an observer, although it is an important fact, e.g. an indicator of the degree of cooperation and motivation of the participants.

In addition, selective perception can be found in language, namely, confounding observation and evaluation. This is obvious because our language contains many words which are semantically considered to be evaluative (Osgood, Suci and Tannenbaum, 1957). Most of our daily descriptions only seem to be descriptions; de facto they are value-oriented judgements. Instead of a description: 'He gave me his hand, shook it for a long time, looked into my eyes, laughed and gave me a pat on the shoulder,' one usually hears: 'He was friendly.' It is necessary, however, for the processes of control and interpretation to hear first an exact description of what actually happened.

28

Only the researcher and not the observer may interpret the incident as being 'friendly'; this may only be done on the basis of the meaning of 'friendly' as determined by operational criteria defined before the study began. To formulate such facts which are simple to perceive leads to problems similar to that of neo-positivism in the 1930s which had dealt with the problem of defining the protocol statements, i.e. the final irreducible observations. The lowest level of observation and perception must be defined for every study according to its problem and hypotheses (see section 4.3).

3.2 The role of the participant observer

The sources of error discussed in the preceding section are of a perceptive and psychological nature, and can be reduced by means of systematic training of the observer. In contrast, the problem of the observer's role is based on the integrative characteristics of social systems which can be identified among others in the roles of the actors.

A peculiarity of participant observation is that over a period of time, an interdependence arises between the observer and the observed. To a greater or less degree, reciprocal influences appear during the process of observation. The observer takes a certain role in his field of observation. While this is happening, the position, expectations and reactions of the observer as well as of his interaction partners change. A social role is defined as a set of behaviour expectations towards a position in a social system (Friedrichs, 1968, p. 125, f). Any change is a process on the intersubjective (observer/observed) as well as on the intrasubjective (consciousness of the observer) level. Because it is possible that the observation field changes, the method of participant observation always runs the danger of not collecting valid data; the influence of the observer can change the field and if this happens uncontrolled, the field will become artificial. Sullivan, Queen and Patrick (1958) showed how the field, a training corps of the Air Force, changed under the influence of the observer, and how the observer was able to adjust to these changes. A change resulting in complete participation was also recorded in the Hawthorne Experiment in Relay Assembly Room (Roethlisberger and Dickson, 1939, p. 72).

The observer should find out, e.g. what *usually* happens in a group and not what happens because of his presence and stops happening when he leaves the group. Since such a feed-back will hardly be completely avoided, the least the observer will be asked to do is to record in his daily log which changes he thinks he has caused. Schwartz and Schwartz (1955, p. 353) talk about a 'continual process of discovery'; Vidich (1955, p. 360) speaks of the 'self-objectivation' of the observer.

29

Of the possible errors in connection with the role of the observer the following should be controlled:

Intersubjective sources of error:
1   Defining the observer's role
2   Choosing key persons
3   Intensity of the interaction
Intrasubjective sources of error:
4   Going native
5   Intrarole conflicts

Defining the role of the observer: Every observation field is a more or less loose structure with positions, expectations, sanctions, institutions and situations. Each observer working in a field is forced to take on a certain role (Paul, 1953). 'Good cooperation is only then possible, when uncertainties in behaviour have been overcome, and when the relationship between observer and observed has become systematised' (Strecker, 1969, p. 25).

The prerequisite for this, of course, is that one finds among all of the possible roles in the field those which are accepted by most of the observed as well as by an observer, and which will 'not cause too great a loss of time and work' (Mayntz, Holm & Hübner, 1969, p. 101; see Paul, 1953, p. 431). That means that it is necessary to find in the pretest those positions which can also be filled by a stranger and in which he can fulfil what is expected of him. It would be difficult for the observer to take over the role of a doctor in a hospital, a warden in a prison, or the director of a youth club. In all three cases, the positions would neither be open to him, nor could he respond adequately to the challenges of situation, i.e. fulfil the expectations of the actors. Even if the positions were available to him, quite a big change in the field would occur resulting from his reactions. It can be generally said that (a) the more specific the expectations toward a position under conditions of (b) a greater differentiation of these expectations according to specific situations at the same time, which implies (c) increasing determination of the behaviour of a position-holder by the position – the less available becomes this position for the observer. The observer can more easily take positions subjected to few expectations where these expectations apply to many situations.

It is especially easy to introduce a participant observer into a position which is continually being held by different people, e.g. in our observation field 'youth centres': visitors and staff were accustomed to students who came to work as trainees, this being part of professional education. The most difficult observation situation can be found in fields which have inconsistent and flexible role structures. Here the participant observer is forced to vary his role. If different social systems (role structures) exist in the observation field, he must be able to change his position and under certain conditions meet the expectations of diverging groups. In a business organisation for example, this is true for the roles of specialists, members of work groups, neighbouring colleagues, and union members; in an urban quarter, for the roles of tenants, neighbours, members of a social class, inhabitants of a certain kind of building, and members of a certain church, etc.

It is also necessary for the roles just mentioned, suitable for the observer, to allow for a large range of individual behaviour. This is because there are few expectations determined by the position. The observer will be able to exploit the tolerance inherent in the position to instigate certain expectations toward him from the actors in the field during the observations by certain behaviour on his part. Typical of this is Teuscher's experience (1959, p. 255) in his research in the Sudan (Africa): 'The role belongs to the social system; society has assigned this role to the observer. By means of clever politicising the observer must try to find a way in the system itself to modify this role and the status bound to it according to need, in order to gain different views of the society.'

Because he is a stranger, the participant observer must first win the trust of the actors. If the position itself which he takes over does not suffice in providing the observed with an explanation for his presence, he must give a plausible explanation as to why he is there and what he plans to do. Giving an explanation in this way has proven especially important in cultural anthropological field research because of the fact that there are not any positions open for strangers to take over.

The way an observer defines his job to the other actors so that they accept him, depends completely upon his personality and his daily behaviour (Dean, 1954, p. 233). Or as Whyte formulates: 'If I was alright, then my project was alright.' As shown by the experience of numerous cultural anthropologists and sociologists (Radcliffe-Brown, 1922, Whyte, 1961, Powdermaker, 1967, Feuchtwang, 1968) it is important for an observer to be frank, act naturally and be willing to give any information. The observer cannot convince the actors in the field with either his position or research task; of vital importance is his behaviour.' . . . the more I gave and the more I revealed of myself, the more familiar I became and the more trusted, so the more I am given and the more is revealed to me' (Feuchtwang, 1968, p. V). Whyte reports similarly (1961, p. 303) that his key person in the field, 'Doc', said to him: 'If people accept you, you can just hang around and you'll learn the answers without even having to ask the questions.' The strategic definition of the observer's role supplies the *structural prerequisites of participation;* individual openness and adaptability in behaviour provide a guarantee of successful participation in a situation.

As a matter of principle, the observer should try not to press his world-outlook on others. He should take the others as they are. On the other hand he need not react with over-conformity. He must only avoid giving the observed the feeling that their 'different' behaviour appears to him inferior (see Schwartz and Schwartz, 1955, p. 347). When Whyte (1961, p. 304) for example began to use obscenities and slang, he was told that one didn't expect him to use this language and that it didn't sound like him. The observer's chance of obtaining information lies in the fact that he is a stranger, asks questions about behaviour which is self-evident for the others, or uses questions to research the past of a group or individual. F. Kluckhohn (1956, p. 104, f) like den Hollander (1965, p. 213) emphasised that playing with his position as a stranger should be regarded as a tool of the observer.

The subjects have qualified the role of the observer via ascriptive processes without his being able to influence them, and for this reason his manipulation of the role is limited. Age, sex and appearance can lead the actors to expect certain things of the observer. Powdermaker (1967) for example, in an ethnological study, had to explain why she didn't bring her husband. The real explanation, that she wasn't married, would not have been plausible for the natives, considering their social structure. So she answered that she was divorced 'because her husband didn't work enough', a reason which was a valid basis for divorce within the society she was studying. The study done by Vidich (1960) showed to what extent the role of the participant observer and the interpretation of this role by the observed reappears for the observer in the form of feedback in his data.

In other situations in which the observer appears as a complete stranger, such qualifications can only determine the superficial attributes of the role which do not additionally hamper the observation. On the contrary, they can even serve to emphasise the clearness of the situation. This is especially useful when one is more willing to give intimate information to a complete stranger than to members of one's own group.

Key persons: The participant observer confronts a quite anonymous group as a complete stranger. If he wants to make successful observations then he has to be accepted. To reach both goals simultaneously, he must find single individuals who accept him and whose trust leads a large number of other subjects to trust him too, because some of the subjects did so at the beginning.

Someone who approaches a group of persons who are strange or not too familiar to him, will first try to build up communication with one person. This one person he will consider as a representative of the group (the person may be considered a representative by the group too) from whom one can learn the patterns of interaction in the group. The stranger tries to find out the expectations of the group on the basis of this single person with whom he interacts. He tries to react correctly in a kind of trial and error process. In the same way, the reactions of the stranger are judged; one tries to discover his goals and finally, to develop relatively dependable expectations of his behaviour. As he is being judged, he will try to find something out about the status of the group member within the group. The higher the status of the other, and/or the more strict the hierarchy of the group, (a) the less the other members of the group will interrupt him, in this way causing a change of the addressee of his statements, and (b) the sooner he will be accepted by the group, as long as he is accepted by the single individual. This might be accomplished by continuing the communication originally instigated by the single individual.

Subjects who fulfil the conditions mentioned above may become key persons for the observer. Lewin (1958) pointed out that primary groups almost always have such key persons (usually the leaders) who have the function of a 'gate-keeper'. They supervise the admittance of new members into the group. If the observer can win the trust of such a key person, like 'Doc' in the case of Whyte's 'Street Corner Society' then he has won an important source of information. The danger does exist, however, that the observer makes a poor choice as to an informant, and as a result receives information which is onesided and limited (den Hollander, 1965, p. 215, f). (See Goffman, 1959, p. 145, ff, Back, 1960, for a detailed discussion of problems involving informants.)

For this reason, the observer should systematically test the quality and reliability of the information given by informants and key persons by carefully observing and classifying them. If he is dealing with persons similar in certain traits, e.g. status or attitudes toward politics, then he will have to regard the information as onesided accordingly.

Following Dean (1954) informants may be classified as:

(a) Problem-oriented informants:
Outsider: He sees things through the eyes of someone from another standpoint, another culture, another group or social class;
Novice: He registers even things which are self-evident, he has no investments to protect;
Owner of a new status: He has changed roles and still reacts insecurely and sensitively toward new experiences;
The 'Natural': He usually informs without reflection but objectively;
(b) Especially willing informants:
Naïve informant: He doesn't know what he is talking about: naïve about the goals of the observer or about his own group;
Frustrated informant (rebel or dissatisfied): He is well aware of the inhibitions of his wishes and desires;
Outs: Informants without any influence in the group but aware of the

goings-on and critical of those who are in;

Routiniers: Informants who are experienced, familiar with everything, and threatened by none;

Leaners: Looking for attention and help by way of the observer;

Subordinates: They must obey the stronger in the group, they develop abilities to get out from under the pressure of authority and feel aggression towards 'the ones at the top'.

Intensity of interaction: It is always being discussed in the literature on the subject, how intensive the participation of the observer should be. Atteslander (1969, p. 40) suggested that we speak of a gradual active and passive participation, since every observer takes part anyway at least with his organs of perception.

Schwartz and Schwartz (1955) and Gold (1958) speak of a continuum 'active–passive' and at the same time suggest a division into four types (roles): (a) complete identification with the field; (b) participant as observer; (c) observer as participant; (d) observer without interaction with the field. Fink (1955) made a similar classification at around the same time, in which she admits that, empirically, all four types will appear together in a research project:

1 Genuine participation: complete integration and adjustment on the part of the observer.

2 Pseudo-participation (F. Kluckhohn): participation is limited by the role and purpose of the observer.

3 Incomplete participation (Malinowski): little integration, but strong emphasis on the observation, which the observer overtly pursues.

4 Techniques of non-participant observation: the observer works indirectly using informants and/or interviews.

When considering these assumptions, it would be wise to test if we are really dealing with a continuum which implies that with increasing participation, the chance of observation becomes smaller proportionately. An alternative might be a two-dimensional model in which the degree of training, precision of the observation scheme and supervision would determine the degree of independence of the two dimensions, participation and observation. Generally the degree of participation results automatically from the desire for a maximum avoidance of obtrusiveness or reactivity (Claster & Schwartz, 1972, p. 75).

For the time being it will remain crucial to decide to what degree the observer can take part without reducing the possibilities of standardising and controlling his observations. For this reason the observer should be told from the outset how he should act. The easiest way to do this is to take a look at Fink's standardised participant observation type 2. Here two intrasubjective problems appear which can lead to errors in observation.[2]

Going native. The more and/or longer the observer interacts with the subjects of his field, the more he loses the ability to observe according to the categories provided by the observation schedule (see sections 4.3 and 4.3.2). He takes on, at least to a certain degree, the values and semantics of the observed. This process has been designated 'going native' (Miller, 1952, p. 98; Paul, 1953, p. 435). The observer's recordings become less and less comparable with those of the other observers. The higher the degree of involvement of the observer in the actions of the others, the lower his impartiality towards them and to the incidents which he is to observe. The observations become inexact and biased, leading to insufficient data recordings.

Intrarole conflicts. The necessary separation of participation and observation leads to intrarole conflicts for the observer. On the one hand, the observer is instructed to act – in terms of Parsons' pattern variables – effectively neutral and specific, according to the special interests of the research. On the other hand, the observer has become a participant which demands of him a contradictory orientation: he must interact with his subjects both effectively and diffusely. He carries the burden of combining both, something which is obviously extremely difficult, according to the final discussion with the seventy-four participant observers in the study of youth centres which made this very clear (see sections 6.2 and 9.2.5). It seems that this kind of assignment is emotionally over-demanding. Probably this is because our socialisation considers it a bit inhuman to look at others as research objects while interacting with them at the same time. The longer the goal of the research demands this, the greater becomes the pressure on the observer.

In addition, the observer must bear the restraints of the observation schedule. If one considers Whorf's statement that language is not only a medium of communication, but also that which structures our experiences, then it follows that the observer is required to perceive in the peculiar way determined by the schedule. This will often differ from his usual perception and modes to classify reality. As Cicourel (1964, p. 51) writes, 'the observer must gain some knowledge of the daily lives of his subjects in order to interact with them; he must also ignore his scientific rationality from time to time, but keep it at hand when describing the actions of his subjects.'

It is very probable that this conflict decreases in studies where the researcher and observer are not identical. There are two ways to reduce this difficulty: the observer is visited often by supervisors, with whom he discusses all problems. The discussions are intended to reinforce his scientific observation. The second way, threatening validity, was also chosen by some of our observers. They divided their observations into parts by sometimes devoting themselves completely to observation, and then completely to participation, not thinking about their observation assignments. The danger of going native arises again here.

Observation phases and roles. Participant observation is, unlike any other method, bound to change in attitude, way of thinking and role expectations of the observer and/or the researcher. He is continually moving within a triangle of relationships, researcher – subjects – others/outsiders. While at the beginning the expectations, and also some of the interests, of the researcher and others are quite similar when compared to the expectations of the subjects, during the research project the distance between researcher and others will increase and the distance between the subjects and the researcher will decrease. The basic reason for this is that the others, such as friends and colleagues, emphasise the voyeuristic elements of the research. This is explained in detail in the report by Weinberg & Williams (1972) about such processes of interaction in field research.

The above-mentioned tendency towards going native is really only one part of a multiphased process in observation and of the respective correlates in taking on roles, interpersonal perception and selective observation in the field. Weinberg & Williams have given a good summary of these relationships (1972, p. 167):

The fieldworker as perceived by subjects, others, and self, as related to the stage of the research.

Stage of the fieldwork	Viewed by subjects as:	Viewed by others as:	Viewed by self as:
Application	Interloper	Voyeur	Salesman
Orientation	Novice	Inside dopester	Stranger
Initiation	Probationer	Pseudo-professional	Initiate
Assimilation	Limbo member	Public defender	True believer
Cessation	Deserter	Expert	Worker who has finished his job

As a result of this analysis, one can conclude that one should not start a standardised participant observation until an observation schedule has been developed on the basis of previous knowledge and pretests, a schedule, that from the beginning will fit the experiences made in the phases of observation. In this way neither information will be lost, nor will the observer's perceptions be changed without some kind of control (see also section 11.3).

3.2.1 *The adequate observer role as basis for reliable data*

Concluding this chapter we should like to point out briefly that the solution of role problems mentioned above is closely related to the availability of reliable observation data. A more detailed analysis of determinants and practical ways of participant observers' behaviour in the field will follow in Chapter 9.

If in standardised participant observation the observer's participation is a methodological prerequisite for the unhindered perception of social properties of the field and thereby a key to validity, then the observer's role establishes concrete scope for the participation. Adequate observer's roles are those roles which are defined in agreement with the given norms and behaviour expectations in the field, i.e. by assuming them, the observer's participation is sanctioned positively, and at the same time does not compromise his scientific role, i.e. guarantees an undistorted observation of the relevant information from the field (see section 3.2). Under this prerequisite, the observer's role passes for a key to reliability.

Kluckhohn (1967, p. 110, f) names three factors, which in relation to other methods, greatly increase the reliability of the information from participant observation:

1 The direct relationship between behaviour and the accompanying rationalisation of this behaviour can be ascertained, whereas this is in principle impossible in an interview.

2 Relevant and comprehensive information, at least, that of a more intimate nature, is supplied by a larger number of persons than by selected informants or those directly questioned.

3 When the participation of the observer is successful, there is little danger that the informants are atypical or maladjusted actors of the field.

The problems of participation and the role of the observer can be characterised as the problem of the uncertainty or indetermination relation of participant observation (König, 1967, p. 37, f). The minimisation of errors by means of standardisation through the observation schedule and the procedure of data transformation is, in principle, limited. In addition, a part of the error variance can be controlled by the observer's role, but only to a certain limit, which is set by the influence of participation on the field. This is related to the fact that adequate observer behaviour can only be rationally planned and foreseen from outside to a limited degree, because the observer's role itself is a result of the social system of the object of observation, upon which the research director exercises a systematic influence only in experiments, which he, indeed, tries to avoid during participant observation.

Because the social conditions of the participation can vary very greatly from field to field, object to object, and situation to situation, a practical strategy on testing level I of the observer's role (see Table 7.4) in a generally binding way can scarcely be specified. Concrete suggestions about this point can, therefore, be gathered only from case studies on phenomena specific to the field (see Whyte, 1951, Bain, 1967, Kluckhohn, 1940, 1967). As a methodological component of the error control over the observer's role, the observer's training, directed toward awakening the social sensitivity of the observers in terms set by the pretest (see section 11.3), and certain compensatory aids through supervision (see section 12) are placed in the forefront.

Notes

1 Here it can be a case of making an inductive conclusion too soon, based on incomplete single observations or just as well a case of an incorrect transfer, i.e. the inappropriate application of a learned meaning context to a situation with a different meaning. See also the problem of creating constants in the perception of *Gestalt* (König, 1967, p. 698, f).

2 See also Schwartz and Schwartz (1955, p. 347), who differentiate between two kinds of participation:

1 Participation as role activity in the research situation; and
2 Effective participation in which the investigator's emotional responses are evoked in the situation. While role participation is controllable to some degree, the observer cannot prevent himself from being affected by the emotional interplay between the subjects or between himself and the observed.

4 Techniques and Instruments of Standardised Participant Observation

4.1 Field of observation

The field of observation is the spacial and social area in which one is to conduct the observation. Since no one area is completely isolated and there is only a gradual changeover from one area to the next, and since situations and processes attributed to this area form a context of mutual influence, one considers this to be a field.[1]

Fields can have different degrees of openness depending upon the extent to which they are interdependent with others. The interdependence can be measured by (a) the number of interactions which exist for persons in one field who then move into other fields and cause effects on the observation field, (b) the degree of spacial separation between the fields. A community or a prison may be spacially or socially isolated. A youth centre or a school is isolated in neither of the above ways. A gang of juveniles could be considered as socially but not spacially isolated.

Further, fields can be judged according to their complexity, i.e. according to the variety of situations occurring in them and the number of persons involved. Seen under this aspect, the observation field 'community' is very complex while the fields 'hospital', 'school' or 'place of work in a company' are relatively simple. Both dimensions of openness and complexity are independent of one another.

In a strict sense, the field of observation is not only the field in which the observation is done, e.g. a prison, a hospital, but also the other objects of the respective empirical class, i.e. all prisons and hospitals which are comparable to the object chosen as a sample. It is then a question of the adequacy of sampling and likewise the economics of the research, as to when and to what degree a chosen object represents its class (the field) in terms of identical characteristics of structure, allowing the results to be applied generally to the set of objects classified as one field.

The standardised participant observation, considering the present state of the method, is best used in fields which are relatively closed as well as relatively simple. (This depends of course upon the problem and the hypotheses of a study.) For this reason we will avoid going into the special problems of studies done on communities (Lohmann, 1937; Janes, 1961; Schwartz, 1964; Whyte, 1964) as well as the observation of larger groups (Willcock, 1943; Ferraby, 1945).

The real observation in a field should be preceded by an exploration which provides initial information about the field. The following structured pretest can be conducted by using studies of literature, contents analyses, interviewing or non-participant observation, or several of these possibilities. If non-participant observation is chosen then it would be a pilot study of the final participant observation (see Atteslander, 1969, p. 134, ff). The pretest is indispensable for finding hypotheses, defining the role of the observer, defining the categories for observation and constructing a schedule of observation, in short, for transforming the conceptualisation of the study into a research design. In order to find out the necessary information about the field of observation, one can use the following paradigm which is an extensively revised version of the one Katz (1963, p. 68) presented:

1   Degree of autonomy of the field or degree of interdependence with other fields.
2   Spatial extension.
3   Number of involved persons:
    (a)   Classification of persons (age, sex, etc.)
    (b)   Groups
    (c)   Relations among persons (formal, informal)
    (d)   Goals
    (e)   Distribution of positive and negative sanctions
4   Degree of organisation:
    (a)   Organisation's goals
    (b)   Degree of hierarchical strictness
5   Modes and channels of communication in the field.
6   Recurrent situations in which persons interact:
    (a)   Number and type
    (b)   Localisation
    (c)   Duration

This paradigm requires a relatively extensive exploration of the field of observation. It will not always be possible to gain information for all of the items.[2] Like any other method of social research, participant observation presupposes the existence of preliminary knowledge and hypotheses formed on the basis of this knowledge.

4.2   Units of observation

Every observation of events in which persons are involved refers to a complex process. Several persons and/or other living beings (animals, for example) and/or material objects are involved. In addition to this, the number, kind, position and location of these participants change with time. König (1967, p. 120) pointed out that the average 'sociological facts' (Durkheim) in such a context are not directly perceivable as well-outlined units. 'On the contrary, they must first be "fixed" singly by combining many details, each of which is again complex and combinable as well as dispersed through time and space, making them difficult to attain.'

A general requirement for the selection of observation units is that every unit should be a part of the field which must be perceivable as a whole, and for this reason must not consist of elements which are dispersed through time and space.

One can hardly find suggestions in literature as to what could be considered a unit of observation. There are basically two types of definition, neither of which excludes the other: one is reductional, the other functional.

The *reductional* refers to the non-participant observation of discussions in small groups (Bales & Gerbrands, 1948; Bales, 1950, 1967). Bales (1967, p. 158) chooses as an operational definition the smallest unit of behaviour, which has a meaning complete enough for the observer to read it or so that it can cause a reaction from a partner when using it in a discussion. This type of unit, however, is hardly applicable to events happening in the street, in a hospital or even in a community. The unit of observation used in the standardised participant observation of such fields must be more complex.

The *functional* definition of units as suggested by Heyns (1948) and Peak (1953) is more appropriate for the complexity of interactions. Without defining it, Peak uses the term 'functional unit' to describe those units which she wants to measure later using scales, factor analysis and other statistical methods. Heyns' approach is more exact. In his article 'Functional Analysis of Group Problem Solving Behaviour', he considers all intellectual statements as a functional unit which refer to the solution of a problem a group is discussing: 'any subject-predicate unit which is classifiable into a single category'. Such units would be, for example, goal-setting, information giving, development planning. They are very similar in content to the above-mentioned categories set by Bales. They get their strictness through their functional reference to the objects to be observed and the goal of the observation. They are functional in terms of the structural functional theory (without explicit reference to this theory by the author), i.e. they contribute in different ways to the attainment of a goal, in this case, problem solving.

Now, it is very difficult to determine exactly the goals and subgoals of a field and then deduce the function of a unit from these goals, without referring to the theories of goal-oriented systems which have been abstract up till now.

For this reason, it seems useful to ask what is being observed during participant observation. This results in the extension of the concept 'functional unit'. Almost always, the sequences of behaviour contain certain regularities or recurrent elements. 'Situations' should be chosen as units under this aspect of a sociological theory of action. A situation is a complex of persons, other organisms, material elements which are usually bound to some extent to a certain location and time period and which as such constitute a perceivable unit. Subunits in such a situation would be expectations, reactions, verbal and nonverbal, sanctions and goals of those persons involved. During the process of interaction these units change. Choosing situations as units has the following advantage: (a) they are relatively easy to outline, (b) the frequency with which they occur gives cues for their importance for the interaction in the field, (c) it is easy to integrate them into sociological theory by means of hypotheses, (d) one can apply the theory of sampling to them (see section 4.2.1).

It will be possible to identify those situations which occur more frequently during the pretests or by other information about the field gathered in advance of the actual field research. Often the spacial location of these situations can be identified. This was the case of the situations in our field 'youth centres', locations being: in the hall during a dance in the evening; in interest groups; in a group in front of the building (parking lot); in a table tennis group in the gym, etc.

The above list illustrates the many abstractions or levels of complexity possible for defining situations. In the same way, the situation 'evening dance' can alone be divided into the units 'admission fee', 'greeting', 'dancing'. The situation 'paying admission fee' can be divided finally into the units used by Bales. Such a regress, however, is a mere possibility. According to the above definition of situation, it is not possible to divide situations infinitely (the situation 'admission fee', for example). The determination of situations, or observation units, is variable only in that several situations can be combined to make a single global one. The necessary level of complexity of a situation should be based upon hypotheses: if the relatively complex situation 'hall' is sufficient for testing hypotheses, then it doesn't have to be redivided into further subsituations or segments. When defining situations, one must of course consider whether they are accessible for participant observation.

It is theoretically possible, and in very complex fields of observation even methodologically necessary, to speak of a situation, then, when several observers are forced to observe sequences of behaviour, which are closely related functionally, at different locations at the same time or one after another; we have a global situation in which the single observed parts are situation segments; the whole situation is made up by coordinating the single segmental recordings. This would be relevant for the field 'community' which is otherwise not dealt with here. An example: In a study done on a community, the (complex) situation 'public festival' is supposed to be observed. Observer A takes part in the situation segment 'parade'; observer B takes part in the situation segment 'festivities tent'; observer C takes part in the situation segment 'reception in the city hall'; observer D takes part in the situation segment 'traffic situation at the market place' etc. The researcher later combines these different segments to make up the global situation 'public festival' and compares it to other situations in the community.

Summary: Prerequisites for using situations as the basis for observation units are:

1   Establishing the relevance of the situation for the hypotheses in the study.
2   Minimal knowledge about the relevance of the situation for the field of observation (the exact relationships to other situations will be explored by the observation itself).
3   Determining the number of, and degree of complexity of, the situations which are to be observed.

Every situation consists of a number of elements or dimensions at which the observation is to be aimed. Just what the elements of situations are has been discussed in works on sociological theory as well as in works on methodology of participant observation (Peak, 1953; Selltiz, Jahoda, Deutsch & Cook, 1962; Jahoda, Deutsch & Cook, 1967). Both seem to be pretty much in agreement, therefore one reaches the following list of dimensions of situations:

(a)   Context:
     (i)   Previous situation
     (ii)   Following situation
     (iii)   Instigator of situation
     (iv)   Frequency of the situation
(b)   Structure:
     (v)   Duration
     (vi)   Persons (number and status)
     (vii)   Other organisms (e.g. animals)
     (viii)   Material objects
     (ix)   Location
(c)   Process:
     (x)   Stimuli and reactions of the persons
     (xi)   Sanctions (rewards and punishments)
     (xii)   Goals
     (xiii)   Media of communication (speech, gestures, mimic, telephone)

(xiv) Possible alternative ways of behaviour, that didn't appear

(xv) Results of the interaction

Those of the above dimensions which belong to the context of the field should be researched during the pretest if at all possible. The observation schedule determines the categories according to which will be observed, as well as these dimensions to which special attention should be paid (see section 4.3).

4.2.1 *Application of the theory of sampling*

As in the case of interviewing, one can apply the theory of sampling to participant observation. The sample in this case does not refer to persons from a population universe, but rather to the times or locations of the situations. If one considers the field of observation from which to draw a sample as the universe, in which everything cannot be observed due to the complexity of the field, then every observation design always implies a sampling from the total interaction in this field. There are many methods available to ensure that the selections made during an observation are subjected to a controlled method in contrast to selections made by the single observer's (biased) interest.[3]

First of all, when there is little preliminary knowledge about the field of observation, one should attempt to use some kind of random sampling from the total of possible time in which observations can be carried out at all. The 'possible' time depends on the field of observation. When doing research in a factory or in a youth centre, one must first find out if the interactions change according to days or months (weekday, month of vacation, etc.). The longest period of time in which all possible events take place could be used as the universe of time, from which samplings of a few hours, days or weeks respectively are made. Prerequisite for this, of course, is that during a longer period, no noteworthy changes take place, otherwise the samples will not be comparable.

This would be a broadening of the technique of time sampling which was used by W. C. Olson and F. L. Goodenough. Arrington (1932, 1937) who refined this technique names a characteristic of the time sampling as being: 'recording of predefined behaviour in terms of occurrence within a specified time interval; systematic sampling of the same kinds of behaviour in selected individuals over a period of days, weeks or months in the same situation' (Arrington, 1937, p. 285). Certain distributions arise from the frequencies of certain behaviours which are comparable from situation to situation over different periods of time. It is possible with the help of simple statistical instruments to figure out the confidence interval and range and variance of interactions within the defined universe. Depending on the field of observation and the amount of time available for the observation, a sample is drawn, which restricts the participant observation to a specific number of observations, each consisting of a certain period of time (a period of thirty minutes, four hours, etc.). When using long observation periods it has been shown that samples of short observation intervals prove better than a continuous observation over the whole period (Hasemann, 1964, p. 812, f). One must then decide which situations it is relevant to observe. It would be advisable to pay attention to everything during the period of the observation. In this way the period of time itself would be a unit of observation. There are, however, only very few fields of observation (for example: conversations between doctor and patient) which have so few situations and so few locations that this would be possible. If one did use a period of thirty minutes, only a small portion of all of the situations and locations would be included in the observation. But even in a longer period, of say four hours, one would have to concentrate on certain units. In both cases, one might say, the unit of observation is not defined by the time period.

The time sampling can be supplemented by a sampling of location or space as long as it is possible to divide the field of observation on this basis. This would apply to participant observations in fields like prisons, hospitals, or a community. One would use random sampling at various levels: observations will only take place in one part of all the rooms and then only in certain, randomly-picked time intervals.

The study made by Tausky & Piedmont (1968) is a very good example of the usage of time samplings in participant observation. Two trained and authorised nurses in the surgical station of a hundred-and-fifty bed hospital observed the behaviour of the other nurses (this being the observation unit in our terminology). The time sample in the first study comprised one week (not including the weekend), from 7.00 a.m. until 6.00 p.m.; in the second (control) study, two days. The observation interval was three minutes long. At the end of this three-minute interval, the activities of a nurse were recorded. If several nurses were present, then each nurse was observed one after the other, the order chosen at random: if, for example, there were six nurses at the station, then after eighteen minutes, each had to be observed once. The two participant observers worked in two-hourly shifts. The 'categories' (observation units in our terminology) were fixed by the researchers; there were fifteen in all. Table 4.1 shows the results of this study. We may dispense with an interpretation of content; of importance here is the comparison of the observation period of two days with that of five days. The five-day period differs significantly in only three categories ($p < \cdot 05$). The short period of two days was sufficient in producing exact results.[4]

Finally, if one has very exact preliminary knowledge about an observation field, then it is possible to take a random sampling of the units of observation.

Table 4.1

Behaviour sampling determination of time spent in various activities, in per cent

Nursing personnel	Behaviour categories*															Per cent	Totals Obser- vations	Days ob- served	Nurses
	1	2	3	4	5	6	7	8	9	10	11	12	13	14	15				
Head nurse	2·4	1·2	3·7	—	4·9	—	14·6	—	—	17·1	31·7	22·0†	1·2	—	1·2	100	82‡	5	1
	3·5	1·7	—	—	1·7	—	19·0	—	—	6·9	24·2	38·0	—	1·7	3·5	100	58	2	1
Registered nurse	11·6†	16·3	3·7	—	13·9	1·4	9·3	4·7	1·4	13·5	13·5	4·7	1·9	2·8	1·4	100	215	5	3
	19·3	14·6	1·4	·5	14·6	4·7	5·7	·5	1·4	12·7	13·7	5·2	3·3	1·4	·9	100	212	2	5
Lic. practical nurse	13·4	17·9	1·5	1·5	10·4	6·0†	4·5	6·0	4·5	14·9	10·4	1·5	3·0	1·5	3·0	100	67	5	1
	13·8	17·2	1·7	—	6·9	13·8	6·9	—	3·5	10·3	12·1	1·7	1·7	6·9	3·5	100	58	2	1
Aide	14·3	16·6	8·5	3·1	4·0	2·7	7·6	6·3	2·2	13·9	9·0	1·8	3·1	6·3	·4	100	223	5	1
	12·3	17·5	5·3	·9	8·7	6·1	10·5	1·8	1·8	17·5	8·8	·9	2·6	3·5	1·8	100	114	2	3

*These categories represent the following behaviour: (a) handling patient's body; (b) use or preparation of equipment in patient's room; (c) communication in patient's room; (d) transporting patient; (e) preparing equipment outside patient's room; (f) cleaning patient's room; (g) communicating about patient outside patient's room; (h) transporting medical equipment; (i) walking empty; (j) off-ward; (k) paper-work; (l) communication of administrative nature; (m) stationary non-productive activity outside patient's room; (n) personal time, on ward; (o) transporting cleaning equipment in hallway.

†Differences significant at the ·05 level or less.

‡The number of nurses observed on a particular shift fluctuates somewhat from day to day, and within periods of a day, because staffing patterns shift with a changing patient population. Thus, what appears as an unduly small or large number of observations for a given kind of nurse is a consequence of staffing pattern.

Source: Tausky & Piedmont, 1968, p. 50.

If within a given field there are N different situations, then a sample of n will be chosen for observing.

Limitations of sampling within participant observation can be found in the role of the observer. He will not be able to enter and leave the field to make random observations in the order prescribed by the sampling. Usually there is a necessary warm-up period during which the observer and other persons in the field define his role. This must be accomplished before he can enter the field and make observations. For this reason, one will have to limit oneself in most of the cases to a continuous observation of sequence. Probably the least difficult is drawing samples of complete situations, i.e. using 'situation' as the sampling unit.

In the first case, there is a possibility for the researcher to use a random sample out of the successive protocols of the observers and then make up an ex post reconstruction of the relevant situations. This sampling requires very careful and exhaustive analysis of data. Further, it requires on the side of the observer to make even, exact and attentive observations. Finally, it also has a methodological advantage: the researcher weights the data according to theoretical criteria (situations with analytical relevance), something which the observer, working continually, is not capable of doing. The researcher is able to ignore those observations which contain repetitions or occurred in unimportant situations. In this way an observation which has been carried on extensively because of the complexity of the field can be structured strictly.

4.3 Observation schedule

The observation schedule is the plan that says what and how to observe. It defines the number and kinds of observation units, the especially relevant dimensions of these units, and it illustrates the language to be used in observing. It is the summary of all of the operational characteristics. The relevant aspects of the observation must be deduced from the researcher's hypotheses and from sociological theory. Before going into this in more detail one should examine some experience gained from experiments in psychophysics which Heyns & Lippitt (1954, p. 400) report:

1 When other conditions are optimal, the human being is more accurate when he makes ordinal judgements than when he makes judgements on an absolute scale. . . .
2 Ordinal judgements are more accurate when there are only two objects to be judged at a time. . . .
3 Ordinal judgements on two objects are most accurate when the objects of judgements are brought close together in space and time. . . .

4 Ordinal judgements of two objects close together in space and time are most accurate when the objects are identical on all attributes except those being judged.

Even if the consequences of such results may apply in different ways to respective observation studies, we still reach a general conclusion: the area to be examined must not be too broad; the narrower it is kept, the more exact will be the individual observations.

In view of the dilemma: a general versus a concrete schedule, this means that one should make the instructions in the schedule as concrete as possible. If the schedule is too general, the observer will be overburdened; more importantly, the reports of the various observers won't be comparable because the information will be registered at different levels of abstraction. The schedule must, however, be general enough so that one can find the listed observation topics at every location of observation or object of a field (for example at every youth centre) and that important topics are not forgotten. A prerequisite of this is, again, a pretest in the field of observation.

The observation schedule determines the content and language of the observation. The aim of the schedule is to standardise situations which are to be observed. This is especially important when two observers are not observing the same units at the same time and the control of their results is only indirectly attainable by giving very exact instructions.

4.3.1   *Contents*

For a start, the units of observation are part of the contents. The number and kind of situations at which the participant observer is to aim his attention are to be determined. Because of the numerous dimensions of a situation, it will probably first be necessary to determine those which seem especially relevant for testing the hypotheses of the study. Of the dimensions given in section 4.2 those concerning 'structure' (duration, persons, other organisms, material objects, location) will probably be indispensable. 'Goals' are probably the most difficult of the dimensions of process to observe because the goals of the subjects can only be indirectly identified by observing those choices of action they may prefer and by refusing others (see Friedrichs, 1968, p. 105, ff).

As a result of this, for all those situations in the field to which the given observation categories are not directly applicable (see below), the observation schedule will have to contain operational definitions and/or empirical examples of dimensions or elements of the situation (see section 4.3.2). These operational definitions can easily be in the form of an openended list of examples if the observer has learned to extend these examples logically according to the respective type of observation. Here the problem is choosing the proper 'indicators' of the concepts, a particular methodological problem of participant observation at the given state of research evidence. According to Opp (1970a, p. 133) indicators are defined as 'those designata, contained in an operational definition which are listed as components of the operational definition'.

To clarify: observation 'categories' (see below) are the smallest units of observation or recording of observations including the attributes of the actors. They refer to individual distinctions of indicators or variables in one dimension, analogous to the categories of a code in the interview or content analysis. An indicator can, as a result, be defined by several categories.

Many of the main sociological concepts are defined very imprecisely so that one is constantly trying to make them operational. These concepts have to be given an empirical reference which in most cases differs from study to study. This can be exemplified by our studies about class-related behaviour at a children's playground (Friedrichs, unpublished) and on the organisational structure of a special prison in Hamburg (Friedrichs *et al.*, 1973) in which a number of hypotheses dealt with the degree of social control present in both fields of observation: parents over their children, wardens over the prisoners. Many detailed discussions were necessary to determine a plausible operational definition of 'social control'. Finally, the following indicators were chosen:

Playground:
  Distance between the parents/adults and the children measured in metres.
  Possibility of eye contact.
  Use of eye contact or reading or discussion with neighbours.
  Intervening in a conflict among children; measured by time span between start of conflict and intervention.
Special Prison:
  Period of time during which the position in a glass cubicle in the hall (from which all halls and doors on the floor can be seen) was occupied by a warden, measured in percentage of the total time the glass cubicle was observed.
  Number of cell doors half shut by the prisoners per day (half shut means that cells cannot be seen into).
An example from the field 'youth centre':
Dimension: Sanctions of the director of the centre.
Sanction: = reaction toward deviant behaviour.

Deviant behaviour of the visitors = an action which is in some way not in accordance with the rules of the youth centre director and/or the sponsors either officially or unofficially. Here are some examples: smoking in the afternoon; playing table tennis in street shoes; coming to the evening dance without paying the admission fee; smuggling in alcoholic beverages; using the photo laboratory without signing up in the office; practising of a band while a discussion evening is going on at the same time, etc.

Examples of sanctions: refusal of admittance for two weeks; exclusion from an interest group; notification to the parents; public reprimanding; warning in privacy; supervision of a group which was previously unsupervised; cancellation of a planned dance; withdrawal of an honorary office; collecting a preset fine; setting up a court of honour, etc.

Validity of sanctions = reaction of the affected group/person depending on the degree to which they accept the sanction. For example: obeys without hesitation or comment; shows disagreement and then obeys; initiates discussion between others and the director; protests loudly in public; threatens with countersanctions of other authorities (police, parents, sponsors); secretly breaks a window; sends others to complain to the director; leaves the centre; tries to convince others to strike, etc.

The chosen indicators seem plausible on face-value. Surely one would consider the introduction and usage by the personnel department of control clocks in a factory as indicators of social control. It becomes difficult when that which has been observed is not an indicator, but rather the result of a behaviour which one was about to record in terms of indicators. A good example of this can be found in the study of playgrounds:

Variable 'conflict':
several children want the same object at the same time; sand is thrown and there is destruction with disregard for playground rules.

Are 'throwing sand' and 'destruction' indicators of a conflict among the children or are they reactions to a conflict? Are they not the results, the logical consequences of the conflict, rather than indicating the reason and kind of conflict? When observing the social status of a person or this person's rank in a group a similar problem of adequate indicators arises (see section 8.3).

Plausibility, then, is only an extremely weak and temporary criterion on which to base the validity of an indicator. Methodologically it is a non-explicit concept-validity (Cronbach & Meehl, 1951): the choice of an indicator is only possible on the basis of a theory, a number of non-falsified hypotheses. In most cases we will have to establish either predictive or concurrent validity. The above-mentioned indicators of social control all imply hypotheses, some of these are: Children are so dependent upon their parents that they adjust their behaviour to the looks their parents give them. The more the parents want to watch their children, the closer they sit to them. The more the wardens allow the prisoners to close their doors half way, the less interested they are in direct social control of the prisoners' private goings-on.

50

Psychological research can better maintain statements of this kind because in this field numerous indicators of nonverbal behaviour have been used to analyse the structures of groups, the interaction in dyads or in research on personality structure. The theory of the process of interaction upon which the choice of indicators should be based like the theory of behavioural sociology (Homans, 1961; Burgess & Bushell, 1969; Argyle, 1969; Hummell, 1969; Opp, 1972), is not completely possible without integrating the results of research on psychology of perception and emotions. Nonverbal behaviour patterns should be given more attention when using participant observation since observation categories deduced from research on nonverbal behaviour greatly relieve the observer from effort and errors in the interpretation and transformation of opinions and verbal expressions of feelings. This function of interpretation is often referred to as a principle of participant observation, a kind of hermeneutic arrangement of indicators into ideas (of cultural meaning) (see Claster & Schwartz, 1972, p. 84, ff).

Nonverbal indicators can be grouped according to channels of communication (see Scherer, 1970):

1　Paralinguistics: voice, tone, length of speech, silence.
2　Facial expressions: dimensions of facial expressions and method of expressing emotions.
3　Body movements: movement of the body or parts of the body; developed by Birdwhistell (1960, 1968) into a research area of its own (Kinesics).
4　Eye contact: direction of the eyes, length of time spent looking at or looking away from, correlation between eye contact and other verbal and non-verbal behaviour patterns.
5　Spacial distance: distance and variation of distance between persons in the time. Micro-ecological concepts like 'personal space', standing and seating patterns of group members.
6　Tactile communication: degree of touching of others during interaction, body areas touched, intensity and duration of touching.
7　Odours.

It is to Goffman's merit that he paid attention to the nonverbal elements of behaviour in his work again and again (Goffman, 1971a, 1971b, 1972); of particular interest are his descriptions of complex situations.

The reason for using nonverbal indicators can be found in the sufficiently proven fact that communication proceeds at different levels at the same time. The sentence 'I won't put up with that!' is usually accompanied by a certain gesture, a certain facial expression and a stamping of the foot. This covariance of communication channels has an advantage in that we may – subject to further research – conclude that a great number of equivalent indicators exist. In addition, they provide us with information about persons and interactions which are less consciously controlled than the spoken work. In many cases one can assume that they give us more valid material about the emotions and opinions of persons.

The disadvantage is that 'describing' such behaviour, occurring at different levels and simultaneously is very difficult for the observer: if he has to give a description, he chooses a few behaviour patterns and usually doesn't have sufficient vocabulary to describe them, as Weick (1968, p. 406) has pointed out. Because of this, a few systems of notation which have just been developed for the naming and recording of the nonverbal aspects of communication should be mentioned: Ekman, Friesen & Taussig (1969), Leventhal & Sharp (1965) for facial expressions; Matarazzo, Holman & Wiens (1967) for speech acts; Birdwhistell (1968), Kendon and Ex (in Argyle, 1969, p. 123, ff), La Barre (1964) for body movements; Hall (1963, 1968, 1969) for several of these channels, among them spacial distance.

A basic problem is the atomistic level necessary for observation and analysis. This will be difficult to overcome for the time being: the blinking rate, number of pauses in speaking, crossing of legs, touching the arm of a communication partner while speaking; just what do such indicators have to say and can they be linked with sociological theory?

There may not be any answer to this imprecise question at the moment, at least not in the sense of a number of tested hypotheses that could be formulated into rules for the use of such indicators in sociological studies. Without doubt, in recording the above-mentioned results of research, we are going in the direction of refining the methods of participant observation and working on a theoretical foundation of interaction.

If sampling of time, location or situation has been made in a participant observation, then the schedule will determine when and how long a situation should be observed or what one has to look for within a certain time period or at a certain location. If the time period or situation has ended, the participant observer doesn't have to leave the group and/or location. Instead, he should continue his interaction without observing. He reduces his double role to simply participating. If he broke off his interaction abruptly, it could result in threatening the role of the participant observer, cause grave changes in the field, and even stop communication between his subjects and himself. As far as the hypotheses and the situation allow it, after finishing his intense observations, the observer can continue his participation by carrying on an informal discussion with his subjects. He can try and learn about their emotions, opinions, attitudes and motives as they appeared in the preceding complex of actions. He should not, however, mix this information with his observation data in the protocol, but rather record it separately (for example in a diary).

Further, the observation schedule should determine at what time during the whole inquiry certain units should be observed. One could make the rule that situations which were identified during the pretest as being complicated in structure and/or contained long processes of interaction will be observed last during the total observation period in the field. It will take every observer a little while to get accustomed to the field after his training anyway and for this reason it seems more reasonable to place the more simple situations at the beginning of the field work. The schedule should contain information as to the time of observation for every unit.

Table 4.2

The interactiogram of Atteslander

				Symbol
A	1	Interaction, not initiated by supervisor		J
	2	Contact-interaction (person of low rank leaves place of job to interact with supervisor)		kJ
	3	Interaction, initiated by supervisor		oJ
	4	Interaction, not directly related to job		I
				(or kI, oI)
B	5	Walking around		U
	6	Walking around transporting objects related to job		Ut
	7	Supervisors inspect work of supervised on place of job; inspection of products or machinery		Bi
	8	Looks, without contact		Bs
	9	Helps supervised		Bh
	10	Trainees supervised		Ba
D	11	Paper work		S
E	12	Own work		Et
F	13	No special activity		N
G	14	Leaves room of work		V
Involved persons and other symbols				
1	Labourers			1–40
2	Supervisors			x, y, z
3	Labourers, not belonging to labour-staff			a, b, c, d
4	Fitter			M
5	Telephone			T

Source: Atteslander, 1959, p. 159 and 1969, p. 149, f.

c

Defining the units of observation is followed by their transformation into behavioural categories which illustrate the smallest units of recording. A good example of this is the *Interactiogram* by Atteslander (1954, 1959). It shows a further development towards a systematised observation and the effort to define behavioural categories as they originated in secondary analysis, based on studies about communities (Chapple & Arensberg, 1940) or on observations in factories (Roethlisberger & Dickson, 1956; Homans, 1960). In a non-participant observation in a factory (Atteslander, 1959, 1969) which dealt with the research of the function of supervisors in work groups, the behavioural categories presented in Table 4.2 were used.

Atteslander and his collaborators only recorded interactions which lasted at least five seconds; shorthand was used to fill in schedules that had already been prepared. In this way it was possible to analyse the individual interactions quantitatively according to their kind and frequency.

This schedule used in a nonparticipant observation is easier to transform into a participant observation schedule than Bales' (see section 4.3.3). Probably the categories would have to be formulated more generally or only short intervals would have to be chosen for observation. One must consider, however, that the usage of such categories in participant observation is principally limited by the situations which usually last longer and by the overt participation of the observer which is of course necessary. In only very few cases will the observer have the opportunity to carefully and only temporarily remove himself from the situation to do his recording, with paper and pencil and unseen by those he has just observed. Sometimes a time up to as much as several hours will elapse between the observation and its recording. The categories must satisfy this condition. They must fit the abilities of the observer's memory and must not overtax it.

4.3.2 *Language*

The possibility of determining exact behavioural categories depends mainly on the number of heterogeneous units of observation of the field. The less different the situations to be observed the more exactly can the categories be defined. For this reason, a schedule with exact categories has not yet been developed for a complex field with many units. The instructions given by Peak (1953, p. 245) or Selltiz *et al.* (1962, p. 209, f) as well as our own list of relevant dimensions (section 4.2) are not detailed schedules with categories, but outlines to help with constructing more exact ones. In most of the studies one will limit oneself to the given categories that are more general. The vocabulary of such schedules is very important in these cases because broad, inexact categories often mislead the observers into perceiving the same events in different ways. Or better said: the chance of reconstructing *one* reality from the number of agreeing observations drops.

The language used in the schedule is different from that of the researcher. The language of observation should be kept apart from the language of analysis and theory since the code of observation is only in terms of an operational translation linked to those concepts which are used in the formulation of hypotheses and in interpretation. For this reason, it is necessary to provide the observers with a certain language. The items given with behavioural categories which are rather inexact should be verbs and adjectives that correspond to perceptible events; e.g. walk, lift, put hand on shoulder, laugh, hit; slow, big, broad. One should avoid giving nouns (friendliness, authority) or even sociological terms (role, power) because there are often interpretations in a broad sense hidden in them.

These problems seem especially relevant for the observation of elements of a situation which deals with processes since here the validity of the observations can be easily impaired. A good test question when transferring concepts and hypotheses into indicators might be 'Can you see or hear it?' 'The observed forms of overt behaviour in concrete social situations can themselves become *indicators* for the direct observation of aspects of the sociocultural system which are accessible nowhere else' (Mayntz, Holm & Hübner, 1969, p. 89).

Nevertheless, irrespective of providing strictly fixed or general behavioural categories, the problem arises of limiting the subjective interpretation of such categories of language. It would be fictitious to assume that providing uniform words for all of the observers would automatically provide similar usage, i.e. a high reliability of observations among all of the observers. Participant observation is generally bounded by the varying usage of language due to the process of socialisation. This can be most clearly seen in describing behaviour which contains more complex individual segments that are not so readily separatable as Bales requires for his categories.

One should try, in spite of this, to reduce the individual semantic variance in the interpretation which results from various language usages among the observers. The schedule and its categories are intended to provide the observers with a specific language and thus, a specific way of perceiving. Assuming that L. Wittgenstein's hypothesis is correct, the meaning of a word is to be found in its usage; then the next step is to determine the usage of the given words too. It is assumed that usage develops during a learning process in situations so that slowly, but surely, words take on a specific and relatively dependable connotation in a semantic space. This semantic space has a quite simple structure and can be easily described in terms of three main dimensions or factors (Osgood, Suci & Tannenbaum, 1957; Hofstätter, 1955, 1966). Every time an observer is trained and whenever certain categories and words are tested, the possibility is given and the attempt is made to develop a uniform usage. One can also refer to such training observations like the one Katz (1953, p. 84) suggested. In a preliminary test, several observers code the same event using the categories worked out as a guide. Only the categories which all observers generally agreed to are kept.[5]

An even more exact test of the language usage for important categories and words can be made by letting the observers judge the words on the basis of a semantic differential before and after the pretest phases. In this way one can obtain a measure of agreement in the usage of the language. (For the method see Hofstätter, 1966, p. 236, ff.)

The given categories also have another purpose: they not only designate what is to be observed but also that which doesn't happen. The greater the number of given observation alternatives, those things one should look out for, the easier it will be for the observer to recognise those behaviour patterns which do not appear in the situation or which he had otherwise overlooked as a matter of course (see section 3.1). In this way, those expectations the observer usually brings into the situation unconsciously, and which influence his perceptions as well as his reactions as a participant, will be reduced.

4.3.3 *Records*

Observations are made hastily: the exactness of memory decreases with time. As proven by the psychologist H. Ebbinghaus and later experiments the following relation holds: that which the observer remembers is inversely proportional to the logarithm of time which has past. In addition it is true that familiarity (redundance) with that which is to be remembered increases the ability of remembering. Since the observed situations usually contain numerous individual events it will be increasingly probable that when a longer period of time passes between observation and recording, only certain actions will be remembered. These are actions which, for example, appeared frequently, or actions which fit together well according to the expectations of the observer.

From this we can deduce some rules for protocolling the observations:

1   The more complex the unit of observation and/or the greater the number of dimensions in the unit to be observed, the smaller should be the period of time between observation and recording.
2   The loss of exactness of the protocol is largest in the time (one or two hours for example) right after the observation. The loss which occurs after this initial time period (one or two days for example) is relatively smaller in quantity. If possible, the recording should take place right after the observation.

These rules imply a certain form for the observation schedule. The more complex the units, and the more exact the protocol has to be, the stricter must be the formulation of the schedule. Bales' (1967, p. 154) schedule of observation fulfils these qualifications in an almost ideal way (see Table 4.3). According to his categories usually several non-participant observers observe the discussion of a group of persons by recording the contents of the remarks of the speaker as well as of the addressee(s). The number of the speaker and the addressee is recorded besides the respective category of the schedule. If for example, person number 6 says to person number 2: 'I don't understand that,' then the observer records under category 7: 6 → 2. If one is using a mechanically moved slip of paper, the *Interaction Recorder* (Bales & Gerbrands, 1948) or relatively long forms then one can also record the location of a statement (interaction) in the sequence of statements.

Bales' method has been applied and expanded very often, usually to make it fit some special fields of observation. We may point to a number of German studies which were aimed at the analysis of behaviour of pupils and teachers in the classroom (Müller-Petersen, 1951; Winnefeld, 1957; Slotta, 1962; Tausch & Tausch, 1965; Roeder, 1965a, 1965b).

Among others, the following behaviour categories were used in three inquiries: *pupil:* reading, reading aloud, writing, watching, listening, drawing, organisational activities (for example sharpening a pencil), group work, individual work, doing nothing; *teacher:* executing discipline, giving a lecture, asking questions about the work, working with individual pupils, being passive, discussion in the classroom. Two observers observed simultaneously one pupil and the teacher for a period of seven minutes. Every fifteen seconds the behaviour of the pupil and of the teacher was recorded in a schedule by using a check. The schedule consisted of categories running vertically and units of time running horizontally (Roeder, 1965a, p. 410).

This kind of elaborate schedule is without a doubt fitting for the complexity of the observation assignment. It provides us with data which are easy to quantify, and upon which refined statistical operations can be applied. Nevertheless, its use is limited to nonparticipant observation. Moreover, in terms of our definitions, the field of observation is identical with the unit of observation; it deals with the single situation 'classroom' alone. In spite of these limitations, such studies may be able to give us hints for possible application within the realm of participant observation (see also Zander, 1967).

A completely different way to observe and record behaviour patterns is to use audio-visual methods. Certain units of observation or parts thereof are filmed according to the pre-prepared plan and the sound is recorded. In this way the material can be observed and analysed by many raters. This method was used by Gesell (1931, p. 51, ff) and later by Volkelt (1934) for the observation of small children. Recently it has also been used in studies of socialisation in kindergarten (Tausch, Barthel, Fittkau & Hübsch, 1968).

Table 4.3

Categories of Bales' interaction analysis

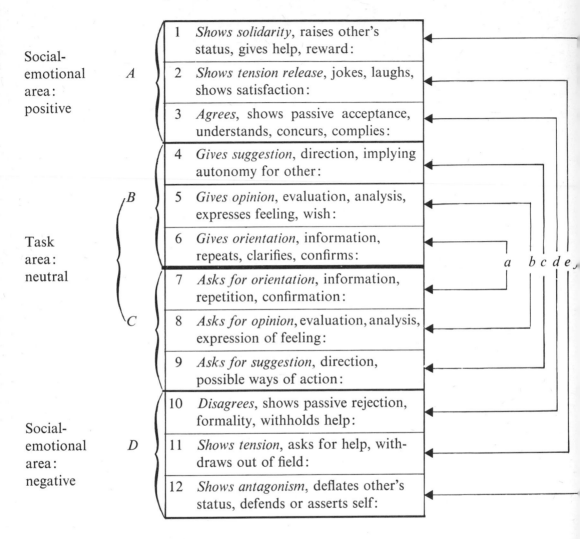

KEY:

a Problems of communication   *A* Positive reactions
b Problems of evaluation   *B* Attempted answers
c Problems of control   *C* Questions
d Problems of decision   *D* Negative reactions
e Problems of tension reduction
f Problems of reintegration

Source: Bales, 1967, p. 154

Even though one is not dealing with participant observation, one should test to what extent this technique can be used at all or at least in relevant parts (e.g. certain situations) of the field; this should be done before the study begins.[6] It is the optimal method of collecting data where the peculiarity of the field makes it possible. 'Peculiarity of the field' means among other things, the agreement of the subjects when filming does not change the field and the theoretical relevance of the situation which is recorded by the filming.

In the greatest number of cases, participant observation must remain dependent on recording observed situations in a standardised way without the aid of schedules used in non-participant observation or films. The observation schedule, a 'questionnaire about reality' has three functions: the guidance of the language, content of the observation, making recording more easy.

It might be suggested that the schedule be divided into two parts: Form *F* (frame) which contains the framework for the entire participant observation, and Form *U* which specifies the instructions for observing every unit of observation. Form *U* can be mimeographed and used as protocol for every single observed unit. The two above-mentioned parts should as a minimum contain the following:

Form *F:* Number and kind of units of observation; when to observe a unit
  (beginning, middle and end of observation period); role instructions for the
  participant observer; time and interval of the observation.
Form *U:* Factual duration of situation; relevant dimensions of the unit (see section 4.2); behavioural categories for every dimension; additional aids (physical traces, drawings, scales).

The schedule taken from a study dealing with effects of social class on the interaction at children's playgrounds (Friedrichs, unpublished) which was mentioned above, also has this form. The Form *U* was further divided into two parts: one Form *PG* to aid the recording of play groups, and one Form *CP* to help in recording children–parent behaviour. The observation schedule for observation in a special prison in Hamburg (see Appendix) (Friedrichs, Dehm, Giegler, Schäfer & Wurm, 1973) also has a comparable graphic structure of behavioural categories and units.

Schedules structured in this way hinder the uncertainties an observer might have about what he should record; moreover, the observations and the material are recorded right from the start in a way relevant for testing the hypotheses. An example of the difficulties which would otherwise ensue is Whyte's (1961) dilemma in systematising his observations in Cornerville. Whyte had the choice of grouping his data either according to topics (politics, church, family, etc.) or according to groups to which the observations referred. He chose the second alternative and added to it a catalogue with key words and a cross reference, since at the moment of his decision, he did not yet know just how he planned to analyse his material. This dilemma was a result of his explorative interest in research and his desire to work as exactly as possible. The Lynds (1929, 1937) chose the other way in their study of Middletown.

Other authors (e.g. Blankenburg, 1973, Humphreys, 1970) have constructed schedules which are organised less analytically. Because of this they represent research plans that are more explorative and descriptive (reprinted in Friedrichs, 1973a). The possibility of including ordinal scales in the recording process (due to a low degree of participation) is useful to Schumann & Winter's (1973) 'Observation outline in the study of trials in the penal courtroom'.

Reiss (1971) chose yet another way to construct observation schedules. It is very similar to the above-mentioned definition of 'questionnaire about reality'. This schedule constructed for the participant observation of police action (Reiss, 1967, 1968a, 1968b) is constructed like a questionnaire; the individual observations and behaviour patterns are recorded by the use of complete questions. This allows for a recording ex post, after the actual observation. As Reiss (1971, p. 11, ff) pointed out this kind of schedule has the advantage of reducing errors of memory. (For an excerpt from these schedules see Appendix.) The other type, used by Reiss, is characterised by a questionlike formulation of items, and therefore permits recording after the observation interval. There is no basic difference between the two kinds of schedule. Nevertheless the schedule mentioned first with the graphic design seems to be clearer and can be filled out faster, especially when one has to record many situations (in other words: units of observation) in a relatively short time. However, this type of schedule requires recording on the spot.

It is rather difficult to discuss the problems involved in recording on the spot versus after the observation interval, because there have not been sufficient studies done using the method of participant observation. From the few there are, only some of these have used standardised observation and recording instruments. It is unfortunate that very few authors deal to any extent with their methods in their publications or even reprint their schedules. As a result of this, not only a cumulative research but also the establishing of reliability and validity criteria is hindered.
Recording of processes.

Does an isolated and recorded action tell us a little less or even something completely different from this same action seen as part of a sequence of actions, based on a stimulus and with a possibly intended effect on a following reaction? I have the feeling that I have missed the most important part, not only because I am able to observe only a few situations, but also because of this supposed inadequacy of the schedule. (Wurm, p. 4)

This comment, made by an observer of the prison study hits the nail on the head; the problem being the recording of complex interactions in a sequence. (It should be added here, that the same observer retracted the criticism he made at the beginning of the study and was able to work with the schedule. Certain processes can be separated into their individual elements for observation.)

Since every participant observation always has the same, sometimes underestimated, problem of necessitating fast recording, the recording of behaviour sequences should not result in new diagrams each time from the observer. The recording of processes – which we are working on now – will probably only be possible by including flow-diagrams in the schedule with fixed alternative routes of action which can be marked by the observer. To be able to do this, however, a very detailed knowledge of the field is necessary.

The more strictly the schedule structures the observations and correspondingly standardises the recording, the sooner will the participant observer forget those observations which may seem important to him but are not provided for in the schedule (e.g. because of lack of knowledge of the field of observation). In order to keep in mind such information, the observer should maintain a diary in which he can note just such observations. The diary has other advantages in that it can correct the schedule and relieve the observer of the narrowness of his role by giving him a bit more scope for unrestrained recording.

Finally other possible aids in participant observation should be mentioned. Among these are the instruments of observation listed in the following section: positions of individual members of a group in spacial measure, facial expressions, gestures, rating scales or other instruments for structurising the data.

4.4   Aids in observation

In every participant observation there are a number of additional methods one can use which are otherwise used in part in other research contexts. Some of them are special techniques used in social research which in this case only have the characteristics of 'aids'. They are only given as examples and it is up to each individual researcher to choose or develop other techniques useful in participant observation. Besides films (see section 4.3.3) and other methods, the following aids which were to an extent already part of the above-mentioned channels of communication can be used:

1 *The spacial grouping of persons.* It can often be useful to observe and record the spacial positions which members of a group have to another whether they stand or sit. Who sits/stands where? How far away from whom? One can assume that the leader or most important member of a group does not stand at the edge of the group, but rather in the middle, and/or that he stands (sits) in a position where he can be seen by as many of the others as possible. From the distance persons are from one another one can even draw conclusions about the social relationships between them and the leader or about the status of others in relation to the leader. Whyte (1961) found that persons having a similar outlook also stood on the same side of the room. He called his method 'positional mapmaking'. These results taken at a micro-level of groups, remind one of the ecological segregation on the macro-level, most clearly recognisable in the unequal distribution of social strata over the parts of a metropolitan area.

Webb, Campbell, Schwartz & Sechrest (1966, p. 123, ff) give numerous examples of how to use spacial patterns of persons as indicators. They quote among other things, a study on the effect of ghost stories on small children. The children sat in a circle and listened. As they were listening, the diameter of the circle shrank, from the first story to the last, from about eleven feet down to about three feet. The authors attributed this to a reaction to induced fear.

2 *Attributes of persons in groups.* Even without being able to understand the language of a group, it is possible to find out something about the individual members and their relationships to one another. Clothing can be a clue to the status of a particular person. For example, wearing an overall or different types of white coats seen in hospital can be indicators of status. The important one here is the observation within interactions of symbols which are 'important carriers of information for the subjects' (Friedrichs, 1968, p. 85). Symbols can be: overt behavioural attributes (verbal, gestural) of subjects, material objects of a situation (e.g. the furniture of an office as indicator of the rank of a person in a corporation), or certain styles of communication. The status of a person can also be documented when he greets or says goodbye to another person. One must pay attention to who shakes whose hand, who stretches his hand out first, or in what order people greet one another or introduce one another. Such behavioural and physical attributes become symbols when they can be connected with certain situations and/or subjects as typical and with a certain regularity. A certain meaning manifests itself in these behaviour symbols (more exactly, a structure based on values and norms) and becomes apparent to subjects as well as to an observer.

62

During the process of discussion in groups with more than four members subgroups usually develop. When trying to discern something about the status or reputation of an individual, one should pay attention to the following: during the discussion of which topics are subgroups formed?; who initiates an interaction?; which member of a subgroup disrupts the discussion in order to listen to the discussion in another subgroup?; (and requests that the other members of his subgroup do the same?); who can interrupt whom constantly without being reprimanded?; who is looked at when he speaks?; if one of the members asks a question, at whom do most of the other members look before the question is answered?

For more information on this topic, we may suggest the studies done by Buzby (1924), Estes (1938), and Taft (1955) (see section 4.3.1).[7]

3 *Rating scales.* In order to improve the reliability of observations rating scales can be included in the schedule of observation, on the basis of which the participant observer is able to classify any parts of observation units. Such rating scales are well established in psychological research. One rates a person according to how intense a certain attribute (hostility, state of health) is, an object (quality of the apartment, general impression of a room) or the intensity with which a certain activity is carried out. The kinds of scales most used are, according to Guilford (1954, pp. 263–301; see also Edwards, 1957; Hasemann, 1964, p. 821, f; Sixtl, 1967):

(a) numerical scales: five or more categories are given to which numerical values are coordinated, e.g. the Likert scale: $5 =$ very pleasant, $4 =$ pleasant, $3 =$ indifferent, $2 =$ unpleasant, $1 =$ very unpleasant.

(b) graphic scales: a horizontal or vertical line, 4–6 inches long is given, the two ends of which represent opposites; in certain circumstances, intervals between the two extremes can be verbalised. The evaluater marks along the line, e.g. the intensity of an action 'How did person A do his work?'

——————————————————X———————————————————————— -

very quickly   normally   very slowly

(c) cumulated points: positive and negative adjectives are given. The positive ones get $+1$ each and the negative ones get -1 each. The observer writes down the fitting adjective for each observation. For example, 'The nurse handles the patients . . . attentively, in a friendly manner, feeling bored, politely, strictly, considerately, excitedly.'

The usage of these rating scales implies that the postulated one-dimensional form of the scale offers the correct attributes of the objects, a requirement which is very difficult to fulfil in a strict sense. If general comparison to other data can be made, then it is useful to work with rating scales. According to the experience made so far they seem to have a sufficiently high validity.

Vidich & Shapiro (1955) had the prestige of 547 members of a small town rated by participant observers on a 12-points-scale with exact verbal references. In addition to this, they had the same rated by interviewing the same persons, using sociometric choices. The agreement between the judgements of the observers about one person and the number of sociometric choices received by this same person proved to be quite good (no correlation coefficient supplied). Kirkpatrick (1933) got similarly good results when he first had the standard of living of 781 farmers (appearance of the farm) rated by observers, and then had interviewers inquire as to their costs of living (rent, clothes, food, etc.). Here the ratings of the observers about the appearance of the farms agreed most with the interviewed indicator 'rent'. Further examples can be found in the scales used by Knauft (1948). In the youth centre study several significant correlations were found between the judgements of the observers and the corresponding characteristics of youth gathered by the interview data (see section 8).

Rating scales are especially important in situations where several participant observers observe the same units of observation either at the same time or immediately after. In such cases the scales become good aids in testing the reliability of the observers. If there is no possibility of having a unit observed by several observers, then it is recommended that the observer and other 'experts of the field' (for example key persons) be permitted to use rating scales in fields which will not be distorted by the measurement. This will provide a comparison similar to that above. In any case, the researcher should be aware of the fact that it is only worthwhile to use this aid when the observers and/or experts will be able to observe the subject *repeatedly*.

4 *Sociometric tests*. The observer can test the distribution of the subjects according to status, popularity or intensity of group relations gained by observation data very easily by using sociometric tests (again, without changing the field). For example: who chooses whom for leader, as their confidant or partner in activities under certain circumstances? (See among others Bastin, 1967; Mayntz, Holm & Hübner, 1969, p. 122–33.) The data from these tests can also be used to help construct quantitative group-indices (e.g. cohesion of the group). If several sociometric tests are given, e.g. at the beginning and at the end of the participant observation, information can be gathered about the change of interactions in the field, something which can be used as an extension or control of the corresponding observation data.

It will seldom be possible to implement an exact sociometric test on a great number of persons. In such cases, however, when random sampling of a smaller number of persons and regular observations of this group are available, the sociometric method can be used to organise and generalise the observation material, e.g.: what relationships in the interaction result from reappearing constellations among the persons *a, b, c, . . . m* and the groups *x, y, z* (see points 1 and 2)?

5 *Physical traces.* Finally we should like to suggest the use of material objects as indicators of the behaviour of persons (see Webb, Campbell, Schwartz & Sechrest, 1966). One can pay attention to the degree to which objects are worn out or used up. One should pay attention to objects which are left lying around, to how new objects are, etc. Melton (1933) carried through some unusual studies of this kind about the relationship between museum architecture and the behaviour of the visitors there. He was able to find an 'exit gradient', i.e. visitors usually took the shortest path between the two doors in a museum room, and they looked at the pictures near the exit less often than at those near the entrance, irrespective of how tired they were or how many pictures they had already looked at. Duncan (quoted by Webb, Campbell, Schwartz & Sechrest, 1966, p. 36, f) measured the attention which museum visitors paid to objects, using the frequency with which the linoleum squares in front of the different objects had to be replaced. Other authors have studied the usage of books and magazines by testing the degree to which the pages were dirty or by slightly gluing the pages together with invisible glue.

All of the methods mentioned here have the status of aids in participant observation. They only then help to standardise the method, when one has exact hypotheses as to what such indicators as grouping, wear and tear, erosion etc. are supposed to measure. If one wants to use them for operationalising single variables of participant observation, i.e. of elements of the unit of observation, then one has to deduce them by specific hypotheses and test them in special pretests. In sections 6, 7, and 8 we will show how some of these aids can be used meaningfully and to what degree they prove valuable empirically.

4.5 Data analysis

Standardised participant observation, used for analytical comparisons and for testing empirical relations implies by definition an intersubjective testable strategy of data analysis. A better testability of the results requires all observation material to fit into a code. One must be able to classify an observed event into an empirically discriminating category, which is one of a number of categories, that make up a description of the relevant distinctions of a one-dimensional variable. The code should be one-dimensional, exhaustive and the categories of the code mutually exclusive. This implies that behavioural categories and coded categories must be identical. The standardised schedule should ideally contain not only all categories of a variable but exactly those later to be used when coding the observations.

This ideal schedule can only be strived at and probably be achieved in such studies which include only very few units of observation which can be observed according to a simple set of categories per variable. Usually, however, deviations from this set or the schedule will be practically unavoidable, and deficiencies will increase with the increasing number of observers. For this reason, the analyst will be confronted with the problem of having to code a certain event on the basis of the material, which is

(a) indicated in different basis protocols under different aspects,

(b) related to different situations (units),

(c) described by using to some degree different categories.

The analyst must, so to say, artificially recombine the variable or event from the individual basic information of the different protocols, and then trace it across through all units (situations). These described properties are, of course, located at a specific section of the schedule. However, in the processes of observation and recording they are distributed successively and situationally. Therefore the operational reconstruction can only be undertaken under the following model conditions:

1   The relevant *variable* must have a clearly defined meaning in the study context; for example, definition of relationships between neighbours in a local area, as (a) communicational incidents of a certain kind between neighbours, and (b) statements about these neighbours and their mutual relationships delivered to an observer or an interviewer.

2   The *dimensions* of the variable which should be observed must be given: which empirical dimensions does the variable belong to? For example 'neighbourly interaction': greeting, a short chat in passing, discussion about a certain topic, lending and borrowing, joint shopping trips, reciprocal invitations, etc., not, however, contact with children or visitors of the neighbours.

3   The *units of observation* (situations) – variables being a part of units – must be given. For example 'spacial ecology of neighbourhood': apartment, window to window, in the entrance house, at the laundromat, on the street, in a store, at the playground, etc. One should also secure information on which units cannot be observed or are irrelevant (e.g. 'shopping' in the situation, 'at the laundromat'). The units of observation must be representative (application of random sampling, see section 4.2.1): for example the window-to-window situation cannot be observed if this form is physically available to only a few inhabitants. A proper methical analysis of the

material will have to conform to the following logic: from m observations in n units using the categories c_x result $m \cdot n$ protocol descriptions of the property x, which contain all the relevant information about x in the object of observation.

4 The behavioural *categories* (or indicators) for x must be constructed specifically for each field, i.e. for all objects of a field and all different units in them. Strictly speaking, these categories must exclusively be predicates of the statements in the protocols of the observers. As a rule, the analyst will accept categories as being sufficient indicators for x if they are similar to those supplied in the schedule. Without such semantic tolerance one would have to demand the language for the protocols to be completely identical for observer and for researcher, free of any further connotations. This is Utopian and it becomes less attainable the more complex the unit of observation and the properties are.[8]

The more these methodological requirements are fulfilled, the sooner will the analysis of the data of a participant observation, which reaches the quality of other social scientific methods, give additional quantitative information about sequences of time.

In this way, the material of a participant observation offers a great number of directions for interpretation. They can be reduced to three analytically independent dimensions: time, unit (situation), and categories. These can be combined to form the model of a cube, analogous to the covariation model of factor-analytical techniques developed by R. Cattell (Figure 4.1). When one dimension is held constant, the empirical covariance or interdependence of the two other dimensions can be examined respectively. From the resulting six different directions of interpretation three are illustrated here as examples:

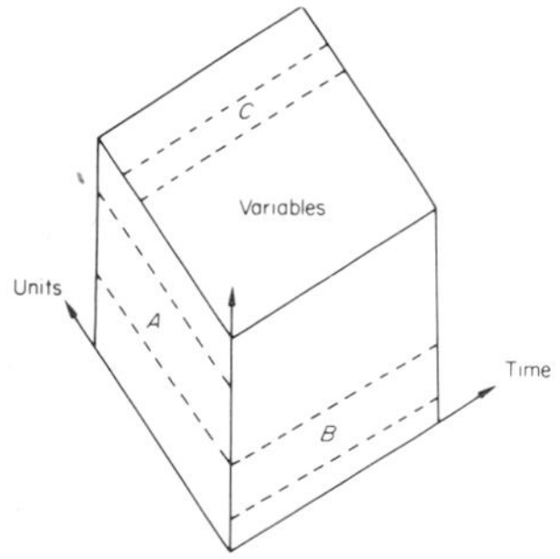

Fig. 4.1   Model of different interpretation directions of observation data

A = Holding time constant; comparison of the categories of a variable across different units,

B = Holding unit constant; comparison of the categories of a variable across different points of time,

C = Holding variable constant; comparison of a unit to different points of time.

Finally, as an additional fourth dimension, a group or a person can be added, allowing further analyses: the comparison of the behaviour of a person (group) in different situations, in a situation at different points of time, etc. In order to use the multidimensional directions of analysis adequately, at the beginning of a participant observation one should decide which direction(s) best serve for testing hypotheses and which corresponding categories, units or points of time, are to be differentiated (see also section 7.1 as well as the section about multilevel analyses).

4.5.1 *Special techniques of data analysis*

We are limiting ourselves here to the presentation of some special techniques with which the raw data provided by the observers can be transformed into codable 'variables' of the field, making it easier to handle them quantitatively.[9]

Basically, the same general methodological principles for coding and analysing the data apply to participant observation as to other research methods used up till now. When considering the methodological specification of standardised participant observation, it seems to us that a rational procedure in the area of data analysis is much more problematic than in other research methods; one must remember that the process of communication between researcher and observer and between observer and field, via the media, schedule of observation and the role of the observer, is much more complicated than comparable relations in other methods.

1 *Ratings by using given categories or checklists.* The most simple form of data analysis is possible, when the schedule aims at a description of the variables which includes the entire period of time of observation. These variables are coordinated to a certain unit and the schedule must contain information about alternative categories which the observer can check, similar to a checklist or rating scale (see de Landsheere, 1969, p. 70, ff). The consistency of the data increases when this is done at different times chosen at random. In any case the observer should justify his use of additional categories not supplied by the schedule by giving additional descriptions of the events. When in doubt, the analyst can check these categories to see if the choice of categories is consistent with the description. The categories marked by the observers can be coded directly, like the closed questions of a questionnaire. This technique was also used with some of the variables of the youth centre research.

2 *Constructing indices.* A more elaborate technique becomes necessary when the individual characteristics (dimensions) of a complex field variable are observed separately. If the values of objects in the different dimensions

have been measured, it may prove useful to reduce this space V with n dimensions in such a way that they form a linear order on a single new dimension: 'By an index we mean a one-dimensional variable, I, with r values, formed by a single-valued mapping of V on I.' (Galtung, 1970, p. 240.)

Mayntz, Holm & Hübner (1969) give the following model as an example: an index of satisfaction with work in a factory should be produced from the observed properties 'job satisfaction' and 'pay satisfaction' (Fig. 4.2).

Job satisfaction	Pay satisfaction		
2 high	d	g	i
1 medium	b	e	h
0 low	a	c	f
	0 low	1 medium	2 high

Fig. 4.2   Job satisfaction and pay satisfaction

The following order of satisfaction at the factory can be set up, based on this two-dimensional property space:

Index Value	Class
4	i
3	g, h
2	d, e, f
1	b, c
0	a

3   *Comparison of empirical and theoretical classifications.* If the predominant part of the raw data consists of diffuse protocols of events and situations because of incomplete standardisation, an analysis is far more difficult. Here one is really dependent upon analysing more complex field characteristics (see section 7.2). The problem lies in comparing relations taken from the basic categories which are not comparable using the help of 'meaningful units'. For example, the leadership qualities of supervisors in a factory are to be analysed on the basis of protocols which were made heterogeneously. In one case, there are records of conversations with colleagues about their supervisor; in another, there are records of discussions between the observer and the supervisor about personnel problems; in yet another, protocol about the interactions between colleagues and their supervisor, etc. The analyst must determine the indicators for each type of data which most clearly relate to the behaviour of the boss towards the colleagues under him in the given context. He then evaluates them according to the frequency of their occurrence.

.These could be in the first case indicators of verbal reactions of the observed; in the second case, they could be indicators of norms mentioned and
attitudes or in the third case, they could be indicators of concrete behaviour
patterns of the supervisor.

It is, of course, desirable that the analyst has a complete schedule of
theoretical classifications of leadership qualities at hand based on hypotheses
and the indicators should extend over all dimensions. The measurement
of the variables is made by comparing the observed with the theoretical
indicators: the leadership qualities L_i are considered to be observed if the
majority of the indicators of the protocols correspond to those theoretical
indicators which define L_i in the schedule.

Eyferth (1966, p. 26) gives an example of the application of this method
in the analysis of child rearing:

> Methods of classification which are useful in the classifying of obser-
> vation protocols were much more thoroughly worked out than the
> attempts at analysing direct observations: Champney (1941) developed
> the 'Fels Parent-Behaviour Scales'. They consist of thirty scales according
> to which the observers classify the behaviour of the parents after having
> visited their homes (this is done according to protocols). Here the
> categories of the variables are recorded by a scale consisting of several
> levels which are established by examples in terms of extreme and medium-
> value categories. This may be clarified by the following two variables:
> (Scale given by Champney 1941)

Activity in the family

Extremely active	Medium	Extremely passive
There is much ten-sion among family members, everybody is nervous, in a hurry, stirred up	Family members walk and work with-out hurry. Alert, but not excited atmo-sphere	The family is indolent, dull and falls flat

> It is interesting to note that among the items, several scales are
> included that do not refer to the behaviour of the parents directly, but
> rather the consequences of their behaviour, the degree of household
> coordination, for example.

The objectivity of this method can be increased when the respective
categories

4   are *judged by several experts independent of another*, whereby the context
of meaning, dimension of observation, and indicators must be known to

them, and where the consistency of their judgements is decisive (inter-rater-reliability). The construction of indices, or the scaling of complex characteristics of a field can also be achieved by:

5   an *empirical analysis using a matrix* which is constructed from the empirical units and indicators and covers all theoretical categories of a variable:

Indicators (categories)	Units (situations) or dimensions of units						
	u_1	u_2	u_3	...	...	...	u_n

i_1	x_1	x_1	x_1
i_2	x_1	x_1	x_1
i_3	x_1	x_1	x_1

:	x_2	x_2				
:	x_2	x_2		x_k	x_k	x_k	x_k
:	x_2	x_2		x_k	x_k	x_k	x_k
i_m	x_2	x_2		x_k	x_k	x_k	x_k

Fig. 4.3   Matrix of indicators and units of observation

Each accepted protocol having the same contents is represented by a certain cell of the matrix. A certain category of a variable is defined by a submatrix; in this way for example, it was assumed in Fig. 4.3, that according to a certain operational aspect, the submatrix (3, 3) represents the category x_1. The logical form of the analysis is: if a phenomenon in $u_r, u_{r+1} \cdots u_{r+j}$, independent of the completeness of the possible combinations, is described by $i_s, i_{s+1} \cdots i_{s+t}$, then follows x_q.

An example:
In a study about the dependence of social relationships upon status, the variable 'reversibility of interaction between blue and white collar workers', is to be measured. The analyst realises that this variable appears in n obser-

vation units (office, stock, assembly line, cafeteria, union session, etc.) and is represented by m indicators of the protocol (1 labourer greets first, 2 white collar worker greets first, 3 labourer does not return greeting, 4 white collar worker does not return greeting, 5 labourer asks for information, 6 white collar worker asks for information, 7 labourer brings information without being asked, 8 white collar worker brings information without being asked, 9 white collar worker gets information from labourer, 10 labourer gets . . . without being asked, 11 . . . after being asked, 12 labourer introduces informal conversation, 13 white collar worker introduces . . . etc.).

The category 'high reversibility' is attributed to the factory i when in the observed situation 'office' the indicators 7, 8, 9, 10, 11; in 'assembly line' 5, 6; in 'cafeteria' 1, 2, 12, 13 etc. appear at about the same frequency. It attributed to the category 'very little reversibility to the advantage of the office workers' when the given and/or other indicators in this and/or other situations described a dominance of the white collar workers in all or almost all interactions.

6   A further possibility in the data analysis of complex variables especially when the empirical relevance of a property dimension is unclear, is the *construction of attribute profiles*. We prefer 'attribute' to 'property' here, since the technique refers to a rather psychological method of ascribing attributes to persons. In addition, methodologically the property to be studied can be considered as a syndrome of the attributes. In such a syndrome, quantitative and qualitative attributes can be evaluated together. This is because the profile, i.e. the relationship among the attributes, is relevant, and not the value of a single attribute.

A fictitious example:
In a slum area, which is to be cleared, a study should be conducted using participant observation, about which influence-groups among the inhabitants might be considered as possible opinion leaders in the process of moving to a new area. The purpose would be to set up a consultation service for the planned move into new housing areas. The observers are to describe aggregates of inhabitants which can be divided into social groups, according to certain attributes, of the following kind.

The analyst compares the profiles of the individual groups and determines the order of importance of social influence of each group in relation to the other inhabitants of the area. He may use a scale of cumulative points, or a classification. If one can maintain on the basis of theoretical framework that the influence increases, relative to the number of following criteria fulfilled: high membership, low fluctuation, frequent meetings, a majority of men, middle age group, central situation within the housing area, activities with a high affinity to the inhabitants of the area or to the general

Table 4.4

Criteria of group analysis	Group A	Group B
1 Numbers of members	3–4	5–6
2 Fluctuation of members	A total of 9–10 alternating members (= medium)	None
3 Frequency of meeting	2–3 times weekly	1–2 times weekly
4 Sex distribution	Men only	Men only
5 Age distribution	65–70 years only	25–40 years only
6 Typical situation of meeting	Bar nearby or benches in front of housing	Parking lot or self-furnished repair shop
7 Typical activity	Card playing	Caring for and repairing of own cars. Conversation about news in housing area
8 Extent of participation in other groups	None	2 members of groups C and D. 1 member of group E

interest of those inhabitants, heavy overlapping with other groups, then one can say that of the two groups under study, group B is to be classified higher.

4.5.2 Multilevel analysis

Standardised participant observation which makes use of the instruments described in the above chapters, deals as a rule with different social objects, more exactly, with statements about the properties of objects at different analytical levels, e.g.:

(a) individual actors are observed in their actions as *persons*;
(b) they are identified within their context of interactions as *cliques*;
(c) sets of cliques produce, according to certain criteria of activities and interactions, *groups*;

(d) different groups are in the spacial context of situations elements of an *organisation*;

(e) several organisations seen as objects of research finally produce the level of local *communities*.

While the observer is basically recording the behaviour of individuals according to elementary categories of a standardised observation schedule, and maybe in addition is recording the respective situational context and the structural antecedents (e.g. size of factory, work or leisure situations, prescribed decision hierarchy) it can be the goal of the researcher, to deduce statements about collectivities (e.g. youth centres, factories, hospitals, communities) from this data. Conversely, he may intend to analyse the pooled random samples of individuals taken from all of the objects of observation (e.g. hospitals) to see what influence certain context properties of the collective have on the observed behaviour. In these cases, the researcher is carrying on multilevel analyses the methodology of which especially Hannan (1970) and Hummell (1972) state in detail. 'It is namely the characteristicum of multilevel analysis, that objects of different order become the object of study at the same time, be it that one considers social units in terms of which subunits form them, be it that when studying the characteristics of individual actors, one pays attention to those social units to which they belong' (Hummell, 1972, p. 13).

If on the basis of material of a participant observation, collective indicators are constructed from individual data (e.g. by constructing indices or using mean values), and these are again related to other individual data, and the influence of independent on dependent individual variables is examined, once with and once without regard to context variables (e.g. belonging to region A, to group structure S), then, in order to avoid ecological, individualistic and other fallacies, it is important to consider among others, the following general principles of multilevel analysis, especially when the given techniques of analysis are used to test equivalent hypotheses:

1 Assertions about the relation of variables designated to individuals (or groups), from different contexts (collectives, systems) need not be valid for single contexts (e.g. hospital X), because the respective internal covariance of the variables can vary among the contexts.

2 The conclusion drawn from collective correlations (e.g. between mean of age and mean frequency of interaction in fifteen groups) and applied to individual correlations (e.g. between age and frequency of interaction of the 200 members of these groups) is not valid, and vice versa. The reason for this is that within each context, its own sociological regularities can exist, causing perhaps the correlations at the individual level to be reversed. (See the classical treatment of this problem by Robinson, 1950.)

74

3 'Purely individual, pure context effects or an additive combination of both can be equivalent to a linear collective regression' (Hummell, 1972, p. 112).

The connection of individual and collective relationships and the method of multilevel analyses is presented by Hummell (1972, p. 91) in the following way:

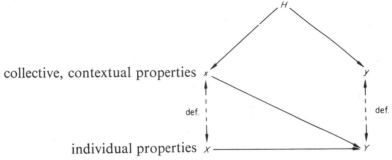

Fig. 4.4   Historical or social causes outside the realm of observation

The broken arrows suggest that the definitions of the collective properties can be deduced from relationships at the individual level.

4.6   Problems of measuring the quality of data

In its standardised form, participant observation is automatically subjected to the same quality criteria of reliability and validity, as, for example, the amply proven psychometrical techniques (see König, 1967, p. 130, f). Undoubtedly, however, substantiating the exact level of quality is much more difficult in our case. Thus, for example, the reliability of the observation depends not only upon the operational clarity of the categories of observation and the choice of representative and consistent units of observation, but just as much on the training of the observers and their appropriate role behaviour (no serious change in the field because of their participation). The reliability of the data is scarcely measurable directly by means of a multivariate analysis of these four factors for which the necessary repeated or parallel observations by different observers in similar, or rather the same situations, would probably have been too costly. As a result, reliability controls over indirect paths were more inviting; such as by the 'secondary' standardisation of the analysis (see section 7) and by indirect testing of the role behaviour of the observers (see section 9).

The same holds true with regard to the validity of the properties observed. Standardised participant observation presents no test to individuals but to complex field situations. The specific structure of this 'test' demands, to be sure, a model of validity which deviates somewhat from that of psychometrics. In this way, both of the main methodological components act as compensations: the complexity of the observation unit (situation) and its variables makes a direct measurement of validity more difficult; the social participation of the observer facilitates the indirect validity rating. Implied is the following relationship: for the variables of the observation (e.g. group coherence: high/medium/low), no suitable criteria for comparison are available in most cases, unless participant observation is supplemented by other research techniques (interviewing, group discussion, experiment), which are capable of supplying relevant external criteria. An indirect inference to the validity of the observation data results, nevertheless, from the fact that the observer himself is a participant in the field, member of the group, role-performer in the object of observation, so that the empirical quality of his records is a function of the degree of his desired participation or his relative integration into the field of observation. The method of participant observation, thereby, takes on regularities from group dynamics and role theory as instruments of control. A certain degree of participation and integration in the field guarantees a certain level of understanding of the field, or rather of the intersubjectivity of the actors' behaviour (*verstehen* as the ability to experience their 'subjectively implied meaning') and thereby an optimal mass of significant information. This guarantee constitutes, first of all, the ability of the observers to give attention to the typical situations and action sequences of the field and to concentrate their observations on them.

It has already been shown that valid and reliable observation consists in a 'deliberate appropriation of the subjective meaning, which manifests itself in the observed behaviour and of its objective social meaning' (Mayntz et al., 1969, p. 88), or rather that the social role of the observer remains linked to his a priori scientific role. Total integration in and adaptation to the observation setting can, for that reason, induce just that emotional bias and mentioned distortion of perception which make it impossible for the observer to regularly keep his distance from the social situation as his scientific role requires him to do. Because participant observation depends on the comprehension of the structure of meaning in the network of interaction observed, without interpreting it according to his own learned cultural prejudices (Vidich, 1955, p. 355; Mayntz *et al.*, 1969, p. 88), the social role of the observer, successfully taken by him, can impede his neutralising these biases. Mayntz, Holm & Hübner (1969, p. 88) write accordingly about this problem:

The acquisition of understanding meaning must, nevertheless, be reflected, at a conscious distance from the appropriated contents. Thus, it is not enough to allow oneself to become naïvely socialised into the sociocultural system under observation, until, in the end, it appears self-evident. Standardised techniques or rules for this process of becoming sensible of other's meaning can scarcely be formulated. In general, it can only be said that, ideally, the interpretation of the observed behaviour should be oriented toward an entirely explicit theoretical model of the sociocultural system concerned.

Even if this statement appears correct in principle, its exclusiveness still requires pragmatic revision:

1   In the case of comparative observations, where there is a separation of roles between research director and field observer, complete knowledge of the observation unit's theoretical model is not to be expected of the observer. Even by the most intensive observation training, important elements of the model can only partially be impregnated in the preunderstanding of the observer.

2   Standardised techniques or rules for that process of learning meanings[10] cannot, in fact, be specified; however, they no doubt can be for the observation of empirical variables according to the situation's operational criteria. Because these indicators (observation schedule) were formulated in connection with the object's theoretical model, the postulated contexts of meaning enter into the observations, which were prestructured in this way.[11] Standardised observation then supplies its findings for examination. It is not suited for the primary exploration of such contexts.

3   Standardised techniques and rules can be constructed, which control the suitability or unsuitability of the observer's strategy by means of checking the observer's role over indirect paths. As a result, two questions provide conclusions about the validity of the data:

(a) Did the observer fulfil the norms of the observation schedule?
(b) Did the observer behave according to a theory of the role of the observer?

A 'theory of the observer's role' is supposed to contain derivatives from empirically confirmed sociological and psychological theorems. The empirical conditions for successful observer behaviour derive from the respective structure of the field (social complexity, degree of accessibility, kind of goals and social control, member status, etc.). If an empirical check of the actual observer behaviour results in agreement with the strategic demands of this theory to a high degree, then, as a result, the chances that the observer has worked in a situation which allowed for an appropriate interpretation of the observed behaviour are good. If, at the same time, he kept to the operational criteria of the observation schedule, then a high degree of validity of his findings is inferred. Examination of the validity and reliability of data from participant observation is, thus, possible on three levels, which can be illustrated in the following way.

Table 4.5

Criteria for checking the data from participant observation

Level	Criteria for checking	Dimension of Objectivity	Validity and reliability*		
			High	Medium	Low
I	Observer's role: strategy of participation and integration	Intersubjectivity actor-observer	+	+ + −	− − + −
II	Observation schedule evaluation: norms and empirical criteria for putting into operation	Intersubjectivity observer-research director	+	+ − +	− + − −
III	Complementary techniques: analogous or complementary variables	Internal consistency of the variables or correlation of different variables according to theoretical hypotheses	+	− + +	+ − − −

*+: criteria of the level being kept
 −: criteria of the level not being kept
The symbols should be read vertically!

The probability of obtaining optimal quality of data is highest, according to this scheme, when all three criteria are sufficiently satisfied (+); it is lowest when only one or none of them is satisfied (−).

Regarding level I: Here the observer's role behaviour is tested, whether he, as participating actor in the field, was accepted and thereby obtained sufficient insight into the relevant patterns of communication. If this is the case, then sufficient reason exists to assume that his records adequately describe the behaviour of the actors, i.e. that the intersubjectivity actor-observer could secure an adequate 'acquisition of understanding meaning'.

Regarding level II: An attempt is made to produce operational consistency between the categories of the research director and those of the observers by means of (a) the observation schedule and (b) the procedure of data analysis through standardisation and observer training. This means an intersubjective clarity of the communication between research directors and observers.

Regarding level III: The 'classical' testing of the quality of the data takes place at this level: testing the reliability by parallel or repeated observations and testing the validity by correlating a property with an equivalent one (external criteria).

Finally, attention is drawn to yet another procedure of data control, that had been suggested by McCall (1969a, 1969b). In order to test the quality of the observation or interview data, McCall (1969a, p. 132, ff) developed at first a catalogue of nine 'categories of contamination', according to which each item (e.g. datum of observation, variable) is analysed; of them, only the three are named here, which are directly related to participant observation: (a) reactive effects (influence of the observer on the field), (b) ethnocentrism (observer interprets the field one-sidedly from his own culture or way of thinking), (c) going native. For each dimension, it is examined how many items are subject to such a contamination (e.g. four) and how many are not (e.g. nine). The quotient from the total number of items and the number of undistorted items (here $13:9 = \cdot 69$) results in the data quality value per category. The sum of the undistorted items of all three categories in relation to the items as a whole then gives us the observational quality index.

In this connection, the data and dimensions can be applied to the statistical testing of the hypotheses of an investigation. In Naroll's (1962) succession, McCall (1969b, p. 237, f) suggests constructing a contingency table of the following form for each hypothesis and field dimension. The respective number of items, checked for errors, are recorded in the cells:

Confirmed hypothesis H

Items according to errors	Yes	No
Dimension A contaminated		
Dimension A not contaminated		

By means of the chi-square test, coefficient of contingency or Fisher's exact probability test, it can be tested as to whether data are too heavily distorted by the participant observer in order to be able to uphold the hypothesis. If a significant negative correlation arises, then only the distorted data are inapplicable for testing the hypothesis and the hypothesis itself can be maintained. If the correlation is significantly positive, then the distorted data hinder testing of the hypothesis; hypothesis, as well as data, should be cancelled. If no significant correlation exists, then the data are not distorted by the respective error dimension: the data, thus, permit a decision to be made on the hypothesis.

One prerequisite for such data analysis is that random samples for the testing of significance are at hand, whereby, once again, we suggest temporal or spacial samplings in the course of the participant observation. The evaluator, when deciding whether an item was distorted or not, is dependent on an objective criterion that can probably only rarely be derived from the observation findings. For the most part, one is, therefore, dependent upon complementary interview data, expert judgements and the like out of which, in turn, the well-known problems from validity testing arise.

Notes

1   See Lewin (1963, p. 273): 'A totality of coexisting facts which have to be regarded as mutually dependent defines a field.' And further (ibid., p. 69): 'Action has to be interpreted by the totality of coexisting facts.' We use the concept field in two ways: (a) as a term for the empirical unity of a large number of elements, and (b) as a term for an area of unchanged social reality which is relatively isolated analytically, contrary of course to the laboratory situation in an experiment and to the verbal communication with each individual in an interview.

2   Arensberg (1954, p. 115, ff) gives another more detailed paradigm for community studies.

3   Webb, Campbell, Schwartz & Sechrest (1966, p. 134, ff, p. 182) and Atteslander (1969, p. 137, f) also pointed out the necessity of time samples.

4   One can see from this that the time sampling within participant observation involves a relationship between numbers of sample units and exactness similar to that of the interview where the reliability of a statement doesn't increase with the number of interviewed persons but rather with the square root of this number.

5   Vidich (1955, p. 359) objected to the preliminary formulation of categories. He maintained that as the observer's familiarity with his surroundings increased, his 'social perspective' changed accordingly. Because of this, he would look at the categories and interpret them differently at different times. This error is reduced, as suggested here, when the researcher and observer are not identical and when the units of observation and given categories in the schedules are not formulated in sociological language. Pretests also help in reducing this source of error.

6   The Institut für Unterrichtsmitschau und didaktische Forschung in Munich has been working with the televising of work in the classroom. The situation 'work group' in a normal classroom, except for the needed equipment, is observed from three monitors and at the same time filmed and recorded. The purpose is primarily to produce audiovisual teaching aids. In addition they are working on an electronically controlled tape-recorder for several observers, with which exact analysis of interactions with the help of a great number of categories are supposed to be achieved. Such an instrument can be used in principle in parts of a participant observation study as well.

7   For information about the problems involved in the observation of behaviour in psychology see also Volkelt (1934), Thomae (1954), Hasemann (1964), Weick (1968), Von Cranach & Frenz (1969).

8   As is known, the neo-positivist-school of philosophy has – in spite of all their attempts – not solved the problem of an empirical base of assertions by requiring 'protocol statements' that refer to physical-psychical phenomena (see Popper, 1969, p. 60, ff). Popper is right when he speaks of replacing the idea of pure empirical experience with objective testability. At a more modest level, this principle corresponds with our suggestion of a primary data control in the phase of data analysis rather than by testing the language homogeneity of the schedule and protocol. This homogeneity should be optimal, but the data analysis should be the final deciding factor over the empirical testability of the results.

9   For information about coding and about the analysis of the data and testing of relationships see especially Cicourel (1964, p. 116, ff), Hyman (1955), König (1962, p. 271, ff).

10   By appropriation of, respectively, experiencing an action's meaning, we do not mean the result of the observer's capability of intuition or introspection, but the application of the *learnt* interpretation of the observed action according to the actor's obvious motives. Successful participation in the social system implies, according to the theory of action (see Parsons & Shils, 1962, especially p. 105, ff), the anticipation of the motivation of alter by ego, i.e. successful role taking by ego implies the anticipation of alter's behaviour expectations in a sort of trial-and-error learning. If the observer qua participation has completed the process, then he succeeds more easily in applying empirical indicators. He describes, for example, the jargon of a clique of young people as communication which provides mutual emotional confirmation, which he probably would have falsely interpreted before as the expression of aggression. In other words: he had learnt, by participating, to attach certain (verbal) symbols to the correct interpretation of action, whereby the former could be valid as objective indicators of the latter (a certain variable).

11   Implied are observation criteria of the following form: the observer should note in which relationship event 'A does x, y, z in the manner S_i or S_k' takes place. According to the theoretical model, this event might signify somewhat of an 'economic behaviour', which means that the model already includes a goal-means-profit motive in indicators x, y, z, S_i, S_k which the observer does not have to disclose or interpret.

5 Participant Observation compared with Other Methods

A complete separation of the individual methods of empirical social research is hardly possible. For this reason participant observation should also be seen as being closely related to other methods. The decision as to which method will be the best, depends upon the conceptualisation of the problem in the study, and upon its transformation into examinable dimensions and specified research plans. The conceptualisation should also serve as an aid in thinking over the relationship between the individual methods and the testing of hypotheses in a study (see a detailed discussion in Friedrichs, 1973b, Chapter 3). Here we will only be able to give a few general allusions.

We have already pointed out in section 1.1 the close relationship participant observation has to other forms of observation. The distinction suggested by Pinther (1971, p. 126, ff) between 'external observation' (the observer is hidden from view), 'internal observation' (the observer is integrated, a participant), 'observation of environment' (observing the objective conditions of the actor's behaviour), and 'experimental observation' (in experiments) appears to us to be rather unsatisfactory, because the separation of the special features in a situation of observation is much too strict since all these features can be relevant for certain research problems in the same study.

When studying the proceedings in a court room (e.g. Lautmann, 1973; Opp, 1970b) or behaviour at a children's playground, we are dealing more with participant or non-participant observation, depending on the role of the observer. One should then consider the different methods as being a sort of continuum. In this way, the aids of the systematised non-participant observation can be applied in studies using participant observation (see section 4.4). In addition, the necessity to use indicators of behaviour, in every kind of observation, is the most important methodological reason for integrating participant and non-participant observation. The only problem here is that the literature dealing with this problem is basically psychologically oriented, i.e. the methods have been developed more for the analysis of personality properties and less for the analysis of sequences of interaction. In section 4.2 we tried to relate some of this literature to the problems of sociological analysis of situations (i.e. conceptualisation plus deduced design). The amount of available information increases with the degree of complexity of the research plan. It can prove necessary to test the hypotheses using a combination of methods and additional aids. Instead of limiting the research, participant observation allows for multimethod studies and sometimes necessitates the integration of different methods. Denzin (1970, p. 186) is easy to follow when he defines participant observation as 'a field strategy, that simultaneously combines document analysis, respondent and informant interviewing, direct participation and observation, and introspection'.

An example of the close connection between participant observation and non-participant observation is the ecological research being done by J. Hoffmeyer-Zlotnik at the Department of Social Sciences at Hamburg University. It is an analysis of the succession in a part of Berlin (Berlin-Kreuzberg) caused by the influx of 'Gastarbeiter' (foreign workers), especially those of Turkish nationality. The topics are the change in the area, the living situation, discrimination and isolation into ghettos of the 'Gastarbeiter'. During the conceptualisation of the problem, it was decided that the single problems could only be handled thoroughly by a design comprising several methods: secondary analysis of statistical data, participant observation of interactions and non-participant observation in the area. During the detailed discussion of the participant observation phase of the research plan, it was discovered that not everything had to be observed in this way; e.g. the number of 'Gastarbeiter' in the streets, their behaviour at squares and number of signs appearing in the Turkish language are all indicators of the process of the succession which can be recorded with the help of photographs taken in a random sample of areas. In addition it is possible to film the activity at some of these locations (whereby the times are again subject to a random sampling of day and time). The precise conceptualisation allows for the use of participant observation only for those problems which cannot be studied with the help of other aids: behaviour in stores, restaurants etc. The hypotheses about the interaction between Germans and 'Gastarbeiter' and between the different 'Gastarbeiter' groups will be tested by participant observation.

5.1 Participant observation and interviewing

The predominant use of the interview in social research is due to the great refinement of this method which was reached during the last decades. The reason why one has so concentrated on the continual development of this method, causing the neglect of other methods, seems to be that the collection of information by using the extensively cognitive medium, language, was easier to standardise. Obviously, validating the inquiry data seemed easier when using preformulated questions than with participant observation which contains greater subjective bias resulting from the strongly affective elements and selective perception. So, one may say that today the biggest mistake of interviewing is not to be found in methodology, but in the fact that it is used exclusively in almost all studies, as Webb, Campbell, Schwartz & Sechrest (1966, p. 1) have put it. The fixation on the interview as the 'royal method' in social research is fatal for three reasons: first, because certain topics are easier to observe or are cheaper to inquire by using the content analysis for example; second, because the other methods can also be refined as the interview has been (including our attempt to refine participant observation); third, because the single methods cannot be used interchangeably, i.e. they are not valid for all areas of research, but rather fit together in a kind of complementary relationship.

The relationship between participant observation and interviewing can be considered from two aspects; generally, in terms of their basic methodological properties, and specifically, in terms of their simultaneous application within the framework of an inquiry.

Basically, participant observation is suitable for research on processes into complex fields of activity with numerous situations and persons, or as a method of exploration to discover relevant variables of the behaviour of actors or in their relation to an organisation; in other words in areas where interview data can be invalid, e.g. because the interviewed subject is uncertain, does not understand questions fully, because subjects are too much involved in a context to see the obvious, because of social desirability effects (Edwards, 1957), or because of social perception (Bruner & Postman, 1951).

Further, not only models of action sequences can be established by participant observation, but also modal situations and modal interaction patterns, in other words, syndromes of one or more actions appearing together respectively. Surely, behaviour syndromes can also be reconstructed from interview data, but only in using more or less complicated techniques of data analysis (overcoding, factor analysis) which involve numerous additional errors of measure. Also, one is often dealing with data which identify opinions and attitudes, in other words only covert behaviour and not overt behaviour as in participant observation, leading to the old dilemma of attitudes versus actions.

Contradictory to all other methods (also to the laboratory experiment to a great extent) by observation methods social activity is studied where it actually takes place. It is in this sense that a thesis by Homans should be understood: 'Some social scientists will do any mad thing rather than study men at first hand in their natural surroundings' (quoted from Madge, 1957, p. 117). This unit of study, the natural setting, is the situation optimally accessible by the (participant) observer, as mentioned in section 4.2.

By inquiring into these kinds of action patterns, participant observation can be used as a complement to the interview or questionnaire. The observed settings always represent hypotheses and concepts in operational form. This could mean that for the interview, a number of the usual opinion questions

D

will be changed into fact questions, in other words into questions about behaviour, if they have proved to be good indicators in observations of further contexts and attitudes. Even situations of field research can be transformed in a shortened form as hypothetical situations into a questionnaire to find out the reactions of the interviewed themselves or their expectations about the reactions of another person in the given situation (Friedrichs, Pongratz *et al.*, 1970). Such hypothetical situations, then, are (a) isolated from the real field context and (b) perceived by the interviewed to a great extent only cognitively, in other words, neglecting important affective elements of the authentic situation. Indirectly, this requires more behavioural thinking in developing the questionnaire so that a closer connection exists between sociological theory and empirical research.

The possibilities sketched out here are also valid for the special case, where within a study the interview and participant observation are used simultaneously. In order to gain a control of as well as additional observation results, a phase of interviewing with a standardised questionnaire can be built into the observation period (this actually happened in the study of youth centres). The beginning and the end of the observation time both appear to be suitable for conducting interviews or distributing questionnaires (see section 8).

If one interviews at the beginning of the observation time, one is able to become better acquainted with the groups within the field of study. The observer gets information about their age, the extent of formal education, their income, denomination, etc. (demographic data) as well as about their attitudes, opinions, class membership, etc. (sociological data). He can, depending on the content of the questionnaire, draw conclusions about the subjects, their characteristics or the degree of their acquaintance with one another (informal groups). These can be used in the further observation. The important disadvantages are that (a) his observations may become one-sidedly directed (selective perception), and (b) his role becomes defined by the interviews, perhaps in such a way that his subjects become restrained towards him. It is just the opposite when one interviews at the end of the observation period: the observer remains more inconspicuous; he can proceed to define his role without exposing the goal of the research; but he loses important information about the subjects of his field.

Whichever alternative one selects, the choice may only be made on the basis of the problems and hypotheses of the respective study planned. It probably would be best to interview at the beginning, this being done by persons other than those who will be doing the observation later.

In certain cases, it can even be desirable to combine the role of the interviewer and observer in terms of personnel and timing: (a) if the field situation is so open and flexible that the role of an interviewer-observer would not be a disturbing factor (e.g. in a group of competitive athletes or test-persons who are accustomed to continuous supervision and scientific control), (b) if the field situation is so restricted that any type of participation of a stranger does lead to changes of the field, the degree of which, of course, would have to be taken into consideration when interpreting the data (e.g. in a prison when the observer is unable to take the role of a fellow prisoner), (c) if the specific research problem necessitates expert information from the subjects in the field, in other words when the subjects can be approached as being experts or co-workers, for example in the participant observation in a new housing estate. Here the data about lodging behaviour and problems of the housing estate were to serve as a basis for planning further apartment houses.

5.2   Participant observation and field experiment

In this book, participant observation is to be understood primarily as a method for discovering the real processes of interaction in their natural setting. In order to reach any kind of standardisation, the conscious or un-conscious influences of the observer on other persons in the field have only been discussed as errors, the number of which are to be minimised or at least made explicit and which must be taken into consideration at the time of data analysis. This proves to be necessary in order not only to attain a valid description, but also to perform exact tests of hypotheses, e.g. making causal propositions about the correlation between situational properties and observed behaviour. One tries to exclude the effects of the observer on the behaviour under study. That does not, however, exclude inducing changes in the field (as in the study by Blankenburg, 1973 about store thefts), as long as these changes are planned and based on hypotheses. The method then becomes either completely, or only in one phase, a field experiment (see French, 1953). Quite a number of such field experiments have been conducted in social psychology, yet the methodology is less elaborate than in laboratory experiments. (See the studies in Swingle, 1973). One of the best known is about the behaviour of young boys in a summer camp conducted by Sherif (1961). Recently quite a few experiments have been conducted regarding bystander effects in situations. One of them was directed towards finding out under what conditions persons are willing to help others, for example when someone suffers a fainting spell in the underground or passes out as a result of too much alcohol (see Piliavin & Piliavin, 1972). These studies have shown that by systematically interfering in a field of action, something only possible in (very) few situations, one can extend the field of participant observation into field experiments inducing behavioural processes.

Decisive criteria for field experimentation is the availability of a study 'in a realistic situation in which one or more independent variables can be manipulated by the research leader and where the conditions of the situation are controlled as carefully as possible' (Kerlinger, 1964, p. 382). If participant observation is applied here as a method of data collection, its operational criteria are the same as in other research plans, except for the following additional criteria:

1 If the observer himself varies the variables as a participant (e.g. initiating the spread of a rumour), if he changes the field, unintended side-effects also caused by him are to be strictly avoided, or they must be handled like the intended influence, as independent or intervening variables.
2 At least two observation phases are necessary, before and after the initiated change. If possible, more sophisticated quasi-experimental research designs should be used (see Campbell & Stanley, 1963).
3 The observation of the independent variables (e.g. behaviour in communication of the subjects, their friendship relations) must proceed according to the same categories in the schedule in both phases.

Zimmerman (1972, p. 195) pointed to the fact that in this kind of experiment, key persons in the field can be of strategic importance: 'One can eliminate effects which are caused by the presence of the research leader (in this case, the observer – F. & L.) when the researcher steps back behind that organisation or single person (e.g. the teacher) who is active in the respective situation anyway.'

5.3   Participant observation and action research

The participant observer becomes even more an agent of planned changes in the field in the methods of evaluation research (e.g. Weiss, 1972), the intervention method (e.g. Argyris, 1970) and in action research (e.g. Haag, Krüger, Schwärzel & Wildt, 1972).

Here one goes completely beyond the boundaries of the basically registering participation of the research for the benefit of a strategy with three principles:

First, the researchers do not suddenly enter a situation to ask people's opinions. They rather slowly take part over a period of time in a social process and help to keep this process going; secondly, they do not work with socially isolated individuals, but rather with groups to which these individuals have relations (something also true of exclusive participant observation – F. & L.). Thirdly, they do not inform these groups about the goals and purposes of the research, but rather give them a part evaluatively in the assessing of the research results. – Action research becomes a process of insight within a process of production. (Haag et *al.*, 1972, pp. 65 and 43).

When dealing with a longer process which is marked by the sequence of phases as Lewin already stated: inquiry – intervention – inquiry – new intervention and the intended participation of the persons in the field in this process of planned changes, very complex strategies of research arise. Examples of this can be found in work done with marginal groups of a slum area or in the organisation and planning of a social therapeutic institution, replacing custodial prisons.

A main problem of these insufficiently tested methods and the respective relevance of the included participant observation, is the question 'to what extent are the researcher and clients willing and able to see the necessity of gathering reliable and valid data about a specific point of time or a certain situation of the action process in order to have sufficient criteria at hand for making new decisions?' The already-mentioned problems of standardisation have to be solved at this point. Perhaps it proves wise to remove one or more researchers temporarily from the roles and communication systems of the field, so that he or they, representing the others, can devote himself or themselves exclusively to the purposes of the participant observation from a more receptive position not involved in the decision processes. Determined adherents of action research as a method sui generis may reject this for being a break in the continuously flowing processes of communication involving all partners. They must, however, be aware of the fact that certain insights into the cause-and-effect relationships, in structural characteristics of the field, in existing power hierarchies, etc. are the more valid, and the perceptions of the observers are freed of distortions caused by going native, or identifying with others. Where the action has priority over analysis of data in terms of hypotheses due to constraints of the field or the situation of the subjects, one should talk of social work and not of science (see Polsky, 1973, p. 74, f).

Obviously it is impossible to examine all the sources of error and refinements of participant observation within the framework of this book ultimately there is a lack of method-critical studies in this field. The further development of the social sciences is likely to be closely connected with the refinement of these methods that have thus far been neglected by the overemphasis of the interview. Within this development, standardised participant observation is also only one step in the direction of nonreactive and experimental methods which will bring about more exact hypotheses, allow for a better isolation of variables and finally allow for a more exact measurement of the relations between variables.

PART II

Practical Field Problems

6 Participant Observation in the Youth Centre Study

The youth centre study, carried out in 1966, (see Grauer, 1973, Lüdtke, 1972, Lüdtke & Grauer, 1973) provides one of the few systematic attempts to apply standardised participant observation simultaneously to a class of comparable objects of observation and to combine it with other methods.

The class of observation objects – the field of observation – consists of institutions of communal or 'free' youth care which possess certain properties of complex organisations, thus, of smaller social systems. Included were clubs and centres with the character of the 'Open Door Houses' which offer a continuous programme of leisure time activities, most of which are independent of those of the youth associations. Their programme is directed at a variety of interests, and, therefore, is supposed to attract a diffuse group of young clientèle. The centres are usually led by a staff professionally trained for this field. Participation is wholly voluntary on the part of the youth; the centres make it possible to form set interest groups or clubs, that is to say, their formation is considered, in most cases, to be of educational value. A detailed description of the field of investigation is not possible here; we refer to the mentioned studies by Grauer and Lüdtke and will limit our description to a short methodological survey.

By systematic quality of the investigation, we mean the attempt to use the material obtained through participant observation to describe the relevant variables of the field of observation, not just to give a purely descriptive analysis. This, in turn, makes an empirical examination of the relations between these variables possible, whereby the conditions named in Chapter 2 must be taken into consideration. Participant observation was used, in this case, as an instrument of social research which contains certain principles of measurement. As can be expected by a first attempt, the research was plagued by many inadequacies and only succeeded in part.

6.1 Short survey

6.1.1 Design and field of observation

Seventy-three youth centres in nine federal states of West Germany, including West Berlin, were investigated. They were selected on the basis of their regional and capacity distribution. All of them conformed to the following minimal criteria of ongoing operations:

1   Open for those youths not organised in work of youth associations at least four days in the week until late in the evening.
2   Availability of at least two rooms or one large clubroom for their open-door work.
3   The presence of at least one responsible centre employee at least twenty hours per week.

The sample was based on the results of mail questionnaires to the universe of centres (research carried out by Grauer), in which the most important properties of the field were studied. The sample of the centres for the participant observation included approximately 6 per cent of all those existing institutions which offered, to a more or less high degree, leisure time pro-grammes. The following features were over-represented: (a) centres in large cities; (b) centres of recent construction; (c) centres in areas of dominant Protestant population; (d) centres which were municipally and ideologically independently supported; (e) 'Houses of Youth' (centralised institutions with differentiated tasks) and purely open-door centres.

The average age of the observed and questioned visitors was about seventeen years; the ratio of male to female visitors was approximately 3:1.

The capacity and level of visitor frequency at the centres observed was estimated to be:

Table 6.1

Capacities and factual visitor frequencies of youth centres

Capacity under normal operating conditions[1]	(N = 73) Per cent	Daily average number of visitors in the evening	(N = 73) Per cent
Up to 75 visitors	25	Less than 20	16
76–125 visitors	37	20–49	45
126–175 visitors	14	50–99	21
176–225 visitors	8	100–149	10
226–275 visitors	7	150 and more	8
276 and more visitors	9		

The distributions show that the complexity of the observation setting (on account of the broad variation in capacity and number of visitors) was quite different for the individual observers. However, the following properties were typical for the majority of the centres: different but simultaneous activities in different rooms with emphasis on informal gatherings, entertainment, games and sports, as well as objectively structured activities; in particular, relatively closed interest and preference groups or courses, occasional larger events such as parties, dances, lectures, etc., a high fluctuation of visitors between rooms and activities, high differentiation of visitors as regards informal groups of regular visitors, cliques, couples, singles, etc. As a whole, the settings were such as to require the observer to be exceptionally flexible, i.e. in which a number of very different locations and reference groups of the observation were possible.

In a narrower sense, the object of the investigation was only the settings, or rather the spacial part of the open-door work of the centres for youth; the work of the youth associations, with children or other clientèle and other areas of involvement of the centres were gathered simply as data of the external system. Emphasis was laid on the evening activities, as in the afternoons the centres are usually frequented only by younger age groups or children.

The hypotheses of the study concern for the most part, the empirical relationship between the general field of orientation of young people in their spare time (their preferences, interests, motives, reference groups, partners and their youth culture) and the institutional-administrative conditions of the centres (external system), on the one hand, as well as their internal system, i.e. their patterns of interaction and activity, on the other, whereby certain assumptions about the selective mechanisms of the centres as complex organisations in relation to the general field of youth in their spare time was examined. The result was a relative variety of research tasks for the observer; besides their actual observation within the scope of visitor activities and groupings as well as the interaction between staff and visitors, they had to gather a series of data about the external system and conduct a standardised interview with the guests.

6.1.2 *Data collection and methodology*

The participant observation was carried out by seventy-four students in March and April 1966. Except for the largest centre (with two observers), one observer was occupied in each centre for a period of six half-weeks; with the exclusion of Sundays and the Easter vacation, between twenty-five and forty days were available for the actual observation period, which in retrospect, proved to be too short. During this time, the students lived at the sites of observation or, in a few cases, nearby.

In the assignment of locations, the personal wishes of the students were taken into consideration as much as possible. The observers, largely in the beginning semesters (average age 23·5 years), were selected from the universities of Hamburg, Cologne and Munich after personal interviews with the research directors.[2] They were composed of fifty-one males and twenty-three females with their study majors represented as follows:

Sociology	41
Psychology	8
Education	8
Others	17

Directly before the research began, the observers were trained in two three-day courses, located in different places and each having approximately 50 per cent of those involved.[3] The course outline covered the following topics:

1   Description of the field and the main problems of the study, illustration of characteristic field settings on the basis of primary experiences and available literature.[4]

2   Strategy of taking suitable observer roles.

3   Analysis of the observation schedule, illustration of the empirical indicators, technique of observation and taking protocol.

4   Simulation of field settings, situation games and taking protocol of them by observer groups according to different aspects, critical evaluation of the protocols.

5   Interview training.

An essential disadvantage for the observer training and its effectiveness later on, was the lack of knowledge of the field; only a small part of the observers had already had experiences with youth work in centres and camps. An exploratory stay in centres or a corresponding excursion before the course was impossible for various reasons; in principle, this should, however, be a part of the preparation for a study.

At many centres the supporting parties and directors had agreed to the form of the study and had been informed by means of a uniform letter. Because mistrust was bound to arise for various reasons (see Lüdtke, 1972, Section 1.1), the letter was consciously meant to appease and in a certain respect reassure. This prior notification bears such significance, because the success of participant observation, the possibility to participate, as a rule, rests mainly on the goodwill of the supporting bureaucratic agencies (municipal departments). Too often the interests of social research are interpreted as means of exerting displeasing (public?) control. For the same reason, the term 'observer' was avoided in defining the students' roles, instead 'honorary assistant', 'trainee' or 'educational assistant' were used. Of course, this could have certain disadvantages for the observer's setting;

in some cases it led to conflicts with the centre direction about the type of duties the students were to assume.

Besides their pure participation, i.e. their participation in the activities of visitors and staff (while relegating official personnel functions to as minor a role as possible), contacting informants (supporting parties, teachers, youth guardians, parents, etc.), taking protocol of the field of observation according to the schedule and keeping a diary outside of this field of interaction, the observers had also to carry out the following tasks, which at the same time show the complementary nature of the research methods:

1 To gather statistical information and analyse documents concerning the physical set-up at the centres (building, layout, rooms, equipment).
2 To interview centre experts (without personnel) by means of rating scales in respect of different centre and visitor properties.
3 To interview centre visitors ($N = 2,334$) by means of (a) a standardised questionnaire for data about social structure, behaviour in leisure time, preferences of activities in the centre; (b) sentence completion tests to distinguish between different attitudes and motivations; (c) semantic differentials for measuring the stereotypes of ten reference groups; (d) Guttman-scales for measuring the attitudes toward visitor groups on the one hand and toward staff personnel on the other.
(See the detailed presentation by Lüdtke & Grauer, 1973.)

The observers were instructed, for reasons of tactic, to carry out visitor interviewing during the last two weeks, in order not to acquire the status of nosy intruders from the beginning. This assumption of status-prejudicing, however, proved to be, for the most part, false. Not only was the interviewing positively reacted upon by the youth as a pleasant change of pace but most of the observers were, also, of the opinion at the end of the research that, (a) the interviewing acted as an especially strong integrative factor in terms of their position towards the youth groups; (b) as a result, they got to know the young people very well, which made the evaluation of their interaction easier; (c) they, thereby, acquired a very clear role which was accepted by the visitors; (d) thus, the interviewing should have been given at an earlier point.

During the data-collecting phase, almost all of the observers were visited once by the directors of the study after it was under way. At these supervisory meetings, most of the problems which the observers and sometimes the centre directors had confronted could be discussed and cleared up. Beyond this, the visits often had the function of acting as an 'emotional feedback' for the observers: the few relatively isolated observers, mostly in new surroundings, could report their personal problems, find advice and recognition and, through direct contact with the study's directors, establish a link with the study as a whole – a need which we had very much underestimated earlier.

After the end of the phase of data collection, two evaluation meetings were held. The meetings took place in order to complete the observation reports, to analyse field experiences, disturbing factors and sources of bias of the observation setting and, finally, in a lengthy taped group discussion, with pertinent questions asked by the directors, to explain the problems which had arisen in terms of the schedule, observer's role and other components of the setting.

6.2   The observation schedule

6.2.1   *Principles and problems*

The observation schedule of the youth centre study must be appraised as an attempt to approach the principles as formulated in section 4.3. The standardisation of the observation with regard to the threefold function of the schedule: to direct the observation verbally as well as in content, and beyond this to facilitate the note-taking, was not perfectly practicable. When research began no complete empirical model was yet available, certain compromises had to be made in the schedule between the generality and specification of the given contents: on the one hand, the observers were supposed to be able to refer back to defined categories, on the other, part of the schedule was to be left open for the protocolling of unexpected aspects and categories of the facts observed. The latter claim arose from the structural variety of the seventy-three youth centres as suggested by the research material compiled by Grauer. We tried to solve this problem in the following manner:

1   For a majority of the observation units (e.g., visitor groups with different activities) incomplete examples or series of different types, property distinctions, or rather, categories of these units were fixed which the observer could complete through further empirical categories.

2   At numerous points in the schedule, the observers were requested to justify their selection of defined categories by special detailed descriptions of the settings. Whereas some observers did without those categories for reasons of uncertainty, it was at least possible to refer back to those, in many cases, much more vivid descriptions in the data analysis.

3   The same was true for the obligatory daily log keeping. For some observers, the daily log acted as a means to compensate for the analytical severity and differentiation of the schedule. This was most often the case

in simply-structured centres, in which the mere absence of centre, personnel or visitor properties mentioned in the schedule would have been frustrating if one were to adhere one-sidedly to the schedule's contents. It speaks in favour of these observers, too, that in such daily log protocols, they made use, in part, of the analytical categories which were suggested in Part III of the schedule for intensive observation of special situations.

As a result of the relationship between the necessity for standardisation and the structure of the field of observation, a fundamental problem becomes clear. In 4.3 we already discussed why a schedule must be formulated in such a way that its categories correspond to the different objects of observation of the classes to be studied, whereby the constancy or consistency of the observations (König, 1967) is guaranteed. Theoretically, this means: if two or more observers in different places at different times describe an observed phenomenon using the same criteria from the schedule, then the probability is very high that this is, also, the case if the observers are alternately exchanged or if the same phenomenon is observed at different places. The more specific the categories are in terms of field and objects, i.e., the more they as a whole contain a hyperdifferentiated model of the field, then the more difficult it can be to arrive at consistency, if a large number of objects are observed at the same time. This holds true because the probability of deviation of an object from the model grows with the increased number of objects, unless one is dealing with a completely homogeneous field. Our observation schedule was very specific in contrast to the *Interactiogram* by Atteslander (see Table 4.2), which lends itself to practically every form of operation, while our schedule refers only to a certain type of centre. Still, at the same time, our field of observation implied an unexpectedly high structural differentiation between the seventy-three centres, although these had been formally selected according to a few clear general uniform criteria. We, thus, realised that our study presented the borderline case in which a high consistency of observation through application of an itemised schedule was still attainable. Therefore, it can generally be claimed:

In comparative and generalising studies with participant observation of numerous objects in the field, a general schedule of categories is to be preferred to a more specific schedule which is directed at an ideal model or an average type, if the variance of decisive structural properties is largely unknown.

If the fixed emphasis of the observation schedule is too specific (i.e. structure of members, goals, frequency, working methods of interest and preference groups with special achievement orientation) then this can lead to faulty direction and insecurity among the observers, if these emphases, in fact, are found to be empirically nonexistent (i.e. in centres without interest group work): it is then possible that the observer tends to interpret the given facts according to these categories, although they ought, indeed, to be associated with other points of emphasis (an informal youth club is described, for example, as a structured interest group).

At the training courses, we had pointed out and emphasised to the observers that possible mistakes might arise because our schedule provided a lot of categorical possibilities among very different centres; however, such warnings are, in effect, no substitution for controllable observation strategies if it is assumed that for an average observer a standardised schedule making empirical claims always demands a certain 'respect', because it consciously or unconsciously is identified with the competency of its professional authors.

One possibility for overcoming this difficulty avails itself to the trained observer by, of the three functions of the schedule, placing the most emphasis on the notetaking, instead of looking in vain for given dimensions in the field, because he knows that the application of correct categories to the units recognised as points of emphasis corresponds to the study's intention: 'Part of the observer's task was to look for help in orientation in the guide before writing in the daily log. . . . The guide became . . . an important means of transferring the perception and research interests of our study to the observers' (Kentler et al., 1969, p. 110). One other possibility could have been to allow each participant observer to give a preliminary test in his specific field (centre) with the observation schedule, in order to allow him to recognise which situations in his field were nonexistent or which demands were not to be fulfilled by him. These problems will be discussed further in the critical evaluation later on.

6.2.2 *Units and categories*

A complete reproduction of the observation schedule used in the study is not necessary here because its characteristics can be inspected in the table of contents and the selection of items which follow.

I The material set-up of the centre:
   A Building and grounds:
      1 Type of building.
      2 Centre-owned grounds.
      3 History of the centre.
   B Centre's spatial accommodations:
      1 List of various rooms.
      2 How are the rooms usually used?
   C Capacity of the centre:
      1 How many can it hold?

        2   Highest possible number of visitors.
        3   Number of visitors on weekdays.
        4   Number of visitors in a month.
    D   Institutional purposes of the centre.
    E   Open hours:
        1   For actual open-door work.
        2   For youth group work.
        3   For other set uses.
    F   The staff:
        1   Composition.
        2   Statistics on the fulltime personnel.
        3   If no fulltime director is available, those responsible for the youth work.
    G   The financing:
        1   Total budgets for 1965 and 1966.
        2   Origin of financial means for the running expenses.
        3   Relation of financial contributions of supporting parties, communal agencies, associations among other groups to one another.
    H   Material stock and lasting supply of the centre:
        1   Furniture and interior design.
        2   Material stock.
        3   Perpetual supply.
II The social structure:
    A   Visitors and programme:
        1   Visitors (exact number).
        2   Individual visits (participation of single visitors according to guest list).
        3   Programme for a single week.
        4   Further observations about this part (results).
    B   Centre director's style of interaction and sanctioning:
        1   General behavioural observations (presence, activities, interactions).
        2   Specific behavioural observations (according to situations and Bales-categories).
        3   The educational and leadership style of the director in contact with youth.
        4   Sanctions of the centre's director.
        5   Effects of the leadership and sanction style – reaction of the visitors.
        6   The educational attempts and intentions of the director – his normative orientation.

7 Effect of the director's normative orientation.

8 How does he define 'deviant behaviour'?'

9 Centre director and co-workers.

C Authority and role structures:

  1 Official centre regulations.

  2 The positions of the centre.

  3 Selfgovernment by the youth.

  4 Visitors' hierarchy of authority and communication.

D Participation in activities and groups:

  1 Survey of the activities actually practised in the centre.

  2 Initiatives for forming groups.

  3 Relations of visitors among themselves.

  4 Visit to the centre and activities.

E Degree of differentiation and appeal of the centre.

F Mechanisms of selection with regard to the body of visitors.

G Centre and surroundings:

  1 The socio-ecological environment.

  2 Forms, means, effects of publicity.

  3 Neighbours and parents.

  4 The relationship of the centre to supporting parties, agencies and boards.

  5 Cooperation with other institutions.

III Intensive observation of specific social situations and interaction:

A Typical situations of centre life:

  1 Classification and characterisation of such situations.

  2 Meaning and scope, frequency and consequences of these situations for the whole social organisation of the centre.

B The specific properties of these situations:

  1 Goal, theme, object of orientation.

  2 Expressed motives, feelings, affects, attitudes.

  3 Form and manner of the activities.

  4 Overtness of the activities.

  5 Mediums of interaction.

  6 Participating persons.

  7 Verbal forms and contents of the interactions.

  8 The whole context of the situation.

C Social processes of the situation.

The actual participant observation was based on Parts II and III of the schedule. Part I demanded, in contrast, gathering data, above all, in the form of statistical registrations, which could be, as it were, carried out when the centre was inactive. Part II, especially sub-division B, was not obligatory but recommended making periodic and situationally possible observations of limited situations more from the standpoint of the nonparticipating observer. In additional information, the level of difficulty and the temporary priority of certain areas of research were mentioned. The observers were supposed to complete Part I first and then gradually turn systematically to the more difficult, and socially more complex, topics.

As made clear by the list, the schedule's classification principle of the highest order was to differentiate between relatively abstract topics or aspects of the centres' social systems and their surroundings. Various situations were then handled within the individual topics. As it turned out, this was doubtlessly a disadvantage. Even these were too abstractly formulated, which led us to make stricter demands of defining set situations to be observed, as named in section 4.2.

Furthermore, our practical experiences confirm the statement that situations should be selected as adequate observation units. Many observers overcame this difficulty by going about it the other way round: they took notes of their observations in protocols which they later classified according to the system provided by the schedule. In such a case, the schedule served, primarily, as a means of classifying the records analytically in theoretically relevant dimensions.

In contrast, Kentler *et al.* (1969, p. 553, ff) categorised their observation guides, in part, according to situational phases of the youth's vacation (trip, arrival, daily programme at the camp, return trip), whereby the time dimension entered the most general of observation units, making the analysis of the vacation process easier. This principle is, above all, especially productive, if used when the participation of the actors in the field is determined by the transitory nature of the situation. The authors, of course, deviated from their classification principle insofar as they selected the participants themselves, occurrences, events and direction as the most general units of the internal social system of the organised social group on holiday. In any event multidimensional definitions of fundamental observation units would have made the observation, as well as the data analysis, much more difficult.

The form of the observation categories given in our schedule, or rather, the indicators for more abstract properties, is illustrated by means of the following excerpt:

> *Structure of authority and communication among visitors:*
> The observations included here concentrate on the properties of the informal structure of the youth. Which authority and communication structures arise from the fact that the centre is a place of social contact between different adolescents in their leisure?
> (a) Leaders and status persons (reference to other sections):

(aa) Instrumental leaders; status persons in relation to achievements and activities.

Expressive leaders; status persons in regard to feelings, emotions, eroticism, conflicts, etc.

(ab) Properties of leaders and status persons (see questionnaire to visitors as well); properties which determine their status and prestige:

*Age and sex.
*Fashionable appearance.
*Physical features.
*Psychical features.
*Social features (behaviour and group membership).
*Formal position in the centre.

(ac) Describe and classify modes of behaviour, functions and status of these persons according to aspects and properties of item (reference).

(ad) Describe the relationship between selfgovernment and informal leadership.

*Identity of positions and persons.
*Complementary reciprocity.
*Competition.

(ae) To which grouping does the status of informal leaders refer? Which groupings do they belong to (cliques, gangs, interest groups, open-game groups, etc.)? What is the makeup of their 'followers'? In which direction and with which means do they direct the behaviour and the activities of visitors?

(af) In which situations does the 'authoritative strength' of informal leaders express itself? When are they typically followed? When do they effectively change events at the centre (see Part III)?

(b) The relation between staff and visitors:

(ba) How do the youth adapt themselves to official centre regulations and expectations of the staff (see experts' questionnaire, reference to other sections)? How do they react to the statements and instructions of the staff in view of the rules of behaviour to be observed?

(bb) How does the staff define 'deviant behaviour' in the centre and how is it sanctioned? (reference).

(bc) Rate the centre's structure of authority as a result of the confrontation of different behavioural expectations and norms: of the youth and the staff. How can the structure of authority be adequately classified?

* The staff's notions about rules are of paramount importance (inasmuch as they differ from those of the visitors!).

* It is dynamic and depends on the situation: the role expectations and interactions of the visitors structure situations in which the youth are amongst themselves, while the staff's norms are relevant in such situations in which the staff actively participates.

* It is largely marked by the expectations and norms of the youth (to the extent that they differ from those of the staff).

* Other structural possibilities:
  Base your opinion on actual situations. Judge which authorities most clearly determine what happens at the centre:

  * the centre director alone,

  * the fulltime personnel as a group,

  * the older parttime employees,

  * the younger parttime employees,

  * youth group leaders from associations;

  * selfgovernment by visitors,

  * informal leaders or status-persons;

  * other authorities.

In which situations does this become especially evident?

(a) Relations of the visitors amongst themselves:

   (aa) Describe typical relations between female and male visitors.
   (ab) Describe typical relations among different age groups and among the groups of the same age.
   (ac) Describe typical relations between groupings, cliques, interest groups, the relations within these groupings and between them and individual young people (level of solidarity, passivity, tolerance, cooperation, competition, distances, conflicts, aggressions).
   (ad) Describe typical relations between the 'non-organised' visitors and those groups of youth organisations which meet in the centre. Which have contact with one another? Which have absolutely no contacts (i.e. as shown by spatial separation; because they avoid one another etc.)? Do some organisations try to recruit members from the non-organised? How can these relations be qualified?

105

(b)   Is there a typical style of social intercourse with one another? Describe this style of communication as extensively as possible with examples (situations, groups, persons).

(c)   Look at your statements in the section 'Educational and sanctioning style of the centre director' and describe its effects on the relations between the young people.

Centre visit and activities:

Make a short evaluation of the visitor and programme statistics you gathered, taking the distribution of the visitor groups with different stays into consideration; number and form (common properties):

* the visitors who come for only a short time in order to see what is happening or whether acquaintances are present;

* the visitors who come to only certain events, programme highlights or interest groups (which ones?);

* the visitors who are regularly present (daily or practically daily) at certain times.

Obviously, the schedule concentrates on:

(a)   differentiating between general observation topics (e.g. authority and communication structures of the visitors),

(b)   identifying the relevant dimensions (or properties) of these topics,

(c)   pointing out to the observers certain connections of these dimensions to other properties (e.g. status of leaders and reference groups),

(d)   asking about situations in which certain properties typically appear, but not using the situation itself as an observation unit,

(e)   supplying indicators or alternative variables characterised by (*) for single dimensions.

Beyond this, a complete observation schedule which was better standardised would have had to provide, among other things, the elementary observation categories, which would have been used as operational basic descriptions in all protocols about the situations which arose. As long as single indicators did not relate to such categories, the observers were dependent upon their own everyday categories while taking notes, which of course, implies a limitation to the reliability of the statements. Uniform elementary categories of the situations were, in fact, intended in Part III of the schedule. However, because of its separation from the other sections and the 'voluntary nature' of its use, they were made in all too non-compulsory a fashion.

Still less compulsory is the observation guide to the youth tourism study. As the following short excerpt (Kentler et al., 1969, p. 558) shows, which limits itself largely to the above-mentioned points (a), (b) and (d):

The participants in total:
Emphases of the observation are:

A Contacts and relations of the participants amongst themselves.
B Configuration of these contacts and relations.
C Significance for the vacation.

Of special interest are:

I Camp practices:
    1 Which practices existed at the camp?
    2 How did they arise?
    3 Meaning and goal of the camp practices.

II 'External relations':
    1 To the natives.
    2 To the staff.
    3 To directors (travel guides).
    4 To other groups:
       (behaviour variants with: German outsiders, foreigners, youth groups;
       differences in behaviour with:
       different social groups, women–men, the aged–young; mutual opinions)

III 'Internal relations':
    1 Tone and style of relations.
    2 Signs of tolerance–intolerance;
       fellowship and lack thereof;
       candour–reserve.
    3 Politeness (manners–external forms, e.g. change for dinner).
    4 Intimacy in public.
    5 Fostering contact with the 'unliked'.

IV Behaviour of opposite sexes to one another:
    1 Forms:
       couples: old couples (arrived as such)–new (founded on vacation), those who wanted to stay together longer (after vacation's end)–vacation couples (couples for a limited time only).
    2 Form and manner:
       Dancing style.
       Flirt.
       Carnival behaviour.

V Group relations:
    1 Cliques (different forms).
    2 Groups of friends.
    3 Outsiders and loners.

4 Cohesiveness as a whole:
Practices and customs.
Conduct regulation.
Joint actions (how they originated; form and manner).
5 Formation of cyclical peculiarities.
6 Opinions about co-vacationers.
7 Opinions about vacation acquaintances.
VI Special incidences:
1 Violation of camp rules ('mutinies').
2 Disputes among one another.
3 Parties.
4 Behaviour under bad weather conditions.
5 Resolution of conflicts.
VII Behaviour in certain situations:
1 On the beach:
(a) getting a tan;
(b) conversations, discussions;
(c) games.
2 Before meals.
3 Evenings.
4 During the night.
5 Going out: in bars – amusement centres – excursions for amusement.

6.2.3 *A critical review*

A few of the deficiencies of the observation schedule for the youth centres have already been mentioned, as well as the complex of problems related to an observation schedule more specific for the field, whose units, for the most part, were not situations and, therefore, related to very different observation situations and objects. On the basis of the results from the group discussions with the observers, the failures of our schedule will now be discussed in detail. Of decisive importance seems to be that most of our observers perceived these deficiencies subjectively as problems of observation and recording, which, on the one hand, speaks for their high methodological sensitivity and responsibility, and on the other hand, speaks for the fact that observation problems of this form, indeed, lie more on the schedule than on insufficient training. It, also, very well could have been the case that the observers, in an attempt to get rid of contradictions between the schedule and the field perception, would have given false data or reinterpreted their situations, the underlying attitude being: 'The schedule is alright, I'm just insecure.'

The majority of the observers (45) expressed dissatisfaction with the form of standardisation. Their criticism directed itself at the following points:

Table 6.2

Observers' objections to observation schedule

Form of statement	Number of observers
1 (a) Items were defined too strictly, the schedule exerted too much pressure, 'inhibition'	6
(b) Schedule, or rather, the implied youth-centre models were too differentiated and specialised; the situations themselves were less specific or diffuse; only a part of the categories were applicable; differentiated observations in the sense implied by the schedule impossible	26
(c) Schedule presupposed interpretation or seduced observers to interpret properties into a situation which weren't even present or to merely cross off the findings which were included in the schedule	11

Form of statement	Multiple specific.
2 Schedule was incomplete or too undifferentiated; youth centre was more differentiated or complex; certain situations were not included	5
3 The statistical part was too all-inclusive; lists and counting (e.g. of visitors) demanded too much time and attention	10

The schedule apparently not only directed the observer, but also asked too much of him: the statements of type 1 imply a sharp discrepancy between situation perception and analytical procedure (e.g. observation categories), the relative differentiation in relationship to the relative simplicity of the situations having been viewed as a source of pressure. It is interesting to note that the criticism is not directed at an overdose of theoretical language in the schedule but at the observation dimensions which they felt were too many. The observers especially had difficulties with the interaction schedule by Bales, which they were not supposed to use – although it was conceived for such purposes – on the one-time individual interactions of the director with the proceedings of a small group, but analogously on the total behaviour of the centre director toward the visitors. Such an adaptation of the schedule to complex situations is apparently not easily done (see sections 4.3.1, 4.3.3).

Furthermore, the classification of leader types and other specialised terms were not always carried out by the observers through means of the corresponding operational contents – despite the efforts of the training courses –

they understood the concepts more in terms of commonsense adaptations. Some of the observers, also, freed themselves of conflict between the constraints of the given categories and the wealth of situations by limiting the observations to topics which were easier to categorise. The majority of observers, however, kept by the research's assumption that the other extreme of a more mono-graphical daily log presentation would probably have led to difficulties in the comparison of data and generalisation of hypotheses.,

Some would have liked only to illustrate the situations, others to mark off 'x's on the schedule alike to a questionnaire. An observation schedule is, however, not a checklist; in that case, it would have to provide very exact descriptions, which first had to be established here (see section 4.3.3).

Our attempt to provide a uniform orientation aid with respect to the single phases of research did not take into consideration that the situations of the individual youth centres were often very different and that, therefore, a single such general solution to the problem of the observation sequence is inadequate. To this extent, the observers were not sufficiently motivated to deviate individually from the suggested succession of jobs. We had the feeling that our suggestions were relatively often misunderstood to be strict orders. Faith in the 'competence of the specialists', which very likely assumed perfectionism on the part of the schedule, may have played a role here.

The statistical part of the schedule is overrepresented in respect of the observation of behaviour and situations. The visitor counts and the putting together of a very detailed programme list and inventory of the centres official activities demanded too much of the observers' time. As a result, observations and facts of a statistical nature should not, if possible, be gathered at the same time and from the same persons; because the statistics – especially at the beginning of the observation – led to bureaucratic adhesion and took a lot of time, it could very easily negatively influence the actual observation by providing an escape from the task to observe complex situations.

From our practical experience with the schedule, the following general requirements can be deduced, which specify conditions for a reliable appli-cation of the standardised participant observation:

1   The given observation units in the schedule should be limited to those field situations which, on the basis of a representative pretest, are viewed as the most typical or probable.
2   Standardised participant observation will, thus, have to be limited, as a rule – at least in relatively complex fields – to observation units whose fre-quency, distribution and significance in the field are fundamentally known. The observation of nontypical or accidental situations and events is, at best, achieved in exploratory research on the basis of a categorically largely open scheme. An example is given in the Appendix.

110

3   If a compromise between both functions is to be attained in a research project, then the standardised and open field observation should clearly be separated into schedule and time sequence. The observer must, thereby, have learned to which point of emphasis he should intensively turn at any given time, so that too much weight is not given to the 'easier' parts of the observation.

4   The higher the variance in properties of the different objects in an observation field, the fewer must be the number of observation units of the schedule in relation to the total number of possible units and, therefore, the more general the operational observation categories have to be. Contrasting extremes are, for example, the field 'a battalion of a branch of the armed services' (little variance because of identical formal structures) and 'informal youth club' (high variance because of different activities, for example, popular music or political discussions).

5   The same requirement applies, to the degree of complexity of the observation units: if the observer interacts with many persons and physical objects in situations, then he should observe fewer different situations according to general categories than if he usually deals with situations which include only few persons (and physical objects).

6   If the research approach is very broad, i.e. as in the case of the youth centre study, the observation by many observers is supposed to cover very different dimensions or units of the field. If the pretest as well as the observers' training suggest, however, that this task is too much for the observers, then a successful standardisation can only be guaranteed by restricting the schedule to those units which do not differ too much from one another with respect to the categories.

7   If the broad research approach, however, is supposed to be upheld, then the following alternatives are to be recommended:

(a)   a *separation* of the observation *into time periods:* first conclude the observation of a part of the units; then (if possible by other observers) the remaining part;

(b)   a *personal allocation* of units: many observers concentrate on only some and different parts of the schedule concerning one object;

(c)   a *splitting* of the units: the observation of individual field objects is concentrated on different units one after another, all units are not observed in a single object; as a whole, however, each unit is observed in at least two objects of observation (e.g. youth centres).

The larger the number of available objects and observers and the more of these alternatives that can be used in combination, the fewer are the mistakes of observation induced by the partition.

6.3 Observers' strategies and procedures

In this section, selected examples will be used to illustrate how the observers of the youth centre study worked in the field and by what means they solved certain problems of the schedule. We have limited the descriptions to the relationship between observer and observation schedule, aids in observation and recording; the special social problems of the participation will be dealt with in section 9. The examples are arranged in order of their degree of generality, not according to the schedule, which for the reasons mentioned could only be adhered to in parts of the protocolling. We have chosen this form of broad illustration by means of numerous examples, in order to show very different possibilities and nuances of the protocol descriptions and, thereby, to demonstrate how very important the structuring of the observation protocols by means of a schedule is, so that a more exact comparison of the properties of the observed objects is not made more difficult or hindered by too many perceptive, receptive and verbal degrees of freedom on the part of the observer.

6.3.1 *Basic protocols of complex situations*

The observers usually described different units within one and the same situation complex with the corresponding overlapping of dimensions. On the one hand, it has the advantage that the significance and connection of the individual elements of the behaviour arise from the same context. On the other, the analyst is presented with the problem of subjecting the basic protocols to a uniform content analysis, whereby according to the schedule, he selects the elements relevant for him out of the total situational context (section 4.5).

The characteristic structure of these protocols proceeds from the examples which follow to the general situation description 'typical club activity':

> No. 26
> The boys usually sit in reversed positions on the chairs which stand in the middle of the room or are grouped around a table. Some of them sit on the floor and lean against the wall. A few (often the girls) use the tables to sit on and let their legs swing. From the loudspeaker beat-music can be heard. The volume can be regulated in each room. If a specially popular song is played (i.e. 'Boots are made for walking'), then it's put on as loud as possible. Some shake their heads to the beat and hit their knees with their hands. The girls often do a few dance steps and like to show they know the song and the singer's name.
> The topic of conversation is usually motor bikes, sports or last weekend.
> The core group in the room consists of an informal group of about

10–12 boys, of whom the large part are present every evening. Their members dress alike: black leather jackets, blue jeans, black boots – very unkempt – dirty hands and shoes. These boys sit very close together and talk amongst themselves mostly. The others, who don't belong to this clique, wear mostly grey or small-checked pants and pullovers. They appear generally better groomed. They come alone or as couples to the centre, take part in conversations and other activities in the game room; they don't get as much attention, however, when they enter as the members of the informal group do. The informal group members recognise one another right away by their walk (boots have taps and on the stone floors are especially conspicuous). 'Robby's coming now,' says one of them upon hearing the steps in the hall. They often are still wearing their helmets when they greet their friends. They hang them carelessly on hooks and join their friends. Almost all of those present smoke and throw the butts on the floor. The cigarettes are generously offered to one another. If someone grubs, then he'll be told to buy his own cigarettes once in a while. For a coke, they often borrow money from one another. Noticeable is the fact that the boys pay more attention to one another when they enter the room than they do to the girls.

Again and again subgroups break away from the group and go into the refreshment room, in order to play games or see what's going on there. Often it will suddenly be decided to go to a bar or get an ice-cream and the whole clubroom is empty for half an hour. By the way, the girls are not asked if they'd like to join them. They sometimes go alone to a place near the centre, because they know that some acquaintances are there.

On the inside of the door to the clubroom has been written in pencil: TBD 'The bloody days.' This name was given to the members of the informal group (youths with leather jackets). They call themselves 'rockers' and emphasise the fact that they are not bums. It sometimes results in fights (according to reports of the youths). Girls from the centre who know hippies are laughed at. A decisive feature of this 'rocker group' is their especially sloppy dress (see sentence completion: 'In the centre people . . . who are dressed well are ignored.') The leather jackets and a good 'buck' (bike) are status symbols within the group.

The informal leader of this group wears a chain around his neck, on which a copperplate hangs with the initials TBD. This plate was made in the centre's metal workshop. Up to the end of my observation period, no one else had copied it. As far as I could see, neither he nor his friends view him as the leader of this group. However, he provides an example for their behaviour.

Example: Three boys suggest going to East Park in order to look at the queers and annoy them. The leader doesn't like the idea because its too cold outside. He doesn't want to go and says it's a crazy idea. As a result, the three members of the group remain at the centre.

Besides, one member of this group told me that when a newcomer enters the centre and is really spruced-up, 'Robby tears him to pieces.'

The observations of this protocol refer to the following units or dimensions of units: club activities, interaction pattern and communication contents, status symbols, core group (and its structure), informal leader. The advantage of this manner of presentation lies in the fact that the observer has already held the time factor constant (through the words 'mostly', 'again and again', 'often', 'for example') and generalised a series of observations of the same or similar processes. The protocol, thus, very likely describes a complex syndrome of constant features of the visitors' behaviour.

This type of generalisation is, in contrast, not found in the following example: it describes completely, by the use of numerous elementary behaviour features, a solitary situation in the club on a given evening, which, however, in view of certain features, might even be regarded as typical (section 6.3.4). Here, as well, several dimensions overlap. The advantage of this extensive description certainly lies in the ability to optimally examine the observer's general assertions according to the items provided by the schedule, by means of the indicators present in the protocol. One significant disadvantage is that empirical generalisations are only possible if a number of such protocols are submitted.

No. 53

I have bar duty. Nine boys between 14 and 15 years old, who belong to the group of idlers, are busy with the table football. After a few minutes, a boy of about 18 years (tall, lanky, friendly, bushy hair, black leather jacket) enters the room. The youths greet him with a loud and extended 'heh'. The newcomer, Franz, sits without uttering a tone on a stool near the game and very indifferently looks on as they continue playing. Five minutes later another boy (the same age as Franz, also tall, lanky, but with a crew cut and wearing a suit with sailor pants) named Gert steps lackadaisically into the bar and sits down on a bar stool. Meanwhile, Franz has left his former seat and sits down next to Gert.

Franz: 'Coke!', turns to Gert: 'You too?' Gert shakes his head slightly, 'Yeah.' Franz to me: 'Make that two!' While I'm busy opening the bottles Gert brings out a pack of cigarettes, which he, without a word, holds in front of Franz. Both then take out lighters from their jackets and each lights his own cigarette. I take the money for the coke which they separately had put on the counter, while they both look me over half astonished, half distrustful. Then Franz begins: 'Just cut out of school;

took a test in bookkeeping; Popo (the teacher) naturally thought I'd have some questions to ask about it. Of course, I said I did.' – Pause.
Gert: 'Erika, the one who used to go with Michael, does she now come to the club more often?'
Franz: 'Yeah. The guys there (the band) are really great!'
Gert: 'The girl you were with on Saturday at the Jazz Festival, is she the one from Gladbach?'
Franz: (shaking his head) 'Yeah, the jerk decided she wanted to have her hair cut off recently. I told her: "That'll be the end for us".' Then, half to Gert half to himself but rather loud: 'Damn dames, always gotta pick 'em up and bring 'em back home!' – Pause.

Miss R., one of the two fulltime workers, enters the barroom. Gert is chewing on a straw. Miss R.: 'Taste good, Gert?' Gert with a slightly ironically meant move towards Miss R.: 'Yeah, great! After all, it's the only free thing around this place.'

After Miss R. has left the room, Brigitte (approximately 16–17 years old, wearing a bright red jacket) enters. We know one another from a lecture. After we've said hello to one another, she takes over at the bar and asks me to remain and keep her company. Both of the boys look at me curiously: bewildered that Brigitte and I should know one another. Afterwards, Gert turns to Brigitte, grins, leans his head in her direction and says: 'Ha, how dandy!' Brigitte, in the same provocative manner asks, 'Do you want anything?' Gert, 'Yeah, but what I want, I won't get anyway.' All three laugh.

Franz plays with a Red Cross button that he is wearing on his jacket lapel: 'Boy, am I ever crazy about a girl with unbelievably long blond hair.' Afterward, speaking rapidly, half to the others, half to himself: 'Hah, but I ain't allowed to be crazy about anyone!' Brigitte, turning to Gert, in a put-on sympathetic tone: 'Heh, Gert, you look really done in! Gone to bed too late?' Gert grinning: 'Didn't look at the time.' Brigitte: 'Were probably too drunk to!'

Franz: 'The Rackets (a band) really steal the show every time: it was wild!'

Brigitte: 'It was really bad last time when Mecki got under the piano!'

Ecki (Franz and Gert's age, long curly hair, slightly scarred face, dressed in bell-bottoms, turtleneck sweater, black jacket) saunters into the room. He's regarded as one of the difficult cases in the centre. First, he goes to the juke box, puts some change in and then takes a seat at the bar. The three already present as well as Ecki: 'Hi.' – Pause.

From the juke box booms: 'Sloopy.' Three of the boys turned off by the selection boo, whistle and beat loudly on the counter. Ecki puts about ten straws end-to-end, then stands up and tries to stick the straws in a coke bottle. Everybody laughs. Then Brigitte, still laughing says: 'Ecki, behave yourself! Otherwise, you'll get kicked out on the spot!' Franz to Brigitte: 'Heh, babe, gotta ice cream for a nickel?' Brigitte: 'There's no such thing.' Franz shakes his head: 'Here I wanted to make a big order for once and you don't have it again.'

Brigitte pulls some pictures out' of her handbag showing her and Angelika sunbathing and hands them to the boys. Franz says: 'Oh no, Angelika! Not on your life? Not my cup of tea! She never looked good!' Gert: 'Brigitte, you look like a circus horse yourself in the photo.' All four laugh aloud. Then Ecki gets ready to leave the barroom.

Franz calls after him: 'Heh, Ecki! You driving to the club now? Can you give me a lift on the back seat (of his motor bike)?' Ecki turns around, shakes his head and says: 'Make it fast! Don't dilly-dally!' Franz to Brigitte and Gert: 'Bye you guys.' Franz and Ecki leave the barroom together.

The opposite extreme is represented by the following protocol: it is, to be sure, too generalised and extraordinarily lacking in information. The points are largely limited to numerical, time and physical data; social indicators of the participants and their behaviour are missing completely. The protocol is limited practically to one unit: 'Form and fluctuation of club activities.'

No. 5

A typical 'idle Tuesday': The room was, as usual, available, a record player and tape recorder installed. In the room about six people were constantly present, of whom four were members of group 63. Two played chess, I played skat with two others, those remaining listened to records. Little by little, more young people entered, who, however, on the average left the house again after five minutes. The large unfriendly room, brightly lit, plastic tablecloths on the tables, wasn't very inviting with only six people there. I really wanted to listen to a long-playing record; because the others, especially the owner of another tape recorder and several tapes, were against it, we went into the centre director's room, continued playing cards there and listened to the records. Mr S. (employee) asked us, however, to go back to the room, in order that at least a few people were sitting there. We moved again, continued playing the records there, whereupon the tape-jockey got annoyed and packed up. A group of eight boys spent about half an hour in the foyer, then disappeared again. Mr S. said most of them only came to see if there was a dance. He objects to the idle Tuesday completely, because it accomplishes nothing.

6.3.2 *Description of social relations*

The observation units 'social relations' and 'persons and groups' (6.3.3) lie on the middle level of abstraction between complex situations and elementary behaviour properties. On the level of social relations (e.g. within the body of visitors in general, between boys and girls specifically, between visitors and staff, etc.), an acceptable compromise between tangibility and abstraction of the assertions can be reached. Because the property dimensions (degree of friendliness, manner of informal pattern, norms, degree of ritualisation, etc.) are less numerous, a few short and usually specific situation protocols are sufficient to characterise a certain property type.

Examples for the dimension 'social relations between boys and girls':

No. 59
The 15–17 year old girls who come to the mixed Falcons'[5] House evening always sit together and from this vantage point converse with the boys. When they wait in the hall at the beginning of the evening, they always sit together, also, and talk to one another. K., the leader of the group, told me that each of the girls was more or less going with one of the boys at the time. The friendships had already changed many times during the years of togetherness. According to him, he has often lent a sympathetic ear to the many heart pangs and woes of the young lovers. For the last six months he has himself been in love with a newcomer (15 years old) and is trying to 'keep her warm', because she is still too young for him (23).

No. 34
The boys compete for the few girls who are regular at the centre. The relations between male and female visitors are to be explained purely in terms of sex. Matchmaking goes on continually. In the centre, selections are made. A circle of ten boys has the best chance among the girls. These youths are, on average, older than the girls. If, as it sometimes happens, they refuse to accompany the girls home, younger boys are sought out to do it. Accompanying the girls home often ends in sexual intercourse, as the youths, to whom it applied, assured me.

No. 62
The younger boys deal with girls of the same age as one of their own, tease, annoy them and make fun of them if they come to the dance class made-up and dressed like ladies. The girls don't let the boys get the better of them, are just as fresh, slap and fight back if they come too close.

The older boys, also, pull the silliest stunts on the girls; they play dirty tricks on one another, still the older boys behave in a more refined manner towards the older girls and are more considerate. The girls take advantage of their sex and try, as a result, to be treated better. But they also know what it means when they're handled a bit rougher than otherwise.

E

No. 39

The girls complain that the boys aren't interested in anything besides ping pong, and cards. They don't have a chance at the records, because the boys play continuously.

Examples for the dimension 'leadership style of the centre director/ relations between visitors and staff':

No. 49

One clique of five boys let themselves into the centre through the cellar window. The centre director forbade them to enter the centre for six weeks. Comment of the youth: (citation) 'And that's supposed to be an open-door centre; if you come through the cellar you're kicked out for six weeks. Tomorrow we'll pull this place to pieces.'

No. 12

The centre director suddenly runs out of his office, brings a boy back who is holding a burning cigarette in his hand. 'How old are you?' – I'll be 15' – 'And the cigarette?' – 'Someone asked me to hold it for him.' – 'Who was it?' –'Don't know him, he was afraid of you.' – 'Where is he?' – 'Outside.' The director goes out into the hall. 'Who gave him the cigarette?' No one says a word. Facial expressions tell the truth: the boy is lying, as he then himself confesses. The director, to a co-worker: ' I think he should disappear from the centre for a while.' The co-worker thinks about it, then nods. The boy leaves without his cigarette. The day before he had mischievously damaged the venetian blinds and before that he was also given a warning about lying about his age – everything is always made note of in the centre's files.

No. 20

This evening there's a dance. The question of dress is typical. Boys without ties and jackets will be turned away. The reaction of the rejected: 'Ridiculous! Old-fashioned. Gotta move with the times and nowadays no one wears ties!' etc. This sort of discussion is abruptly cut off by the director of the centre who sits at the cash box. A motor bike gang in typical dress (crash helmet, leather jackets and pants, beatle hair-dos) is turned away rather sharply. To support his words of dismissal, the director takes out a rubber club from under the desk. The gang, which apparently wanted to provoke trouble, left after a few defiant remarks. Four strong older centre visitors, who demonstratively stand near the cash box, approach the entrance way in such cases. In answer to my questions, I learned that, by these means, all trouble was avoided at the centre. But, of course, it has already happened that visitors to the centre have scuffled in front of the centre.

No. 47

The director of the centre is sitting lazily in the easy chair, drawing on his cigar. A whole line of boys run up the stairs from the cellar, slide over the stone tiles of the front hall and hurry to the exit. The director, who is sitting there and can be seen, looks at the first one who slides by and keeps quiet. As the pack, screaming loudly, slides after him, a distinct, 'Heh!' is heard from the easy chair. No reaction. The next ones show their sliding skill on the polished floor. From the easy chair comes another 'Heh!', but this time with a much stronger ring. Otherwise, no movement. This time an astonished side glance on the part of those called after. The easy chair takes on exact contours and look! It's the director! Disconcerted, they continue sliding without really having understood what was going on. Only after the third drilling 'Heh' are the 'athletes' shocked into stopping. They've got the idea with a shrug of the shoulders and turn to go. The director remains in his armchair, doesn't stir a bit, does nothing and after a few seconds of quiet, shouts after the boys that he's going to get a polishing cloth right away so that they can erase the marks from the floor.

No. 57

Jürgen, who is always having difficulties, has won a great deal of self-confidence ever since he was made percussion player for the 'Vampires'. When I asked him about the 'Rackets', he said to me verbatim: 'Me, I never get together with them. What a bunch of blow-hards! Whatever their percussion man does with his hands, I do with my feet!'

He recently needed money and, thus, wanted to sell his instrument. The centre directress told him he was crazy but he pawned it anyway. The next Saturday the band wanted to play and Jürgen needed his instrument again, but he didn't have any money to pay for it. The directress handed him the money – 200 marks! He thinks she's a great lady!

Even if they refer to very different situations in a centre, protocols of this form, for the most part, clearly define a specific type of relationship, whereby two complementary property dimensions are described: (a) the quality of leadership style of the centre direction, and (b) the corresponding reaction pattern of the visitors. The evaluation can, as a result, follow analogous to the methods Tausch & Tausch (1965) used in the classification of teacher and pupil behaviour.

6.3.3 *Description of persons and groups*

From the observers' findings, it follows that, in comparison with other observation units, they have obviously been most successful and complete in empirically identifying subgroups, key persons and leaders (besides the position of the centre director). Of course, this is to be explained by the special visual tangibility of these units. Thus, the description of external and behaviour features is, also, dominant in the protocols about these persons and groups, while the descriptions of their position and their behaviour in relation to other persons and groups in the centre is incomplete in comparison.

Descriptions of leaders and status persons are often in the following forms which merely reproduce symbolic attributes:

No. 59
The clothing of youth with the highest status: P always wears pants, whose broadly cut legs fall to the floor, and a blue-black jacket. Most of the time he wears black suede shoes (with buckle), which have already been the object of admiration many times.
D. often wears a pink-coloured shirt, snug-fitting or bell-bottom pants and half boots (which along with his stalking step bring cowboy boots to mind).
H. changes clothes after school and in the centre wears (intentionally) frayed snug-fitting pants, in order to adapt to the others: most of the time he, also, puts on a fashionable ski sweater, which heightens his youthful looks even more.

Protocols of the following form describe certain tendencies in the behaviour of key persons as well, yet the presentation remains strongly interpretative, because there is no explicit connection with concrete indicators and situations in which this behaviour and the position of persons can be observed overtly:

No. 30
The instrumental leader is 18 years old, masculine, dressed as a rocker with blue jeans and jeans jacket, sometimes with fur jacket, coloured glowing shirts, long hair, athletic build. He seeks contact with the centre staff, likes to talk to the observer, he seems to me to be unstable in character, but open to reasonable arguments and basically well-meaning, very sarcastic and ironical. Thought to be a very good billiard player. He belongs to a larger group of friends, who think a lot of him, somewhat isolated because of his often aggressive (when irritated) behaviour (threats with bodily punishment). He finds himself in a crisis to the extent that he must come to an understanding with the new director. He provoked him, opposed him until after a discussion of views the relation improved markedly and could almost be called good.
No. 47
A visitor of long standing who is formally a member of a youth group: he likes to play the 'sunny boy', needs to be looked up to and popular,

in order to feel alright and would like to be the centre of attention everywhere. But his actual intelligence and leadership ability are limited. He never gets any further than loosely belonging to groups which often change. The others like to have him around, but the group itself limits his actions by either not going along with him or contradicting him strongly. Thus, this youth tries to strengthen his status by getting on good terms with the centre management (shaking hands, frequent talks) or by frequent contact with children with whom he plays fatherly games.

The desired characterisation of such persons in the context of the situation of interaction, their following, their influence and form of sanctions is included in the following protocol, which simultaneously provides an almost optimal compromise between completeness of description and brevity of presentation.

No. 35

An important clique in the centre is 'the clique around Rolf'. Rolf is 23 years old, wears mostly turtleneck sweaters, or white shirt and a jacket, Saturdays a blazer. He is small, athletic, has otherwise no special physical traits. At the centre he has a quasi co-worker function. He is a master mason, now a lorry driver. He decides, for example, whether his clique remains at the centre until closing time or whether they should leave earlier in order to go to another place. When he is the barkeeper, everybody gathers at the bar. Once when he happened to be barkeeper, two girls were sitting on the bar and he said to them: 'You could wash the dishes for once,' which they did. When a conflict once arose between the centre direction and the clique (otherwise they have a very good relationship), Rolf was responsible for the departure of the whole clique which left without even having helped to clean up. To a large extent, he feels obliged to the centre rules, which shows itself, for example, in the fact that he expressly emphasised that all the boys must appear at the centre in a shirt and tie.

With similar differentiations, the typical visitor groups were described too, mostly, however, in distinct connection with other persons or groups:

No. 43

The regular billiard players are, for the most part, young people who make a quiet, concentrated and well-groomed impression. Many of them are secondary students. Age 15 to 19 years. The majority of loafers are between 15 and 18 years old. Above all, they give one the impression that they only come to the centre in order to meet their intimate circle of friends. They repeatedly hang around the office doing nothing. The office is the gathering point for this age group and for these loafers, like a cozy corner. These visitors always go to this room first when they arrive. Here they greet one another with a handshake, exchange a few words, then from there they go, if at all, to pursue other things. These 'regulars' are well known to the staff. The staff greets them daily. From this group, five are members of the Visitors' Committee.

No. 26

An informal group of friends of about fifteen boys between 15 and 18 years old is typical for the centre. They come to the centre every day. They wear blue jeans, black leather jackets and boots. Shoes, shirts and hands are extremely dirty. Most of the time they sit in the club room and talk to one another, they smoke cigarettes and drink coca-cola. They often play table football or fool around on the floor. They leave the centre for a while in order to drink a beer in a pub or to get an ice cream, but they come back to the centre. Six girls are also in the same rooms where the boys are. Two pairs of girl friends and two single girls. The girl friends always go together through the centre. If they don't meet any boys to talk to they talk to one another. One of the single girls always hangs around with the boys and does not even speak to the girls. The other one sits or stands around alone. If she doesn't make contact with the loafers she goes upstairs to the tape recorder group.

No. 66

For the first time since I've been here, there was a larger informal group in the reading room – because there is no comfortable clubroom. I was with the 'proletariat clique' in this room. This clique of apprentices and workers is not a solid group; they just play ping pong together. Outside the centre at least four workers form a clique, or more accurately a gang, among themselves. They are always together, have, also, already gone camping together and are slight lawbreakers (Home for Wayward Boys because of motor bike stealing). This group of about eight boys is separated from another group, the beat boys from the high school, who hang around in the large room only, which the others do not enter. The secondary school pupils and non-secondary school pupils don't even know one another's names for the most part (in this village!). The proletariat clique is completely isolated. None of them participates in other activities (except table tennis).

The exact and representative description of key persons and especially prominent groups of the field in relevant situations is of such methodological importance, because, in general, it can be assumed that the most important social processes crystallise around these persons and groups. For an observer who is sensitive to this, the chance is very high that he, also, actually catches the relevant situations. If the behaviour of these persons and groups and the form and manner, by which they structure the situation, can systematically

122

be followed from situation to situation in the observation protocols, then a special form of reliability control arises as a result.

6.3.4 *Collection of elementary properties of behaviour*

An exact comparison of field situations, relations between actors and groups is more possible the more descriptions of elementary properties of behaviour are contained in the protocols on the observation of these units which can be elucidated according to simple categories. In the above-cited situation protocols, there are a number of such property descriptions, yet their dimensions vary considerably with the individual observer. Here, as well, the dilemma between the demand for completeness and uniformity of the categories applied and the methodological advantage of presenting the different properties in their situational contexts is apparent. If this manner of presentation within the context is supposed to guarantee an exact comparison, then the dimensions of the unit and the number of the properties to be observed must have an appropriate relationship to one another.

The observers of the youth centre study made various uses of the possible methodological margin of play available to them. Some of the typical expressions of the visitors gathered by them follow:

> No. 12 (comments on a piece of music on the radio)
> 'great,' 'swingin' beat,' 'he knows what he's doin',' 'shaky,' 'groovy,' 'cheap imitation,' 'weak improvisation.'
> (comments about girls)
> 'bedroom eyes,' 'what a bomb,' 'a real doll', 'a dishrag,' 'what a handful,' 'witch,' 'washed-out Marlene,' 'homesick chick,' 'out of this world.'
> (greetings)
> 'Well, Chick?', 'Pining away?,' 'Just got up?,' 'The fire still burning?,' 'Got a dime to lend or is your Dad a Scot?,' 'Bad times,' 'You contaminate this whole place, two minutes ago it was fun here, but now!' 'I was hoping you'd go again real soon!' 'When you come, I can go,' 'They already let you out?' 'I'd almost forgotten how gorgeous you are', 'You really got a handshake there.'
> (parting)
> 'Watch out crossing the street,' 'Don't speak to strangers!,' 'Don't fall into a manhole!,' 'Gotta piss off?,' 'See you to the grave.'

This collection of characterisations of the property 'subcultural jargon' can be complete or incomplete; it includes at least a description of the typical characteristics of the jargon in different partial situations. Total situations and the moment of the observation are held constant, of course, so that a comparison is possible only by reference to the unit centre without weighing the situations as such.

Other observers describe elementary behaviour features of the visitors within the context of specific situations. Examples for the observation unit 'pattern of interaction between boys and girls' by use of diffuse behaviour features:

No. 34
Today Rainer bought two bottles of coca-cola for Ruth and himself. He placed them in front of the girl, then went back a few steps and looked around bored to tears. Ruth looked at him, without understanding. A bit later he sat down next to her. He took a large gulp from the bottle, bent over towards Ruth, kissed her and slushed the coke around in her mouth. At first she was surprised, even made a disdaining gesture, but then she wanted more, so that Rainer scarcely was able to cover her requirements. This happened openly in the clubroom. There were only a few present, a few of whom laughed about the gag, others took no notice of it whatsoever.

No. 35
When a tall thin girl comes into the centre and calls Ronald BWW (Board with warts), the centre directress responds in fun: 'You'll get a whole pound right away.'

No. 59
The underestimation (externally) of the young ladies by boys, who hit them on their upper arms with their fists in a form of perpetual body communication between boys and girls, is apparently a ritual among them. Harry's (16 years old) and Rita's (13) greeting took the following form on several occasions:

'Hello Rita, already here?' – Harry gives Rita a hefty punch on the arm. Rita takes hold of her arm and follows Harry making a half-smiling, half-injured face. Harry sits down on a bench, Rita next to him. Harry: 'Come on, show me!' He takes the arm as if to check it over – and hits Rita hard (at the same time) on the knee. Rita begins to push. Harry hovers in the corner. During the whole thing Rita's girl friend is standing nearby and watching it all with interest. The three of them go upstairs and mix with others. The greeting lasted about ten minutes.

The following example refers to an even more specific unit: 'ritual by games'.

No. 57
Four boys sat in the clubroom today where they were playing 'sick-trick'. The small T. (15 or 16 years old) lost and had to follow his fellow players' wishes. He wanted to get away immediately but U. and W. held him tightly, while J. pulled the tightly pressed together pack of cards across

his knuckles with heavy pressure. The small T. almost cried out in pain and anger while the others grinned. This seems to be an old game, because W. pulled a large roll of bandage tape out of his pocket, from which many strips had already been cut. Of course, the entire skin of T.'s knuckles had been torn open as far as the sinews or bones, apparently by very strong persons.

Taking protocol of this form is well suited to the empirical illustration of general assumptions, not, however, for checking the hypothesis 'centre A differs from centre B in terms of the behaviour syndromes X, Y, Z'. The test would require a complete sample of observations and consistent dimensions, on the basis of which the construction of a syndrome of elementary behaviour properties is possible. An approximation of this requirement is illustrated by the following compromise between the generality of the situation and the elementary description, whereby the specific nature of the situation and the moment of observation are held constant in favour of the unit 'typical behaviour patterns in the daily club setting'.

No. 50 (with a strongly subjective interpretation by the observer)
Mostly fooling around, talking nonsense or flirting, often two boys with two girls, serious flirts were never witnessed, aren't usual at the centre, but a fun-loving, frolicking, kidding tone, one doesn't show he cares.

The typical style of social intercourse is that which is typical for young working men and craft apprentices. They greet one another with a care-free handshake – 'Hi, Herbert! You old idiot!' – They behave in a manly, sluggish way; they laugh at one another freely and don't show their weaknesses but brand the 'pithy' type: this type is not the cowboy, but the successful elegant big city type, a James Bond, for example. On the one hand, this becomes apparent by the sweet teen elegance of the youth with high status and, on the other hand, by the prestige value of phrases from the language of the sales trade. Everything is 'in terms of' work, 'in terms of' kilometres, looks etc.; besides that, everything is 'from the beginning': 'I couldn't stand him from the beginning,' 'the BMW was bad from the beginning.' Besides shaking hands to say hello and good-bye there are rules of communication or interaction; often many people speak at the same time and try to make themselves heard by talking loudly. Verbal fights often turn into harmless fist fighting or laughter; communication and interaction are mostly spontaneously motivated and change very easily in their form and direction.
No. 12 (by using fewer elementary indicators)
The facial expression of the young people is as sloppy as possible, apparently indifferent, bored, chewing gum; avoids excitement as much as possible. This is, especially, true of the girls present. No one wants to

show weaknesses; to get excited is taboo. Conflicts; verbal arguments with big words; whoever loses his cool first, has lost; the winner prominently takes his seat, which he had before – whereby, at the very most, the girls take notice or show recognition while the others pay no attention at all.

Of course, shop talk leads to rather lively discussions and standpoints are heatedly presented. Whether disinterested or involved in heated debates one has the feeling that their world view is being expressed.

One drinks soft drinks like 7-up or coke, listens to the radio, mostly rock music, waits for contact with others, new arrivals must say the first word, otherwise they won't even be noticed. Girls are angered by being touched, messing up their hair-dos; blowing smoke in their hair; winning everyone's attention for a short time and then it's bored quiet again; chewing gum, listening to music, with half-closed eyes if possible. Cigarettes aren't offered to others, everyone smokes his own brand – unless someone asks another for one; this is guaranteed without objection.

6.3.5 *Aids in observation*

The largely ad hoc applied aids of the observers illustrate attempts to record complicated circumstances, to disclose additional information possibilities or to deal with unforeseen field problems. The following examples demonstrate the variety of possibilities for application. If such aids are supplied as binding as the schedule, these aids cannot only be looked at as means for interpretation of the data, but, also, serve as analytical instruments for the comprehension of such field dimensions, which cannot be adequately illustrated in verbal observation protocols (see section 4.4).

1 *Lists.* In order to make the analysis of the structure and fluctuation of the regular visitors easier, the observers were asked to keep a list of the daily visitors as follows:

Date:

No.	First and family name	Age	
			Afternoons
			Evenings

As the basis of these notes, a daily guest list was to be used, in which each visitor signed in at the entrance, which was already obligatory in many centres or could be introduced during the observation period. Unfortunately, this proved illusory; it could not be expected that a large number of the visitors to the open youth centres would regularly sign-in on such a list, and some of the observers had to make great efforts to prevent conflicts by insisting on enrolment. The list, however, could have offered the analyst the opportunity to follow the individual composition and groupings of the daily visitors over a longer period of time and, for example, to identify constant loners or visitors in cliques. By means of a synopsis of the visitor lists and the situation protocols, the behaviour of persons and groups in the centre could have been placed in relation to the patterns of frequency and groupings of their visits. Such a list can also be helpful to the study of formal behaviour criteria (frequency, duration and partners), as well as the reliability and validity controls of the situation descriptions (identification of persons).

2 *Sociometry*. Some observers conducted sociometrical tests among the regular visitors. By this means, they were able to isolate certain cliques and sociometrical visitor types (marginal persons, stars, 'hedgehogs'), and were, thus, in the position to characterise these types, accordingly, in their situation protocols. The tests, thereby, proved useful as a means of acquiring indicators when describing interaction processes.

3 One observer found the group structure of his centre to be in a critical state of deterioration. Among the regular visitors, he carried out *informal tape-recorded interviews*, in order to obtain information about the reasons for this development, the motives and referees of the visitors as well as their ideas about the future of the centre. In this way, he made allowance for the effective change of the field of his very small and clearly arranged centre and spared himself, at the same time, involved research. The main advantage of his strategy lay in the fact that with the statements of his informants he could reconstruct a lapsing process (the centre was about to close down), whose factors and results would probably have remained unknown to him by merely observing the present situation.

4 Another observer recognised, in the course of his numerous contact talks with different informant groups which contradicted one another, that his observation object was in an unusual state of tension, i.e. conflicting interest and relations due to inconsistent policies on the part of the supporters. In order to be able to present appropriately the observed interactions and statements, he created the following model of his experiences giving an overall view of the general social network of the centre and its environment (see Figure 6.1).

5 One other observer proceeded somewhat similarly by producing an original quantitative illustration of the visitor groups (Figure 6.2). Because

the groups had been described in detail in another part of his protocol, this presentation of groups as sets gives exact evidence about dominant, middle or marginal positions of the groups in terms of their members, the overlapping with other groups, their influence and their activities. The interaction processes presented in the situation protocols could then be drawn upon to test empirically such hypotheses as the following: a group is more influential, the more members of other groups it includes, whereby the measure of its influence is judged on the basis of the consequences of the interactions.

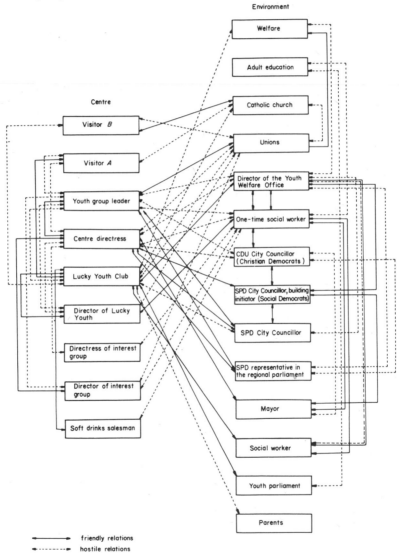

Fig. 6.1 Description of intrigues of a youth centre and its institutional environment (no. 47)

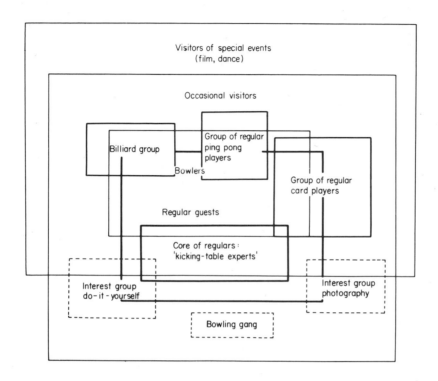

Fig. 6.2 Visitor groups of a youth centre described as sets (no. 58)

The last examples were helpful not only as sketches of the existing relations but for the data analysis as well. The observation material is not only analytically structured, but standardised according to a general standard of comparison – a function of the technique of data analysis.

Notes

1   The activities excluding special events for all in the halls or larger rooms, e.g. parties or concerts.

2   We must confess that no objective criteria for acceptance was at hand. The more or less subjective criteria for the decisions were, in particular: personal likings, 'youthful looks', or rather, the anticipated ability to adapt to youth groups, earlier experiences in youth work, relative to knowledge of the field, empirical practice, 'well-meaning' after learning of the working conditions, willingness to waive personal advantages such as special allotments, working together with members of the opposite sex in the same place.

3   Friedrichs and Lüdtke were each members of one of the teams directing the two training courses.

4   For this reason, a capable instructor with expertise in centre practices was placed in each of the teams of directors.

5   The 'Falcons' are a West German youth organisation whose members identify with the Socialist Movement.

7 Data Analysis

7.1 Data control and index construction

In a case such as the study of youth centres, in which the standardisation of the participant observation and, especially, of the schedule is incomplete, the special value of separating the research director (evaluator) and the observers is made clear in the codification of the data; he can then test the different observers and objects in regard to their methodological comparability and establish the attained level of completeness. If the material is incomplete insofar as it deals with only a portion of the units and dimensions to be covered or is structured differently in terms of contents or form then the codification has to be adapted to the changes as far as is justifiable in terms of the study's approach, or only those parts of the schedule would be evaluated which were universally gathered by all of the observers. In each case, the research director determines through his data control the form and depth of the analysis and, thereby, the extent to which the empirical findings can be proved (see McCall, 1969a, 1969b).

Because, in general, deviations from the given schedule abound, it is most often appropriate to reformulate individual observation units or categories for the analysis by means of content analysis. This means that the analyst makes use of the observers' new common indicators in the categorisation of the material. Having well-learned observers at one's disposal this need not be a disadvantage, as long as their working methods imply sensible adaptations to unexpected situations of observation and not departures from the contents derived from false interpretation. Another possibility in analysing incomplete data lies in broadening the level of abstraction of the observation units or categories. If, for example, in our case, the observer, for various reasons, is not always in a position to make observations according to the aforementioned elementary categories and, instead, uses general indicators, then the codification of data ensues according to the general indicators or, as well, leads to an increase in consistency in terms of multidimensional units of coding. If, for example, the behaviour of the centre's director with different groups was supposed to be classified according to Bales-categories, while the observer chose to make more extensive descriptions of the behaviour, then the analyst would not classify his behaviour according to elementary categories, but would choose to make a more general statement of the quality of his leadership style at the time. In other words: he chose a more complex field variable than an elementary interaction variable.

By manipulating the data in such a way, the loss of fundamental information due to this departure is, of course, not recovered, but one retains at least the exactness and systematisation of the analysis. For the sake of emphasis, let it be said again that the correctness of the analysis does not depend on the complexity or simplicity of an item, but on the methodological and operational premise of the analysis. In principle, the frequency distributions and variances of styles of leadership or group structures can be measured as exactly as those of elementary interaction variables within the same observation complex. It is then possible, on the basis of certain assumptions, to proceed from the interaction variables to indices by means of the observation categories, as already illustrated in section 4.5.1.

In more extensive participant observations, the attributes of variables necessary for the development of an index will not always be directly available, but may first arise after a multi-stage transformation of various crude data. Depending upon the form of object under study, depth of observation, level of standardisation and creativity of the researcher, many various possibilities are plausible. We would like to show one such possibility for developing an index, based on an example taken from our study of youth centres.

The 'structure of activities' in the youth centres was to have been measured. The observation schedule included exact empirical categories for differentiating between the contents of activities. The observers' task was to carry out a daily count of visitors and to classify them according to participation in single-activity areas. Hypotheses on the proportions of the different areas of activity in terms of participation were on hand; the rule for measuring a centre's structure of activities should, however, be of an empirical nature, i.e. it had to proceed from the distribution of property values in the entire sample.

Steps of the analysis:

1 For every centre and each day of observation, the visitors to three activity areas including all empirical activity categories were tallied up from the observation lists, which noted the visitors' daily participation in activities.
2 Then the average daily number of visitors to each centre was totalled according to area of activity. The same values were determined for the sample of the seventy-three centres. The average values (in percentages) of the areas of activities (number of participants in percentages of the average daily total number of visitors) formed the basis for developing the index.
3 The three areas of activities could now be codified per centre accordingly.

Table 7.1
Diversity of activities

Area of activity	Index value (code)		
	0	1	2
Club activities, informal contacts, amusement, play, consumption	less than 58 per cent	58 – 66 per cent	67 per cent and more of the daily visitors
	n 25	18	30
Sport activities	less than 20 per cent	20 – 28 per cent	29 per cent and more of the daily visitors
	n 29	17	27
Achievement- and learning-oriented activities	less than 11 per cent	11 – 17 per cent	18 per cent and more of the daily visitors
	n 25	14	34

4   The construction of the index of diversity of activities could then proceed through accumulation of the index values per activity area; operational definition: sum of rank values of participation in the activity areas. Codification:

Table 7.2
Activity structure (diversity)

Code	Sum	Meaning	n
0	1 – 2	Undifferentiated	23
1	3 – 4	Slightly differentiated	43
2	5 – 6	Highly differentiated	7

133

A look at the validity of the measurements provides the following significant correlations between activity ·structure and other variables: capacity
($\cdot 27$), attractiveness of the material set-up ($\cdot 33$), fluctuation of visitors ($\cdot 35$).
Further information about the multistepped index construction is to be
found in sections 7.2 and 8.4.

If one were dealing with a complex variable such as an ecological property
of the field in a community study, which cannot easily be reduced to
analytical dimensions, then one would have to do without multistepped
index construction and would be forced to turn to a complex estimation of
the property distinction on the basis of multidimensional protocol description.
The youth centre study afforded one such case:

In part G1 of the schedule the task was defined to ascertain strength,
location and function of other relevant agents in the system of leisure
activities close by the centre ('natural area' of about one kilometre radius),
and to describe their influence on the behaviour of the visitors to the centre
and the reaction of the staff members to them. The protocols of the observers
were judged by the research directors according to the degree of the effects
of these agents (successful competition) on the centre, while taking the
following criteria into consideration: (a) number of leisure time agents;
(b) manner and meaning of their offerings in relation to that offered by the
centre; (c) use by visitors to the centre and comments about them by the
juveniles; (d) reaction of the centre to these offerings.

This form of assessment of a multidimensional phenomenon gave the
following results:

Table 7.3

Ecological effects of the leisure time agents in the vicinity of the centre

Code		n
0	No recognisable effects	25
1	Slight effects	29
2	Strong effects	19

Examples:

No recognisable effects (case 12):
In the direct vicinity, there is one pub, one cinema, one coffee shop, the city
library and parks.

The library is looked at as a supplement; thus, their own library is rather
small. The large parks and playgrounds still act as substitutes for the centre
to many children, but the many game and activity possibilities of the centre
attract more and more children.

134

The nearest place to dance ('Teenager') is one subway station away. There is no theatre in the near vicinity. Youth programmes of the nearby churches are unknown to the visitors.

The young people from quarter *B*, who really live near the youth centre *x*, come in large numbers to our centre, because, ostensibly, more is going on here.

The centre's programme in no way reflects these agents, except in terms of the volume and form of the library; nor does the centre's propaganda. The centre's management comments with reserve about the pub, because this still attracts some of the youth after 10 p.m. The visitors themselves are indifferent; for most of them, the centre is much more interesting.

The immediate area within one kilometre of the centre has nothing to offer in terms of varied leisure activities; except for a football field, pubs and two cinemas, there are no other possibilities for the young people to occupy themselves unless they go to dance halls farther away.

Slight effects (case 5):
Churches: Protestant church with nursery school, children's centre, sectarian community hall, assembly room of the Catholic church.

Others: city youth home, French Cultural Centre; special events are organised, for all those interested, in cooperation with the adult college and the Arts Board of the precinct (more for adults); sport field indirectly next to the centre, park across from the centre.

Amusements: not including cinemas; two or three, dance hall 'Zillertal', offering a rock programme for young people three times a week (band 'Star Lighters'); numerous pubs, some of which have corrupting tendencies.

Children's activities of the church are well attended, could be competition, if the centre seriously took on such practices. Assembly room of the Catholic church is felt to be complementary; young people who go there are, also, supposed to come to the centre. Dances at the 'Zillertal' are well attended; an opinion as to whether the centre would be fuller without them was, however, not possible.

As a whole, the other institutions are not seen as competitors, because they always include groups other than the potential population of the centre. One competitor for those youths particularly interested in cultural activities, could be the Cultural Centre, because what it offers, as well as does the adult college, is qualitatively better.

The centre's programme depends upon it; no reaction to other agents.

Mr N., representative of the supporting institution, has a positive opinion of the other offerings, because conflicts rarely arise. As might be expected, he has his hesitation about the dances at the 'Zillertal'. He fears that the young people might take on certain modes of behaviour there, which could

135

rob them of other possibilities of occupying themselves. Mentioned on the side, was the possible danger of prostitute bars, too. First of all, however, the police can intervene there; secondly, the owners themselves are careful not to permit minors to enter; thirdly, of the young people, only a few are attracted.

According to Mr M. and Mr N. the mentioned institutions, for example, the confessional ones, are not competitors. Earlier, there were conflicts with the youth groups when it was feared that the centre would take away their young members. This question is, however, of no actual importance today, because the centre did not absorb many of the young people.

Because I never heard any comments about other leisure time agents by the visitors, I assume that they're indifferent to them. Jutta was the only one. She gushed about the dances at the 'Zillertal', but she probably has a special liking for them.

Of course, the youth also frequent other places but these cannot be localised specifically in the vicinity of the centre.

The centre's director never spoke of other leisure time agents, so that I, also, assume indifference on his part. As a whole, his opinion could not have been very different from that of the supporters. Mr O. views all leisure time programmes, which attract many people, as positive, including the dances at the 'Zillertal'. He campaigns in the centre to adopt the same methods, so that the centre will be full. This view is based, primarily, on the absence of any educational intentions and the desire for 'good' statistics.

Strong effects (case 23):
In the neighbourhood of the centre there are:
1 city youth centre, 1 Catholic youth dormitory and centre, 1 community house with rooms open during the day (preponderantly for aged people) as well as 1 further day centre for young people of the Protestant church; 1 swimming pool in a primary school, 3 playing fields which are managed by clubs; 1 pub with several slot machines, 3 coffee shops, no parks.

Dancing is offered in 2 larger places and in 1 avowed dance hall ('Studio 65'). The number of pubs can only be guessed at, probably between 40 or 50. Of those, only five are regularly frequented by the centre's visitors. There are no cinemas.

The only real competition is presented by the sporting clubs, pubs and – above all – the city youth centre on A-Street. Undoubtedly, many of the leisure time agents play a complementary role, especially because the centre is closed on Saturdays and Sundays. This affects the centre to the extent that when there are dances at the city youth centre, and on pay days, few visitors are to be met at the centre in the evenings. Beyond this, because of the different standards of the two youth centres, departure of certain groups

136

from our centre is taking place. This movement includes, above all, the female visitors.

No attempt is made to coordinate or contrast our programme with those of the other agents. During the period of observation the only publicity agent came from the municipally published *Meeting Point*, which offers a calendar of the youth activities and events in *D*, and upon which the individual centres exercise no influence.

The supporters' representative is only incompletely informed about the centre's programme and practically not at all about the offerings of the other leisure time agents. In view of the quality of the visitors, he believes that working out a larger, more demanding programme would simply be a waste of time and money.

The staff is very well informed about the offerings of the other centres and agents, but dismisses them, however, partially because their standards are too high, partially because of one's own limited personnel and material possibilities. The centre direction has the feeling that they are isolated from the parish and the city centre, and for that very reason, finds cause to continue in the same manner with their visitors.

There are two groups with contrasting attitudes towards the city centre. A smaller group which is present at their dances and other such events, and a larger group, which rejects the centre including its direction, or rather they are not allowed to enter. Beyond this, there are young people who usually avoid *A*-Street and only appear at dances. Those who reject the city centre especially feel the pressure to adapt to what, in their opinion, are unnatural manners and dress codes. As a result, a provoking hostile attitude often arises.

The variable effects or pressure of competition exerted by other leisure time agents in the area correlates very significantly with:

Supporting institution (public $+$; private $-$): $r = -\cdot32$
Institutional dependence (upon supporter): $r = \cdot30$
Degree of organisation (see 7.2.2): $r = \cdot30$

It is interesting to note that no relationship exists between this variable and type of community (number or residents) or industrial differentiation of community.

With these results, the hypothesis could be confirmed, that with increased internal organisational forces and dependencies, the youth centres tend to be less attractive competition for commercial and specialised leisure time agents.

Undoubtedly, the observation of ecological fields could considerably be refined in order to construct more exact indices. Thus, for example, the structure and fluctuation of visitors of leisure activity centres or of recreation areas could be researched by means of temporally and regionally stratified random samples with regard to the following dimensions: demographic composition of visitors, means of transportation used, frequentations of the agents (pubs, parks, swimming pools, etc.), length of stay (e.g. by finding out the fluctuation of parking spaces), outdoor activities of groups, etc., which are very well suited to index construction (see Catton, 1966).

7.2 The role matrix as a special instrument of analysis

7.2.1 *Application and construction*

In connection with the youth centre study, an instrument, the role matrix, was developed by Lüdtke, which makes it possible to analyse certain structural data of social systems, and to subject it to quantitative analysis. This instrument is well suited to the classification of observations in complex organisations, e.g. such systems where an institutionally regulated extent of division of labour and functional differentiation of status-positions avails. This includes, e.g. business organisations, administrative agencies, youth associations, union groups, hospital departments, schools, closed and open educational or welfare institutions, etc., as well as less bureaucratically organised, more informal systems, as long as they involve groupings of longer duration and are observable in terms of a relatively fixed allocation of competencies and transactions among certain positions according to functional requisites: e.g. clubs, tourist parties, planning teams. Such empirical observation data gathered, pertaining to the following questions, can be rationally arranged in a role matrix: (a) which institutional positions can be differentiated in the observation object and arranged in a complete rank or set (for example, according to occupation, qualifications, competence, authority, membership status, achieved indispensability, task, charge)?; (b) during the period of observation, which typical and regularly repetitive elements of transactions or duties (functions), relevant for the system as a whole, can be distinguished and arranged completely in order of rank?; (c) How are these functions typically distributed among the positions available?

The role matrix thus reflects the structure of the observed allocation of typical functions among typical positions in the field. Above all, it is well suited for a structural comparison of differing goal-oriented systems.

The main methodological problem in creating a role matrix lies in determining the positions and function dimensions independently of one another as much as possible. This is often impossible when classifying the empirical set of elements because in the description of a position (for example, by name of occupation) certain functions of its incumbent might be inseparably

138

involved. When certain questions are asked about the observations, it might even be desirable to compare the list of positions with a corresponding classification of functions, so that certain functions correspond to certain positions. The empirical frequencies in the role matrix could then be called upon for the analysis of the deviations of the actual role allocation from the theoretical model of positions-functions-congruity.

In principle, the instrument is better qualified for application in comparative analyses than in explorative studies. What this means is that the complete lists of possible positions and functions in the field are given and known to the classifying observer, without first having to differentiate them in the course of his observations and, as a result, be subjected to tautological bias. Especially by a comparative observation of a number of objects of the same class (for example, youth centres), the classification should be made according to a general model of possible positions and functions.

Of course, this presupposes a certain familiarity with the object. In a case in which complex organisations are the field of observation, the blueprint of the object can also serve as the model prototype. The role matrix then becomes the instrument by which the official role system and actual role pattern are compared.

The role matrix itself already presents a systematic abstraction from the data. Thus, it assumes a multistepped process of data collection and transformation, of which the following strategy gives account:

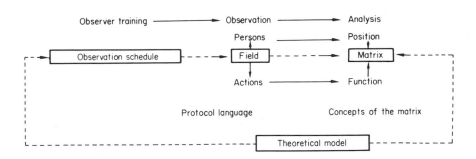

Fig. 7.1   Paradigm of the operational steps of producing a role matrix.

1   The observation schedule includes instructions for the long-term observation of persons and their actions in situations typical to the field (time-sampling).

2   The persons observed over a period of time are individually associated with positions given on the observation schedule. The accumulation of

	Role Matrix of Centre no. 12	Positions	A Staff				B Quasi-staff					C Visitors					Sum of occupants (P)	Held positions (N_p)
	$Bu = \cdot59$ $O = \cdot47$ $Coo = \cdot49$		1 Director	2 Educational assistant	3 Trainee	4 Custodian	5 Leader of organised group with staff member status	6 Voluntary adult assistant	7 Contracted internal group leader over 25 years old	8 Contracted internal group leader up to 25 (also visitors)	9 Regular visitor with delegated co-worker functions	10 Chairman or speaker for the visitors to the centre council	11 Elected member of council	12 Informal leader (expressive)	13 Informal leader (instrumental)	14 Average visitor		
	Functions / Occupants		1	2	2	1			3	3	31	1					44	8
A Executive functions	1 General direction, programme planning, coordination and control		1	1							5	1					8	
	2 Sanctioning of deviant behaviour (e.g. expelling visitors)		1	1													2	
	3 Formal direction of group activities		1	1	2				3	3		1					11	
	4 Supervision of activities		1	1							5	1					8	
B Administrative functions	5 Administration of rooms, money, material; service		1	1		1					5	1					9	
	6 Work in the office		1	1													2	
	7 Information, parent guidance, publicity		1	1							5	1					8	
C Integrative functions	8 Active cooperation in task-oriented groups at the visitors' level										5	1					6	
	9 Collegial communication in group of visitors (club activities)																	
	10 Personal guidance of visitors		1	1													2	
	11 Delegated representation of visitor interests										6						6	
	12 Informal expressive leadership or initiative in group of visitors																	
	13 Erotic leadership in group of visitors																	
	14 Informal instrumental leadership or coordination in group of visitors																	
	Sum of roles (F)		8	8	2	1			3	3	31	6					62	
	Functions exercised (N_f)																	

Fig. 7.2 Role matrix of centre no. 12

different positions by any individuals is possible. In accordance with their observed action sequences, the persons are, likewise, associated with functions given on the observation schedule, which were empirically implied in these action sequences. For more complex observation objects sometimes a limitation to a few dominant functions is advisable. The accumulation of different functions by any individuals will be normal.

3   The operational indicators for both forms of listing are described in the observation schedule and/or explained during the observers' training period by means of empirical examples.

4   In the role matrix, the individual pairs of categories are finally combined, so that a cross-tabulation of the positions held and the functions exercised is made. Any occupied cell, thus, tells the number of holders of a certain position, who exercise a certain function. The pattern of these cells can be called the empirical role pattern of the object of observation. Role is defined here as the combination of a held position with an exercised function.

As Figure 7.1 shows, the observers of the youth centre study did not start with theoretical positions and functions but with observed persons. Their task consisted in finding out the persons acting in a certain way according to a list of given jobs in the centre, describing the formal and informal status of these persons and associating them with the observed tasks (sequences of action).

Based on these data the persons were classified according to positions and status in the role matrix.

In Figure 7.2 the role matrix of a youth centre, based on the observation data, has been reproduced.

7.2.2   *Role matrix analysis in the youth centre study*

Numerous possibilities for analysing role matrices mathematically and statistically are conceivable depending upon the empirical questions asked. In the following sections only the form of the evaluation is presented which held true in the youth centre study. In so doing the basic intention was to arrive at some structural properties of the seventy-three studied centres.

The following parameters were used:

P = number of possible positions
    (numbers remained constant on hand of a theoretical model)
N_p = positions actually held
f = number of possible functions
    (numbers remained constant on hand of a theoretical model)
N_f = functions actually exercised
i = a certain sector of the list of positions
j = a certain sector of the list of functions

F =   sum of roles = sum of the allocations of functions to available position holders

F_{ij} =   sum of the partial matrix from position sector i and function sector j

P =   sum of the position holders

P_i =   persons in position sector i

The following indices can be deduced:

1. $\dfrac{N_p}{p}$ = position plurality

2. $\dfrac{N_f}{f}$ = functional complexity

Assumption 1: $P \leqslant F$: Persons able to take over certain functions are always too few.

3. $\sqrt{\dfrac{N_p}{p} \cdot \dfrac{N_f}{f}}$ = measure of multiplicity of roles: the average chance of a position holder to occupy a role of the model. The higher this probability, the more complex the organisation of the roles is.

Assumption 2:

decreasing division of labour = increasing chance of accumulating tasks:

maximal division of labour: no difference $F - P$:

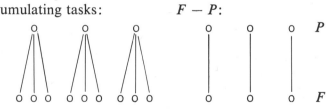

Thus, it follows:

4. $A = \dfrac{P}{F}$ = degree of division of labour

Because this measurement does not take the differences in the multiplicity of roles into account, it must be weighed accordingly.

5. $O = \dfrac{P}{F}\sqrt{\dfrac{N_p}{p} \cdot \dfrac{N_f}{f}}$ = degree of organisation (maximum = $1 \cdot 0$)

From the role matrix, a few more variables can be deduced. In view of this we were interested in the following questions:

(a) To what extent do staff and quasi-staff members limit themselves to executive and administrative functions? To what extent does the staff exercise integrative functions?

On the basis of these questions the following variable was constructed, which should apply to the measure of the degree of bureaucratisation (in the sense of ritualism in staff's behaviour) in the centre.

In this case, the quotient from the sum of roles (staff) for executive and administrative functions and the total sum of roles (staff) are of use:

6. $\dfrac{F_{1-9/1-7}}{F_{1-9/1-14}}$ = relation of the executive/administrative roles and total roles of the staff including the quasi-staff members.

The exercise of certain roles by the staff, however, depends upon the degree of division of labour among the members of the staff, because the lower it is, the greater is the limitation of their taking further roles according to assumption 2. As a consequence, the quotient is weighed with the value A (for the staff):

7. $Bu = \dfrac{F_{1-9/1-7} \cdot P_{1-9}}{F^2_{1-9/1-14}}$ = bureaucratisation of the staff's behaviour.

(b) To what extent are executive and administrative functions connected with visitors' key positions (nos 9–13)?

On the basis of this question, the following variable was constructed, which can be used as a measure of the influence of visitors in key positions on decisions, or rather as a measure of their integration or cooperation:

8. $Coo = \dfrac{F_{9-13/1-7} \cdot P_{9-13}}{F_{9-13/1-14} \cdot P}$ = cooperation between staff and visitors – on the premises of

Assumption 3: Visitors' positions are filled relatively independent of the degree of the division of labour in the centre, because the organisation of the centre is not dependent upon the voluntary participation of the visitors.

The following significant correlations between the three variables deduced from the role matrices and other variables were ascertained:

Table 7.4
Correlations of some variables derived from the role matrices ($N = 73$)

	O	Bu	Coo
Index of accessibility of rooms	−·23	−·25	
Time of opening for open-door activities versus work of youth associations	−·23		
Average age of visitors*			·32
Percentage of visitors in school or college*	−·32		
Proportion of sport activities		·24	
Proportion of achievement and educationally-oriented activities			−·27
Diversity of activities		·23	
Friendliness of visitors' attitudes to staff*	−·28	−·32	
Discrediting behaviour of male cliques to many female visitors	·23		
Institutional dependency of centre			−·28
Effects of socialisation and leisure time agents in the vicinity (pressure of competition)	·30		

* These variables were measured in terms of average values derived from interview data.

The theoretical relevance of these results for an analysis of the structural constraints present in youth centres cannot be discussed here. The correlations sufficiently demonstrate the usefulness of this relatively simple-to-use instrument for participant observation, which allows for a fairly exact empirical analysis of some properties of social structure. Because of their complexity, the measurement of these properties has otherwise been looked at very sceptically.

8 Validity and Prognostical Power of Observation and Interview Data

8.1 Observers' judgements versus informants' judgements as indicators of reliability

In the youth centre study, the observers were given the task of having several complex properties of the centre, the behaviour of its director and of its visitors judged by several experts, intimately familiar with what took place at the centre, on the basis of eight rating scales (see Lüdtke & Grauer, 1973). The scales consisted of statements about qualitatively different distinctions among the respective variables; the statements were partially formulated in such a way (e.g. 'The centres' programme is one sided and fixed on only a few leisure time activities'), that subjective evaluations were supposed to be involved in the ratings. Because the observers, likewise, had to order their opinions according to these scales, their ratings could be compared with those of the experts. The differences per scale were tested by chi-square and the coefficient of contingency (C). Four of the scales gave rise to significant differences. Table 8.1 shows the results of this testing. The scales were ranked according to the homogeneity of ratings. Those distinctions of variable which were strongly overemphasised by one group, in proportion to the other, are specified.

Table 8.1
Observers' versus experts' judgements

Rank of homogeneity	Dimension of scale	C	P	Overemphasised properties	
				Observers	Experts
Highly homo-geneous 1	5 Direction of centres' welcome for visitors	·04	·80	–	–
2	8 Socialising functions of centre	·09	·30	–	–

Table 8.1 (*continued*)

3	7 Behaviour tendencies of visitors	·11	·10	Over-adaptation; passivity	Initiating cooperation with staff and innovation
4	3 Group structure and social cohesion	·14	·10	Weak cohesion	Absence of structure; disintegration
5	1 Authority and communications structure	·19	·01	Normative instability (minimal structure)	Integration; democracy
					High formalisation and rigidity
6	6 Class selectivity	·22	·001	Over-representation of lower-educated and workers	High representativeness in terms of social structure of centre's near vicinity
7	2 Director's characteristic mode of interaction	·25	·001	Lacking initiative, holding a marginal position	As a good fellow, integrating
8 Highly heterogeneous	4 Diversity of activities	·30	·001	One-sidedness, lacking alternatives	High diversity

It is telling that, as a whole, the items specified by the observers and deviating from the ratings made by the experts correspond more nearly to the results of the study than those ratings. The observers were apparently able to maintain greater distance and objectivity than the more deeply involved experts. None of the staff members could, by the way, be regarded as experts because of being exceptionally emotionally attached to the centres' affairs. As Table 8.1 shows, the experts interviewed over-emphasised those items within the lower four scales, whose implications are desirable as real properties of the centres according to official youth policy. We are, therefore, tempted to read into this result an evidence for good reliability of observers' judgements in the terms set by levels II and III of the scheme above (see Table 4.5).

8.2   Validity of the actors' observed attributes

On account of the multi-dimensional and complementary nature of the research techniques employed, the youth centre study offers a good chance to compare observation and interview data, in order to examine their validity, the operational consistency of different variables, the prognostic power of one variable relative to another. If such a comparison is successful, i.e. relevant correlations between variables measured by observation and interviewing can be proved, so that either measurements are indicators of a latent variable, then a reciprocal validation of the different indicators thereby is given. In this way it can also be demonstrated that by comparative participant observation, the measurement of elementary variables is possible as is the study of situational contexts.

Moreover, the examples taken from the study serve to test the following questions: (a) To what extent are observation data about individual actors sufficiently suited to predict or explain behaviour variables measured by interviews? (b) In which manner are observed field variables connected with individual behaviour variables? (c) Can aggregated interview results (e.g. average values per indicator) be handled as variables of the corresponding object of observation (youth centre)?

After each interview with a visitor, the seventy-four observers were asked to include on the same questionnaire a description based on the following questions:

To be filled in after the interview:
37   Physical properties (relative to age):
   (a)   tall / medium / short
   (b)   athletic / slender / corpulent / atypical
   (c)   physically advanced / normal / retarded
38   Conspicuous external properties:
   (a)   hair-do and appearance
   (b)   clothing
   (c)   conspicuous bodily features
39   Social properties:
   (a)   sociometrical type at the centre
       'star' / 'hedgehog' / marginal / yes-man / atypical / no judgement possible

(b)   can the respondent be regarded as a key person in the centre?
yes / no / don't know
in case of yes: in which positions?

(c)   which conspicuous modes of behaviour or qualities affect his social status in the centre?
positively (higher status)
negatively (lower status)

(d)   which informal groups (e.g. cliques) does the respondent belong to? Describe the size and position of this group at the centre.

Thus, the data issuing from these questions deal with actual observations, which supplement the interview data. Because the interviews took place in the last phase of the observation period we could assume that the observers knew the greater part of the questioned visitors well enough, after approximately four weeks of continuous field observation including intensive communication, so that they could describe some of their individual characteristics. In so doing, we were interested in information about individual and status properties, which were probably of significant social relevance in the centre situation, within the body of visitors, and could be considered as independent or intervening variables of the behaviour. The indicators of these properties had been illustrated in the introductory courses by means of numerous examples.

From the data to questions 37–39, the following four variables could be extracted (data from $n = 2,334$):

Conspicuous external properties (ExtProp)	Per cent
Constitutional, physical features or deficiencies	7·9
Physical merits and attractiveness	1·7
Fashionable symbolism	4·5
Other conspicuous properties	1·1
No conspicuous properties, no comments	84·8
	100·0

Sociometrical type (SocTyp)	Per cent
Atypical, yes-man	46·2
Star	12·1
Hedgehog, marginal	13·5
No comments	28·2
	100·0

These types only present analogies to the types of choosing behaviour as a result of sociometrical tests. The actor's typical position within his visitor group should be specified as a result of the interactions between him and the group.

Key position at the centre (KeyPos)	Per cent
No clear key position	66·5
More formal key position	6·6
More informal key position	6·6
Other key positions	1·1
Several key positions	0·6
No comments	18·7
	100·1

Relevant status criteria (Stat)	
Positive:	Per cent
More instrumental abilities	4·8
More socially integrative abilities or individual prominence	7·5
Demonstrative symbolism or erotic qualities	2·4
Other properties	0·9
Combination of properties	2·7
Negative:	
Lack of sociability	2·3
Disintegrative behaviour	3·2
Other properties	1·9
Combination of properties	0·3
No comments	74·0
	100·0

It was understandably too much to ask the observers, above all, those in large and complex centres with higher visitor fluctuation, to describe Stat, because this variable is only ascertainable by continual observation of relatively smaller groups. Nevertheless, the numbers of specifications, as the following tables show, are sufficient for the analysis of various relations.

Internal consistency and validity of the variables:
With regard to the correlations of these four variables, the following hypotheses can be formulated through application of several theorems of group dynamics. These were tested by chi-square (coefficients of contingency):

Hypothesis: ExtProp versus Stat: individual external properties have a complementary or strengthening effect on the criteria for positive or negative social status recognised by the group.

Table 8.2

ExtProp versus Stat (in per cent)

Stat	ExtProp				M
	Const. defic.	Phys. attr.	Fash. symb.	Other	
Positive:					
Instrumental	13	7	18	19	14
Integrative, prominence	28	14	14	13	20
Symb., erot.	3	36	18	25	15
Other and combinations	11	25	18	13	16
Negative criteria	45	18	30	31	35
	100	100	98	101	100

$p = \cdot05$ $C = \cdot43$ $N = 171$

Hypothesis: SocTyp versus KeyPos: a dominant position in the group increases the chance of holding key positions in the centre; a subordinate or marginal position in the group will decrease it.

Table 8.3

KeyPos versus SocType (in per cent)

KeyPos	SocType			M
	Atypical, yes-man	Star	Hedgehog, marginal	
None	91	25	88	80
Formal	5	25	6	8
Informal	2	42	5	9
Other or several	1	8	2	3
	99	100	101	100

$p = \cdot001$ $C = \cdot53$ $N = 1495$

Hypothesis: SocType versus Stat: an actor's position in the group will deviate from the average position more or less according to the special status criteria which he represents.

Table 8.4

SocType versus Stat (in per cent)

| Stat | SocType | | | M |
	Atypical, yes-man	Star	Hedgehog, marginal	
Positive:				
Instrumental	23	15	7	17
Integrative, prominence	27	40	11	29
Symb., erot.	7	13	8	9
Other and combinations	12	22	4	14
Negative criteria	31	11	70	31
	100	101	100	100

$p = \cdot001 \quad C = \cdot47 \quad N = 519$

Hypothesis: KeyPos versus Stat: the representation of high or low valued status criteria of the group will strengthen or weaken, respectively, the holding of a key position in the centre.

Table 8.5

KeyPos versus Stat (in per cent)

| Stat | KeyPos | | | | M |
	None	Formal	Informal	Other and several	
Positive:					
Instrumental	19	14	18	14	18
Integrative, prominence	20	49	33	41	29
Symbol., erot.	10	3	11	9	9
Other and combinations	8	20	26	18	15
Negative criteria	44	13	13	18	30
	101	99	101	100	101

$p = \cdot001 \quad C = \cdot45 \quad N = 540$

All values of total chi-square are significant, for the most part, even highly significant, despite some relatively small numbers of cases[1], the other two tables, not rendered, as well: ExtProp versus SocType ($p = \cdot001$, $C = \cdot27$), and ExtProp versus KeyPos ($p = \cdot05$, $C = \cdot26$). The hypotheses can be considered confirmed, even if partially only in terms of the tendency.

Because the operational indicators (categories) of the various variables overlap in their contents to a certain extent, (e.g. formal/informal key position and prominence), relatively good validity measures are provided by the co-efficients.[2] Obviously, there are good chances for participant observers, even in relatively complex fields, of observing and classifying actors in a greater number in terms of refined individual and social categories.

Observed properties of social status versus behaviour variables measured by responses in interviewing:

As intervening variables of their behaviour in the youth centre, the attitudes of the visitors were measured by means of Guttman-scales (a) toward the visitor group, (b) toward the centre director, whereby different dimensions of the attitudes were scaled (see Lüdtke & Grauer, 1973). According to the study's hypotheses, we assumed that the attitude of an adolescent to both of these reference groups in the youth centre, as a whole, varies with his status in the homogeneous age group, and that, specifically, adolescents with a high status (high integration) express a more neutral attitude toward the centre director than those with low status. If the measurement of the four observed components of status is valid and the assumed relationships hold true, then empirical relationships found in cross tables of the status components and the attitudes should confirm them. In fact, significant differences in the dis-tribution of the attitude values arose in the majority of possible cross tables, which can be traced back to the influence of status variables as assumed beforehand This is illustrated by means of two examples:

Hypothesis: status-furthering qualities of an actor are linked to a friendlier social opinion of the group than status-diminishing properties.

Table 8.6

Stat versus image of the social behaviour tendencies of the other visitors (in per cent)

Stat	Score:	Image (friendliness)			*M*
		0–1	2	3–4	
Positive criteria		62	70	75	70
Negative criteria		38	30	25	30
		100	100	100	100

$p = \cdot05$ $C = \cdot27$ $N = 574$

Hypothesis: adolescents, who call special attention to themselves in the group by means of special (attractive) properties, show a greater social aloofness towards the centre director than those with conspicuous constitutional, physical properties and deficiencies.

Table 8.7

ExtProp versus social distance from the
centre director (in per cent)

| ExtProp | | Social distance | | | | |
	High	0–1	2–3	4	Low	
Constitut. deficiencies		15	42	43		100
Phys. attractiveness		22	51	27		100
Fash. symbolism		19	50	31		100
Other conspic. properties		32	41	27		100
M		18	45	37		100

$p = \cdot025$ $C = \cdot26$ $N = 322$

The efficacy of the independent variables of social status observed, though to a small extent, to explain or predict attitudes of visitors, held true, for some variables of their leisure time behaviour, too, as inquired into by interviewing. For this reason, the following illustrations are cited:

Hypothesis: status-diminishing properties of an actor lessen his chance of interacting with other group members.

Table 8.8

Stat versus interaction with other visitors outside
the centre (in per cent)

| Stat | Units of interaction* | | | | | |
	None	1–5	6–12	13–28	29+	M
Positive	59	73	69	72	71	70
Negative	40	26	32	29	28	30
	99	99	101	101	99	100

$p = \cdot025$ $C = \cdot29$ $N = 577$

*Product of frequency of interaction and number of partners.

Hypothesis: the more central the position of an individual in the visitor group, the more frequently he visits the centre with best friends.

Table 8.9

SocType versus visit to centre together with best friends (in per cent)

| Joint visit to centre | SocType | | | M |
	Atypical, yes-man	Star	Hedgehog, marginal	
None	15	16	19	16
Sometimes, seldom	30	22	39	30
Most of the time	54	62	41	53
	99	100	99	99

$p = \cdot 001 \quad C = \cdot 14 \quad N = 1623$

Hypothesis: adolescents holding key positions – especially formal ones – in the centre tend to participate more considerably in specific group activities than those without key positions.

Table 8.10

KeyPos versus participation in specific group activities in the centre (in per cent)

| Participation in specific group activities | KeyPos | | | |
	None	Informal	Formal and other	
No	86	7	6	100
Yes	73	9	18	100
M	82	8	10	100

$p = \cdot 001 \quad C = \cdot 28 \quad N = 1728$

Hypothesis: adolescents with status-diminishing properties tend more to social and consummatory activities, less to achievement-oriented activities than those with status-furthering properties.

154

Table 8.11

Stat versus activity preferences at the centre
(in per cent)

Preferences	Stat		M
	Positive	Negative	
Informal communication, parlour games, consumption of mass media, dancing	42	52	45
Centre sports, field and gym sports	42	36	40
Achievement and educationally-oriented activities, cooperation in the administration of the centre	16	12	15
	100	100	100

$p = \cdot 001 \quad C = \cdot 37 \quad N = 585$

8.3 Validity of complex field indicators

To show how valid complex observation data can be, the youth centre study will be used as an example. In so doing, variables measured by means of different techniques and from different parts of the observation schedule are intercorrelated. We are concerned here with a validity testing on level II (see Table 4.5). A part of the significant relationships of this form are included in the section about the role matrix. The variables to be quoted represent, as most of the quantitatively analysed data in the youth centre study, more or less complex structural properties of the youth centres. Thus, they partially relate to generalisations from series of observation situations, however, not to elementary interaction units of the form found in the Bales-categories. The characteristics of these variables can be defined as follows:

1 The variables are descriptive results of long observation series in various situations of the field.
2 Their operational criteria originate in part from different data fields and parts of the observation schedule.
3 They are constructions set up by the analyst and based on different crude data from the field observation.
4 They are the result of two standardisations on different levels: the standardisation through the observation schedule and the standardisation or rather coding of the evaluating process.

In principle, these characteristics increase the error variance of the variables. They show, however, as well, one of the main possibilities of comparative participant observation: the ex-post construction of comparable complex variables from relatively unconnected records of numerous observers (see sections 4.5 and 7.1).

Observation data versus observation data:
Using both diversity of activities and attractiveness of the material set-up variables, the validity of different observation data dealing with the same object will be demonstrated. The first variable was measured in two ways:

DIVERSITY OF ACTIVITIES
1 directly by observers' ratings on a scale of statements expressing the following alternatives (see dimension 4 in Table 8.1):

		n
0	One-sidedness, lacking alternatives	15
1	Medium diversity, few alternatives	48
2	High diversity	10

2 indirectly by the multistepped index described in section 7.1.
The coefficient of correlation between both rank orders over the 73 centres was ·45.

ATTRACTIVENESS OF THE MATERIAL SET-UP OF THE CENTRE
With this variable, it was attempted to measure the symbolic and affective valences of the centres' material set-ups (rooms, furniture, interior design, inventory) which were related to the relevant activity dimensions. The easiest way to make them operational was by means of observers' ratings on the following scale:

	n
0 not stimulating visit to centre	7
1 slightly stimulating visit to centre	17
2 moderately stimulating visit to centre	33
3 very stimulating visit to centre	16

The second way of measuring this variable arose from a complicated step-by-step combination of interviewing and observation data as follows (see the extensive description by Lüdtke & Grauer, 1973):

1 Scaling intensity values (*z*-scores) of favouring different set-ups by means of pair comparisons: a random sample of visitors to a large city centre were asked to rate, in this way, 10 different dimensions of equipment. The visitors were instructed to give their judgements about these 10 complexes of

156

empirical examples according to their correspondences with an ideal centre.

2   Valuing the 10 dimensions of equipment according to the degree to which certain objects of inventory and rooms were available as having been recorded by the observers. The following values were used: $0 =$ nothing, $0 \cdot 5 =$ few, $1 \cdot 0 =$ medium, $1 \cdot 5 =$ many.

3   Weighing the scores of favour by means of the respective degrees of observed availability of objects per dimension and centre.

4   Summing up the scores, in this way obtained as products, of attractiveness for all dimensions to arrive at a total score of the attractiveness of the centre's material set-up.

Distribution of scores:

	n
up to 12	5
13–22	14
23–32	33
33–42	14
43 and more	7

The coefficient of correlation between these scores and observers' ratings amounts to $r = \cdot 48$. The correlations between attractiveness (cumulative scale) and another variable, valence of architectural atmosphere amounts to $r = \cdot 49$. The latter was measured by the sum of observers' ratings in a semantic differential whose scales indicated different dimensions of positive and negative valences of this kind.

If the multidimensional and synthetic approach of the operations above is taken into consideration, then the observers' judgements can be viewed as valid to a high degree.

Observation data versus interview data:
These last two examples are supposed to show how indirect validity inferences arise from a comparison of observation data with interview data which refer to similar property classes. The correlations cannot be defined as genuine measures of validity because the variables do not belong to an identical property class. If this had been the case, then closer correlations would probably have been the result.

1   In the interview the young people were asked how long they had already been visiting the centre. Their answers given in months on an average per centre could be regarded as an inverse measure of mean visitors' fluctuation at the centre.

In the schedule the observers were requested to identify (dichotomously) rejecting behaviour on the part of male regulars (clique of perpetual visitors)

157

towards girls. The correlation of both variables amounts to $r = -\cdot36$. It verifies the fact that the rejecting tendency of the regular visitors moderately decreases with increasing fluctuation, because the rise of regular cliques is rendered more difficult in centres with high fluctuation.

In the same manner, an index of the frequency of visits was constructed from the responses of the visitors. It correlated with the observation variables, diversity of activities ($r = \cdot30$) and institutional dependency of the centre ($r = -\cdot34$): with growing diversity of activities and autonomy of the centre in relation to control by supporting parties the average frequency of visits increases.

2 The mean scores of the visitors' attitudes toward the centre's director were used to measure degrees of friendliness in the field of interaction between visitors and staff. This variable correlates significantly with degree of organisation ($r = -\cdot28$) and bureaucratic tendency in the staff's behaviour ($r = -\cdot32$), two measures of the role matrix (see section 7.2.2). With increasing bureaucratisation the emotional distance between the visitors and the staff grows.

It should be clear that these relationships refer to contextual properties of social systems, not to individual properties, i.e in order to avoid ecological fallacies, there is no reason for inferring analogous relationships among individuals from those among the centres (see section 4.5.2).

Notes

1 Because in the case of missing statements, the observers frequently failed to say whether they meant 'could not be judged' or 'without special properties', only the cases with substantial data could be taken into account. The sharpness of the findings is, as a result, of course, very limited.

2 The coefficients naturally cannot be interpreted as linear product-moment-correlations. Experiences show that in the case of normally distributed marginals, C is more often lower than the analogous values of r, so that in spite of everything, with C an approximation is given. Hofstätter (1957, p. 292) writes, 'that, also very carefully developed tests only seldomly possess diagnostic validities, which lie over $r = 0 \cdot 60$'. In general, values of $0 \cdot 40$–$0 \cdot 50$ are already regarded as sufficient validities (Sader, 1961).

9 Problems of Observers' Roles in the Field

9.1 Determinants of observer behaviour

1 Duration of role finding

The assumption of a suitable participant role, i.e. the social integration of the observer, is a dynamic process and dependent on the specific nature of the situations. König (1967, p. 37) writes for that reason, 'that a more or less long period of "infiltration" is needed in every case, until the participant observer has reached that position, which allows him to participate somewhat adequately as well as to exercise a systematic observation.' The success of this 'infiltration' depends on entrance into the field at the right time and place (Jahoda, Deutsch & Cook, 1967, p. 88), i.e. in a normal and relaxed setting of the field happenings. For the observer, this starting period signifies a gradual probing into the various behaviour claims on him in a relatively reserved and waiting manner, whereby he tries out the appropriate modes of behaviour by trial and error which guarantee a methodically unproblematic participation. In this first phase, systematic observation tasks should either be withdrawn or at least extended to only those dimensions which can be experienced especially clearly and are accessible, because the phase of finding a role limits the reliability of the observations.

2 General and specific roles

Kluckhohn (1967, p. 98, ff) differentiates between general and specific observer's roles. General roles are those which are not played by individuals as such, but are defined in the social system according to the fundamental aspects of sex, age, class affiliation and the like (e.g. occupational roles), while specific roles have their meaning in the observer's interaction with individuals or groups. In view of both of the role areas, the position of the observer in the field must be clearly defined. The assumption of specific roles is, thereby, relatively free of problems: the observer internalises them through social sensitisation in interaction with certain persons in certain situations. Of course, their acceptance by the actors presupposes, above all, a successful definition of a general role. However, at the same time, the research role of the observer is of decisive importance. If the observer decides to hide his research intentions, then the question still remains open as to which general role or roles he wants to play. Thus he must find out the social meaning of both of the determining factors of general roles (age and sex) prevailing in the system in question (Kluckhohn, 1967, p. 100). From that which has been said these general conclusions can be derived:

(a) The more the actors in the field are *instrumental and goal-oriented*, the more important become general observer's roles as to the dominant activities and, therefore, the more the observer must correspond to the achievement expectations of the actors or simulate these achievements by taking on a covert research role (i.e. business: role of co-workers with the same occupation; prison: role of average delinquents with corresponding offences).

(b) The stronger the *informal-expressive* orientation in the field is the more important different specific observers' roles become. However, the observer must not, thereby, run the risk of falling into a marginal position through his sex, age, social background, appearance, etc. In view of these attributes, he must comply with the norm as much as possible. (He must not be conspicuous, i.e. in a slums area by middle-class living habits; a woman in an all-male tourist party; a Babbitt-like adult in a youth club, etc.).

(c) If the research tasks of the observer are supposed to remain hidden and if he deviates noticeably from the average actor in terms of general attributes, then a compensatory general role should be assumed by him so that the transitory participation of a stranger appears plausible and acceptable to the actors. In our society the roles of visitors, guests, trainees, aides and the like often offer such an opportunity.

(d) In such fields, which are hierarchically structured into positions of power, the acceptance of a middle position should often be avoided, because it very easily becomes the source of conflict and change (i.e. a foreman's position in a factory). Thus, it is recommended, depending on the research aim, to take a higher or lower position of power, which guarantees the greatest general view over the field.

3   Integral versus peripheral roles

Kentler *et al.* (1969, p. 109) refer to this differentiation without going into further detail. We can define integral roles as those which are especially important elements of the social structure of the field; in contrast, peripheral roles are those of subordinate importance. Integral roles are, accordingly, bound to the area of central and middle positions, while peripheral roles belong to the marginal positions of the field. General as well as specific roles can be of integral or peripheral importance. At this time we cannot present any empirical typology of both forms of roles, because the structural importance of a role is dependent on the specific nature of the social structure and the situation. Thus, e.g., the general role of the average visitor of a youth centre can be of integral importance, whereas the average member in a union might be of peripheral importance. In general, it can be said that as a rule, next to the pronounced leadership roles, the roles of instrumental experts (specialists), expressive leaders, helpful colleagues, good neighbours etc., are of integral importance, i.e. they reinforce the institutionalised patterns of the system. It seems that a compromise is desirable for the behaviour of the participant observer: he should, on the one hand, experience the 'normal' events in the field as intensively as possible and in representative situations but, on the other hand, perceive structural tensions and changes, as well, without taking part directly in their outbreak and solution. That presupposes, without a doubt, the assumption of strategically favourable, thus, mostly integral roles. As a general rule it can be said: *the observer should attempt to proceed from peripheral to integral roles, however, only to the extent that his behaviour does not give rise to uncontrollable impacts and power effects, which change the social structure, or to affirmations of a given party in the field.*

Special situations for the study can be imagined in which a contrasting strategy might be necessary. If, for example, in a social field of tension, more specifically the situation of marginal groups or minorities (foreign workers, students, coloured inmates in a lodging house), are to be observed, then this should take place under circumstances conforming to the positions and roles of these groups, i.e. by the assumption of peripheral or marginal roles or rather roles defined as deviant. At this level the participant observer can best naturally perceive the 'normal' restrictions of the environment to which these groups are exposed. If, in such a case, the participant observers first introduce the marginal positions by being themselves, e.g. by coloured students, as participant observers, moving into a community, then the observation becomes a part of an experiment, by which the relationship between conditions at the start, induced influences on the reactions of the observer and the observed, or rather, changes must be strictly controlled.

4   *Overt versus covert observation*
In principle, the participant observer is asked to keep the actual research task hidden from the actors. Most authors of such methods agree on this point. It is, for that reason, that Kentler *et al.* (1969, p. 106) characterise it as 'covert participant observation', too. This principle might, of course, prove to be abstract in practice. For instance, the actors might not be satisfied once and for all with a 'plausible' explanation by the observer for his presence (see section 3.2). It must often be repeated on different occasions in varied forms. Also, it cannot always be avoided, that the observer becomes somehow conspicuous by 'curious' questions, always being there, making notes, etc. Beyond this, he usually remains a stranger. No matter how he behaves – it's hardly avoidable that he is given, or rather, granted, a special status.

In view of this, a practical compromise between the overtness and covertness

161

of the observations must be found. This depends upon the respective facts of the field. As Jahoda, Deutsch & Cook (1967, p. 89) write, there are many situations in which the observer would be found to be a disrupting stranger, if he does not exercise a function appearing plausible to the actors. As a result, the complete disclosure of the research intention to the actors might be rational in an extreme case, if the observer succeeds in proving to be a 'normal', integrated, honest and liked participant of the group. This was doubtless the case with Whyte (1961); also Bain (1967) explained his thesis to coloured workers, of course, as he comments, without explaining what it really was. The majority of the observers of our youth centre study would have likewise preferred a situation in which the visitors as well as the staff were better informed about the purpose of the investigation.

Because, as already discussed in section 3.2, the social estimation of the observer depends more on the everyday social behaviour than on some external reason for his presence, which at any rate remains abstract to the actors, the principle of covert observation should not be overvalued. Recording an observation must, of course, remain covert but the research purpose can be disclosed. In order to make it plausible, it is often sufficient to make a partial explanation somewhat on the following lines: 'I would like to look around here for a while, in order to get-to-know the people and what they do, so that others might sometime learn what happens here.' As a general rule it can be formulated as such; *The observer gives reasons for and realises his participation in such a way that the actors in no situation find reason to suspect they are being used as objects of a doubtful interest directed against them, or of an unknown control board.*

5 *Active versus passive participation, intensity of the interaction*

General information about this problem was already given in section 3.2. We only need to repeat here that, in general, the compromise 'pseudo-participation', limited by the observer's tasks, is recommended. However, practically speaking, the degree of participation depends on the respective social structure of the situation. In a system of high-levelled specialised roles, the observer might be forced to come to terms with a very passive participation while he possibly is forced to continuous intensive activity in a youth club with high flexibility and emotional-expressive colouring of the interactions, in order not to appear as an outsider.

Furthermore, the participation is objectively determined by the goals and the power structure of a system. In this way, the participation in activities of the supervisory board of a bank is almost impossible, while participation in crimes of a gang of criminals is by itself forbidden for ethical and security reasons (Jahoda, Deutsch & Cook, 1967, p. 90). These authors are right to believe that an intensive participation recommends itself in the following two contrasting extreme situations: (a) if the object to be investigated is totally new to the observer, so that he cannot draw upon his own experiences in life for the missing links of information, and (b) if it is so familiar to him that he almost only regards it by looking back on his own life, in case he doesn't intentionally assume another role which allows him to experience the finer differences in it himself (ibid., p. 89).

Beyond that, the intensity of the participation is a dependent variable of the assumed general role. The observer must, to a certain extent, interact according to the institutionalised behaviour expectations of the actors towards him. If this role is more important in certain situations (e.g. where specialised competency comes into question) than in others (in the case of a specialised general role), then he must expect to come into closer contact with certain groups than with others. In order to avoid resulting observation distortion, the observer must then try to interact suitably with the other groups by means of his specific roles. Thus, a relative equilibrium of his social relationships may arise in the field.

As consequence, the observer, by himself, can manipulate his own behaviour to a limited extent along the dimension of active versus passive participation. The alternative, *initiative of versus response to interaction*, is methodically more important and can be better controlled by him. In general, it can be stated that an adequate observer, in principle, should rather reciprocate interactions initiated by others than the other way round. If the observer's activity shifts in direction to dominant initiative, then the danger exists that he becomes an influential key person who changes the field unwillingly. Part of the special methodological abilities of the observer is to seek to increase the information value of the interactions initiated by others for himself, by e.g. using his response as a reason to direct questions at the communication partners without giving them the feeling that he is taking the initiative.

In connection with this strategy the following statement by Kluckhohn (1967, p. 102, f) is important: 'To me, the assumption seems justified that one can experience more from a person, if this person believes that one would like to be as he, rather than if he suspects that one wishes to find out why he is different from us' (translated from German version).

9.2 Empirical analysis of the participant observers' role performances

In the preceding sections, the youth centre study was drawn upon for the illustration and application of procedures of data control to the levels of testing II and III of Table 4.5. In the same manner, some possibilities for analysis of the observer behaviour (level I) will be demonstrated as well, by which the youth centre study again was reanalysed in terms of indirect testing procedures as suggested in section 8.1. We have, thereby, arranged the material for this purpose according to five sources. of errors in participant observation, as discussed in section 3.2.

9.2.1 Role definitions

The definition of the observer's role in the youth centre study had, for the following reasons, proved to be quite difficult to state beforehand:

1   The centres are characterised by a dichotomous role structure: the young visitors, on the one hand, have the status of voluntary participants in contrast to the director and the staff (full and/or part-time) of the centre with the status of members and formal authority (see Lüdtke, 1972). The holding of middle positions is only possible in small measure. The observers had to be introduced to the responsible staff as trainees and honorary co-workers, because, on the one hand, the staff is perhaps the most important communication partner and these positions are considered fundamental in the centres and, on the other, because it would be unrealistic to assume that the youth would accept the, on average six years older, observers as their equals without restrictions (see section 6.1.2).

2   According to the structural complexity and type of centre director, the authority structure of centres varies remarkably: it stretches from autocratic direction to partner like integration. The role definition had, to a certain extent, to be adapted to the respective types so that predictions were not possible.

3   Because of their quantity and for various other reasons, the group of centre visitors, or rather their inner structure, was the prominent object of observation. Thus, despite the formal limitations, an observer's role with high affinity to the visitors' roles or at least in relation to a middle position between staff and young people was desired.

Analysis:

1   *Data of the role matrix* (*see section* 7.2)
The following self-assessments by 40 observers about the functions which they exercised were compared with the corresponding findings for the staff and the visitors from all 73 centres.

Table 9.1 demonstrates very clearly that the observers have taken over far stronger visitor-centred than staff-centred roles in terms of their duty allocation. More than half of the assumed tasks can be characterised as integrative functions, thus lying in the narrower field of the visitor group. A further fifth of the entries falls to neutral administrative functions, to services rendered for the visitors and the staff. Only about one fourth of the entries falls under the category executive function, thus under the real domain of the staff. This distribution of observer tasks can be judged to be appropriate in terms of methodological premises.

Table 9.1

Roles of staff, observers and visitors in the youth centres under study

Functions (roles)	$n = 73$ Staffs		$n = 40$ Observers		$n = 73$ Groups of visitors	
	$a*$	Per cent	$a*$	Per cent	$a*$	Per cent
Executive	13·2	51	0·9	27	4·0	26
Administrative	6·0	23	0·6	18	4·1	26
Integrative	6·6	25	1·8	54	7·4	48
	25·8	99	3·3	99	15·5	100

*Average of individual functions per centre which fall to the given occupants of positions respectively.

A test of the relationship between sex and functions of the observers gave rise to a significant difference: the female observers assumed stronger administrative tasks than integrative and executive functions (see Lüdtke & Grauer, 1973). This could be designated as a 'withdrawal tendency' on the part of the female observers, which is to be traced back to the fact that in the centres male juveniles very strongly dominate, making the integration of a strange female observer more difficult. Their more distinctive service roles (e.g. bar duty, issuance of games, among others) could then be considered as appropriate, traditionally predetermined general roles.

2 *Data of the group discussions*
The result from Table 9.1 (visitor-centred role definition) was confirmed in both of the group discussions carried through during the evaluation meetings of research directors and observers. The statements of the observers on corresponding questions of the research directors could be evaluated in the following manner after an additional control on the basis of the observers' diary notes:

Table 9.2
Affinity of observer's status (self-ratings)

	n
Status tended more to the part of the *staff* (as a person of authority or held in respect, assistant of the staff)	14
Status tended more to the part of the *visitors* (successful adaptations to the behaviour of the juveniles, as a recognised group member, without identification with the centre directions, etc.)	26
Ambiguous positions, in-between positions (different positions according to the situations)	7
No explicit specification	26
	73

The statements of the observers about the tensions and conflicts which arose between them and the other actors in the field agree very much with these self-ratings. From the only 13 positive entries, 2 fall to conflicts with youth as opposed to 7 such conflicts with the centre director and 4 with other co-workers and representatives of the supporting parties.

3   *Observer's status versus climate of attitudes between staff and visitors*
If the friendliness of attitudes toward the centre director, as measured by a Guttman-scale as a part of the interview, is placed in relation to the observer's status, then the following significant relationship results:

Table 9.3
Observer's status versus climate of attitude
between staff and visitors

Mean score of friendliness in visitors' attitudes	Per cent Observer's status				
	Staff-centred	Ambiguous, no explication	Visitor-centred	Total	n
−3·4	(0)	(6)	(27)	12	9
3·5–4·2	(71)	70	38	59	43
4·3 +	(29)	24	35	29	21
	100	100	100	100	
n	14	33	26		73

$P = $ ·05 $C = $ ·36

166

The tendency is, thereby, demonstrated that the observer's status in the centres showing less friendly visitor attitudes toward the staff had a higher affinity to the visitor group.

Result: our analysis supplied different evidences for an optimal definition of the observer's role and for a successful integration of the observers in the field in the terms of the methodological postulates.

4 Specific factors of role-taking and integration of the observers

Because the youth centres, as a rule, are relatively open and dynamic systems and are not fixed one-sidedly to instrumental orientation, it was to be expected that very different causes and factors would be important in the process of finding roles for the observers, as they arise in situations with dominant expressive, informal and subcultural behaviour patterns. We mentioned already in section 6.1.2, that the process of interviewing gave reason to the youth to clearly define the general role of the observer. Beyond that, the following characteristics of successful integration on the part of the observers were brought to light: transformation from formal to personal relationship in terms of the form of address, footing in pubs, ascription of symbolic attributes (nicknames) and much more, primarily informal mechanisms in age groups, as the following illustrations from the diary notes verify:

No. 20

I had big difficulties the first three days finding any contact at all. Although the centre staff was addressed informally* by most of the visitors and in turn the staff did the same, I was spoken to as 'Mr' by the staff even in the presence of the young people. Although I had been immediately invited to play cards the first day, the attitude remained sceptical, reserved but not aggressive or unfriendly. When I then went with the large part of the visitors to a nearby pub, many visitors lost their mistrust. With many of them I had a warm friendship-like relationship and was addressed by my first name. One part of the visitors remained, however, reserved; contacts limited themselves completely to greetings.

The youth were willing to participate in the interviewing. I also told them that I would have difficulty in carrying out at least 30 interviews. For this reason some of the youth went around to mobilise their friends who otherwise also frequented the centre but on this day were not present. *Consider here and by some of the following protocols the modes of addressing persons, peculiar to the German language: addressing 'informally', by the first name, or getting to a close relationship, refers to the intimate mode of 'thou'; addressing 'formally' or by 'Mr' refers to the mode of formal 'you'.

No. 9

With the young people of my age I became quite good friends after I

167

had told them enough about myself. I was thoroughly recognised as one
of them after I gave my official footing as well some time ago. I am also
very regularly invited to go with them to a pub and accept this invitation
very often (to the disadvantage of my bank account).
No. 25
Since the interview with Frank, I am for him only 'Miss Test', an honour-
able step up from 'Spy' and 'Auntie M'.

Informative as to the integrative importance of external causes is the
following example:

No. 9
On the way to the centre a 'hippie' sat down in the bus with long hair and
an old worn-out army jacket. A man of about 35 years asked him to
stand up: 'Hey sonny, stand up. You can just as well make room for
others.' 'You could just as well call me "Mr"', I am, after all, 19 years
old.' The man reacted furiously and an argument about manners and
long hair and hippies ensued. Finally, I got involved and supported the
hippie by saying that the adults could just as well be more polite, too, and
address the young man properly. Thus, there were two parties in the bus, the
hippie and me on the one side and the grown-up passengers on the other.
That evening in the centre two girls remarked that I had really 'given it' to
them. They were – unseen to me – witnesses to the incident. As a result of
this whole story, I made contact with the girls for the first time. They had
probably always greeted me before, but nothing more.

Some observers experienced difficult interaction with a few groups despite
being relatively well integrated on the whole. Here, differences in age and the
lack of familiarity with the field became noticeable:

No. 1
Some of the youth already greet me with a handshake; many were
mistrustful of me at first, especially as a result of having to sign-in on
the visitor list; but in many cases, the mistrust vanished when I tried to
explain the reason for the list and my function at the centre (student, who
must get practical experience for his studies). I have difficulty in finding
contact with some of the youth: those who come to the centre to kick
up a row, who often talk to one another in filthy language and like to
make as much trouble and noise as possible. I really don't know how
I could approach them.

In some cases the observers sensed that certain changes in the behaviour
of actors or in the situation were introduced by their presence, e.g. by the
observer's sex, by the unusual position of the trainee or, as well, by interpreting the observer as a 'control official'. Such cases might, for the most part,

be exceptions, which the observer has to resolve individually, which, however, the research director should expect occasionally.

No. 15 (female)
Because very few girls frequent the centre, my assignment is, for the meantime, a welcome change for the boys, to put it more mildly, a new plaything. They are there wherever I am and paint with the children, whenever I paint with them. The suggestion to play cards is applauded, with a loud 'yeah', and immediately a large, much too large group forms to play cards. I very clearly have the feeling that my appearance has brought unrest into the centre, and that the visitors behave differently than otherwise.

No. 34
I am asked if I will be the new centre director. I take pains to explain that I am a student who is doing his traineeship as a guest at the centre. They don't quite accept it: there has never been a student in this centre; the role of a social worker trainee is new to them. I am afraid that I am being identified with the role of the centre director, his assistant or of an educator. *A*, 17 years old, later expresses his surprise that I had not been planted by the 'top', as he had suspected.

No. 20
The centre staff seems to have adjusted to my presence. The visitors were repeatedly called to order ('this time sit down properly', 'pick up the paper there!' etc.) but always with a side glance to me, as if to see whether I was also taking notice of this intervention. The reaction of the concerned (grins, dumbfoundedness) clearly shows, that it otherwise proceeds somewhat looser here.

In the few cases of a staff-centred status, the observers felt, for the most part, this to be a disadvantage. Some made attempts to compensate and this reached the limits of the centre's authority structure or their own social capacities:

No. 13
Unfortunately I detect that the centre visitors view me as a member of the centre direction and, therefore, are especially polite, well-mannered and quiet towards me. If 50 visitors come to the centre in the course of the evening, I shake about 40 hands for it seems just as normal to personally greet the centre director and the co-workers, no matter whether the youth is coming only for a short ping-pong match or a round of cards.

No. 3 (from the group discussion)
I was introduced as a trainee and the trainees are called 'Sheriff's

Deputies' by the youth, and their attitude was about the same. For quite a time it was extremely difficult to even get them to call me by my first name. At first they continued to call me 'Mr', and when, some time later, after a good time, I asked them again to call me by my first name, they then treated it as a gift; and in spite of it, the authority gradation remained. They were already too caught up in it. All of the other staff members were addressed formally, and I simply continued to be identified with them. A close relationship could never arise. Simply because I had a 'Deputy Sheriff' function.

9.2.2 Selection of key persons

Because the youth centres are, for the most part, a relatively easily comprehensible field with situations, narrowly limited in space and time, the selection of suitable key persons scarcely presented a methodological problem. Despite the high fluctuation of visitors, the observers were able to differentiate between the most important single groups and their leaders and to observe their behaviour after a time. It was, thus, unnecessary to obtain information connecting individual observations through means of systematic communication with representative key persons.

For structural reasons the difficulty arose in individual cases to find contacts with leaders of nonconformist marginal groups or isolated cliques. These persons had to be observed and judged from a relative distance.

Viewed as a whole the field represented no 'strange culture' for the observers to the extent that they were not dependent upon intensive explanations by special informants for adequate interpretation of the social processes. The youth and the student observers might represent in fact partial 'subcultures', but not total contrasts to the usual patterns of behaviour and motivations.

Special key informants were necessary in terms of some properties and relationships of the external system (organisation, supporting body, budget, municipality, etc.). The easily accessible members of the staff, officials and supporters offered their services for this purpose.

As to the additional interviewing of experts (see sections 6.1.2 and 8.1), the observers were handed exact criteria for the selection of informants: people intimately familiar with the centre (honorary workers, youth guardians, pastors, visitors of long standing and the like).

9.2.3 Intensity of the interaction

For at least three reasons as intensive a participation as possible on the part of the observers in the activities of the young people was desired: (a) because the situation of a youth centre was unknown to the majority of observers; (b) because the social patterns of these centres, as is generally the case among youth groups of the same age, are dominantly expressive in manner, i.e. there is continual and strong mutual emotional reinforcement; (c) in order to overcome the barriers of authority between observers and centre visitors possibly set by a formal definition of roles.

The danger that an observer could be overintegrated by too intensive interaction or become an informal opinion leader, was considered low because of the age difference and the relatively high fluctuation of visitors and activities.

Analysis:

The question as to the appropriate activity and intensity of the observer's participation can only be tested by very indirect means when no specific testing procedure is available. It was, also, partially positively answered already in section 9.2.1.

1   *Change of the stereotype of the relevant reference group*
If the possibility exists to projectively measure the social affinity of the observers to the relevant actors, then, in order to estimate the interaction density, one can proceed from the following simple theorems by Homans (1960; translated from German version): (a)   if the frequency of the interaction between persons increases, then the degree of their inclination for one another will increase, and vice versa (ibid., p. 126); (b)   the more a number of people resemble one another in their social rank, the more frequent they will interact with one another (ibid., p. 188).

The same semantic differential with 32 descriptive pairs of attributes of 'juvenile centre visitors' was presented to the observers as a stimulus at the end of the introductory course (before the beginning of the research) as well as at the evaluation meeting (after its conclusion). Visitors to the centre, it could be assumed, had to be relevant for the students not only as research objects during the period of observation but, also, must have presented an important reference group as generalised by other social situations in the centre. If one, furthermore, assumes that elements of social affinity in relation to this group fall into the stereotype measured in such a manner then a comparison of 'Before' and 'After Profile' must give information about the changes in attitude among the students on the basis of social experiences during the participant observation.

Because the 32 pairs of attributes encompass a broad variety of dimensions, the correlation between both profiles was, as was to be expected, high; it amounted to $r = \cdot 90$ by the one course group and $\cdot 91$ by the other.

We have now selected those 14 pairs from the semantic differential which, in our opinion, dealt most nearly with an *affective social classification* of the object, and tested the changes of the classification in the course of the participant observation (see Table 9.4).

171

Table 9.4

The change of the stereotype 'juvenile centre visitors' by 74 observers

	Before observation*	Change in direction to the right side	After observation*	
Hostile	3·75	1·05	4·80	Friendly
Strange	3·55	0·90	4·45	Familiar
Affected	4·05	0·75	4·80	Natural
Closed	3·65	0·70	4·35	Open
Conceited	2·60	0·55	3·15	Modest
Ill-humoured	3·70	0·50	4·20	Cheerful†
Sad	3·95	0·40	4·35	Gay
Vague	3·30	0·30	3·60	Clear
Old-fashioned	4·80	0·25	5·05	Up-to-date
Rigid	3·60	0·15	3·75	Flexible
Versatile	3·80	0·15	3·95	Stiff
Controlled	2·35	0·10	2·45	Moody
Fair	3·65	0·05	3·70	Unfair
Cool	3·30	0·00	3·30	Feeling

*Means of ratings on a 7-point scale from 0 to 6.
†Differences Before-After on the first 6 scales are significant to the ·05 level.

The attitude changes, as made apparent in the change of the profile mean values, are significant by the first six scales. They can be interpreted as an increase of social affinity of the observers to the young people resulting from increased intensive interaction with the reference group. By applying both of the theorems by Homans, we can indirectly conclude that this result is probably a consequence of desired intensity of interaction and fewer differences in status between the observers and the visitors to the centre.

2 Attitudes of the visitors toward the observers

This assumption can be re-examined and confirmed by classifying the visitors' attitudes towards the observers, as they were perceived by the latter. After every interview with the visitors, the observers were obliged to note the reaction of the respondent to the observer in the period of participation preceding. The distribution of the findings is as follows:

Table 9.5

Reaction of the visitors to the observers

	Per cent
Very positive – on friendly terms	19·4
Friendly – collegial	39·8
Indifferent–neutral	25·3
Negative, avoid contact	3·5
Strongly negative – aggressive	0·6
No comment	11·4
	100·0 (n = 2334)

The reactions of two-thirds of the classified visitors were judged by the observers as 'very positive' or 'collegial' and only less than 5 per cent as negative or aggressive.

Between the judgements of the male observers and those of the female observers arose a significant difference: the females classified the reactions of the youth as somewhat less positive. In turn, the effect mentioned in section 9.2.1 (point 1) becomes noticeable here; the female observers had a more difficult time being accepted as participants by the dominantly male visitor groups.

9.2.4 *Going native*

We have not found any reason to believe that the observation material in individual cases was subjected to a systematic error effect by going native. Certainly, errors of this kind can only with difficulty, be controlled ex post facto. Nevertheless, it bears no relevance for the youth centre study for the following reasons:

1   The period of observation (25–40 days net) was too short for the observers, in order to (a) maximally fulfil the fixed tasks assigned them in the observation schedule and (b) to make an excessive involvement in the actions of the actors possible. The observers were much too busy with the cognitive seizing of the field (see section 6.2.3) and the role-finding in the time available.

2   The observation tasks were oriented to the structural heterogeneity of the field, i.e. to the variety or the contrast of positions and groups (e.g. staff versus visitors). The observers not only had to find their role within this multiplicity or between these contrasts, but also had to take them into

consideration within the observation units. It seems to us that these circumstances offered the best possibility of hindering going native: in socially heterogeneous and tension-filled fields the observer is constantly forced to approach the different reactions of the various actors very sensibly. Diverging or complementary perceptions make it extremely difficult for the observer to become absorbed, so to say, in the homogeneous reactions of one group and thereby impair his ability to maintain cognitive distance from the social happenings.

3 The danger of going native especially exists there where observation is done (a) exploratorily, (b) unoriented, i.e. without scheme and analytical categories, and (c) in a situation of total existential dependency of the observer on the field (in a 'foreign culture' without deviating surroundings). None of these conditions were given completely for our observers.

In some cases the observers experienced highly social integrative, easily comprehensible centres with stronger cohesion.

The fact that the observers here became especially active or even became key persons can be viewed more as a structural consequence than an individual deviation from the standard role.

9.2.5 Role conflicts

The observers' role conflicts in the youth centres were related to discrepancies within one role (between role segments: intra-role conflicts) as well as to such between different roles (interrole conflicts). This differentiation will be handled more carefully in section 12.2. Both of the major origins of role conflicts consisted in (a) a methodological omission, and (b) a structural discrepancy.

Concerning (a): in the definition of the observer's role (see sections 9.1.1 and 9.2.1), respectively, the instructions to the observers to keep their research tasks concealed as much as possible, we had overseen that it would have been beneficial to differentiate between the reactions of the staff and those of the juveniles.

As it turned out, more explicit information should have been given to the staff (e.g. by notifying them that the observations were related to the young people). The actual observer tasks naturally did not remain secret to the staff. In a field with insufficient professionalism among the position-holders (see Grauer, 1973), this led to insecurities and misunderstandings on the side of the centre management. Thus, the observer sometimes fell into the negative role of the 'secret spy'; for some of the observers this, also, implied an intra-role conflict (covert observation versus overt participation) – indeed only in relation to the staff:

No. 31

I do not have the impression that I have gained the centre director's confidence. I believe the instructions from the course have confused me more than helped me. I don't trust myself to ask any questions; I always think about how he doesn't even know exactly what I am investigating. Contact with the young people is good, but not with the director. I have been trying now for a week to ask if there is an official layout of the centre, but I don't dare because when I asked him whether I could evaluate the receiving list, he appeared to be really cross.

No. 22

The definition of the observer's role is not credible, even for me who, in my first days, immediately showed a great interest in engaging in centre activities. I am broadening the definition with care, without even mentioning the function of assistant. The centre director seems to have become insecure. I openly report on the investigation, go into details, making believe that the investigation is complete, which apparently has good success. Contact with the visitors was actually good from the very first day on. Most of them are extremely approachable, talk about themselves without being asked. I answer their first question as to the reason for my presence correctly: trainee during semester break.

No. 15

I slipped somewhat into the role of the part-time assistant, once in awhile I make such comments as 'don't do that, leave it be' – Concrete: In the 'Western cellar' silly jokes were being told. I requested that they be dropped as I didn't enjoy them. Next day the centre director told me that I had been called arrogant. The young people, however, have not changed their behaviour toward me – despite the new tag.

On the same evening, the student, Helmut, along with 3 other youths drove me home. The director told me on the next day that Helmut would not bring me home again. I didn't understand. I had said nothing in the car. I also said nothing to the director at this time. In his presence that evening the first thing that Helmut says to me is: 'Can I bring you home again this evening?' I take up the topic with the director who disputes it and can do nothing else but laugh. It is clear that he envies my good standing with the young people because he knows his own is very questionable. This is strengthened by a second fact: the director recommends the people to be interviewed, who – as it turned out in two cases – liked him and not so much the others. Perhaps I should really include the director in more work to combat what I sense to be an inferiority complex.

Concerning (b): in various autocratically structured centres, the middle position of the 'young trainee', who was valued by the staff as a loyal co-worker, and by the visitors as a solidifying member of the group, was not foreseen. Up to this time, one had either taken this or that position. This led in some cases, to conflicts between two roles, because a role was defined by only one of the groups (staff or visitors). The following (extreme) experience is an example for this:

No. 17
(The director of the centre, 3 assistants and the observer are in the conference room). Suddenly Mr G. says: 'Mr M., a direct question – we all just happen to be together now – On your "ride" Friday with two of the youths you drank the pledge of "brotherhood"; how did you come to do that?'

The tone of his voice expressed such displeasure, it sounded as if I should have bid his permission beforehand. 'Did you do it on the basis of certain educational considerations or do you promise yourself, thereby, special success in terms of your work? We are a group of fellow workers, to which you also belong as trainee, at least in the eyes of the youth. Do you think that a close relationship would, also, be a possibility for us?' I explained to him that I had had no educational training and that the friendship was of a purely private character. Two weeks ago I was asked to spend an evening alone with them and not, as usual, accompanied by someone from the centre direction. I was, also, asked on earlier occasions if I would allow them to address me by my first name, which I would have rejected at that time. As to the question whether such a friendship between the centre management and the youths might in general be answered positively, I cannot answer that. But the question is probably not even relevant as the staff members are all much older than the youths, whereas with me the age difference is not so great.

The staff members unanimously declared that addressing one another on intimate terms among staff and youth was completely excluded as a possible form of contact. Once again it was even pointed out that my conduct was disapproved of.

A variation of this problem is depicted by a third type of role conflict. In the first example, the specific thuglike behaviour of a type of visitor stands in contrast to the demanded conformist behaviour according to the pattern: 'A trainee does not do that.' The observer's solution led to limited contact with the specific group (rejection of a specific role):

No. 16
My contact with the visitors does not consist of amusement and conversations. I would have to sit just as rudely around the table and push

176

the ashtray back and forth. That would, without a doubt, be frowned upon as 'impossible' by both the staff and the visitors. Above all, I play chess with some of the younger visitors and few of the older ones, besides ping pong with those interested. I find recognition in both games, but only with those few with whom I play.

In the second example, the foregone conclusions of the staff stand in contrast to the 'analytical inquisitiveness' of the observer. An intrarole conflict of the participant observer is herewith presented:

No. 7
The fact that I make a fool of myself with certain questions, which I know, however, I am obliged to ask, has as a consequence conflict between two different sorts of goals to be attained: building up of my own position which is difficult to unite with the optimal fulfilment of the observation tasks.

Because I don't know which questions will move the staff members to make merry (and the Berliners anyway tend to make fun of others) and, more because of certain deficiencies of tact, don't realise the limits of insult, I have become insecure as a consequence.

For example: I say: 'Do you sometimes organise propaganda for the centre?' Director: 'Yes, you know, we hand out little pieces of paper to all the people on the street and tell them they should drop into the X-Street sometime!'

My impression: Publicity is found to be ridiculous here! Still there is a prospectus about the centre.

An interesting special case is depicted in the following experience: here an intrarole conflict becomes articulated ex post facto in the course of time. The observer perceived a transformation from going native to judgement from a distance:

No. 3
In my attitude toward the centre and its management, I have experienced a transformation, which by the end of my observation stay was still in such flux that I don't know in many points whether I should judge and answer them according to my earlier, more positive attitude to the centre, and its management or according to my present, more sceptical-negative attitude. At the moment, I would take an even more critical standpoint on all questions which contain a judgement as to value, than one, two, or three weeks ago. By having to answer the questions of the schedule bit by bit from the beginning my statements might gradually have taken on different colourings, or downright contradictions might even arise,

between which I would not like to decide in the present state of my information.

An exact assessment of the methodological consequences of this conflict of roles is very difficult. For various reasons, we believe that they are not to be overestimated as sources of systematic errors, or rather that they lie within the boundary of uncertainty, which was set by the deficiencies of the observation schedule and the differentiation of the field anyway:

1   Only a minority of the observers gave the appearance of role conflicts.
2   Role conflicts in relation to the visitors, on whom the observers concentrated, were of lesser frequency and importance.
3   The solving of role conflicts was clearly to the advantage of the visitors (see section 9.2.1). Corroborating this statement is the fact that in the group discussions 18 observers expressly emphasised that their relation with the visitors had been positive during the period of observation, remained positive or was characterised by a decrease of tension – only one observer noted an opposite tendency while the corresponding information in relation to the staff read: 11 (positive): 8 (negative) statements.
4   As to the question of the attitude, on the whole, of the staff toward the research tasks of the observers (which, at the observer's introduction to the field, were partially described while avoiding the term 'observation') the following findings were made:

	n
Positive interest, agreement, sympathy	25
Neutral attitude, disinterest	4
Rejection, negative interest	10
No specification	34

178

PART III

Instruction and Supervision of the Observers

10 The Adequately Trained Observer as Methodological Component

In the first part of the book, the reasons for which a separation of researcher and observer(s) was felt to be sensible, were given. The problems of such a division of labour, as illustrated in the second part, now make it necessary to provide an especially intensive training and supervision programme for the observers.

By no other, as yet, successfully applied method of social research does the reliability of the data depend so very much on the behaviour of the research staff as by standardised participant observation. It makes no difference whether you are dealing with an interview, depth interview, group discussion, an experiment or non-participant observation: the participant observer is always concerned with a higher complexity of the object, more difficult conditions of communication, more differentiated research tasks, longer and perpetuating work in the field and other problems, most of the time with several of those simultaneously.

These problems become even more intensified, because the participant observer is at the same time supposed to follow methodologically appropriate norms of behaviour which are fundamental for the other methods named, and this even more so, the more intensely he has to apply additional means of assistance and complementary techniques: thus, he is supposed to, e.g. register verbal statements just as objectively as the interviewer reacts to them without exerting influence, to evoke information just as skilfully and systematically as the depth interviewer, to control the changes in the field by his behaviour just as precisely as the leader of a group discussion directs the effectiveness of the discussion by his statements, to observe the effects of new field determinants as exactly as possible and to make judgements like the experimenter, to be just as attentive as and to command an apparatus of categories like the non-participant observer, and much more.

This, inevitably, results in, among other things, the following additional demands on the participant observer, whereby it must be said that we always refer to the observer, who is not identical with the researcher: (a) higher scientific qualifications in terms of methods and research goal; (b) stronger motivation to cooperate and identify with the project; (c) greater intellectual ability to successfully combine personal and instrumental-functional behaviour

181

G

in the field, or rather to act responsibly according to the demands of the situation; (d) greater input of sociability in terms of observer's role, social integration, interaction with strangers, friendliness, or rather, relative reserve toward actors; (e) higher expenditure of physical energies by: more intensive interaction in the field, overcoming emotional barriers towards actors, working out diffuse experiences, mastering the overlap of the situation in question and the privately behaviour disposed, life in the 'unknown' etc.

Undoubtedly, the main methodological problem which the participant observer has to confront is the participation in the field itself, because of the sources of error which are least controllable by the direct approach (see sections 3 and 8). If one views the relationship between researcher and observer as a process of communication, which (a) goes through training, data collection and data analysis phases, as well as (b) operates on two levels: the observer 'questions' the field, the researcher questions the observer, both being united by the observation schedule, then the decisive middle phase of the field work as well as the first level signifies a 'black box' for the researcher (and for psychological reasons also for the observer himself, to a slight degree), i.e. an unknown complex of possible distorting factors in its particulars, which he does not observe directly, and of which only input (schedule, observation instructions) and output (protocols, notes) are at best known to him. Thus, the researcher can only actually rely on the effectiveness of the preceding training and before the analysis of the data, experience some of the sources of errors from the observer's perspective. The empirical analysis and assessment of these sources of error is, however, again more difficult than, for example, the analysis and assessment of a systematic set of responses by an interview or by reactions to attitude scales (see the example by Campbell in section 3.1). For the time being, it must probably be limited to various indirect methods of error control such as those set forth in section 9 with regard to the observer's role.

Therefore, of paramount importance is the minimisation of anticipated disruptions. As a result, the following statement is valid for standardised participant observation in general: *Besides the instruments of the observation schedule and the protocolling, the observers' training in the instrumental and social-functional modes of behaviour as well as their supervision is a decisive component of the method.*

In view of the multiple behaviour constraints in the schedule and field it is necessary to sensitise the observer's perception capability first. Moreover, the fact that the observer himself participates, that is, is affectively and cognitively taken into the process of data-gathering, makes supervision requisite. The task of the supervisors is to discuss the observer's conflicts of roles and tasks, in order to relieve him of them. (Finally, a detailed discussion on the instrument of research, the observation schedule, must be taken into account.)

The following sections have been arranged chronologically, according to the appearance of these three problem areas.

11 Behaviour Training and Pretest

11.1 Perception training

Most everyday observations, as already explained in section 3.1, are characterised by two things: a voluminous, largely unconscious choice of situations to be observed and the interlacing of observation and evaluation. For the most part, both of them contribute to error-making to the extent that ensuing discussions about the observed situation, e.g. a playground for children, soon focus on the contradictions in the observations made. The talk then shifts to the evaluation or the criteria for evaluation of the persons observed. Thus, it becomes clear that it is impossible to base differences in selection and evaluation on the language used in the protocols. This is probably possible only on a meta-linguistic, or rather psychological or methodological level. Such distortions become most distinct when persons are evaluated. Attempts are frequently made to characterise people in empathetic terms, i.e. sympathetic understanding of the other person. Psychological studies have unanimously shown that the evaluator's own projections and cultural stereotypes enter into just such judgements, which moreover render insufficient recognition to the judged person's specific characteristics (Bender & Hastorf, 1950; Hastorf & Bender, 1952; Gage, 1952).

In contrast, participant observation is dependent upon the observers who, only in small measure, make such mistakes. For that reason, it is requisite that observers be allowed to experience their distortions of perception by being confronted with their own biases. Only after the observer has been sensitised to his direct, everyday surroundings, will he be in a position to observe his new and strange field of observation more precisely, with fewer inhibitions and fewer judgements as to value.

Thus, perception training has two complementary functions: (a) the primary psychological function as mentioned and (b) based on the acquired sensitivity of the observers, the function of enabling them to apply reliably the given observation categories.

In this regard, the following statement is significant: when *situations* are used as the units of observation then certain difficulties arise for the observer in identifying the properties of the objects of observation. As a result, his observation is directed toward definite categorical properties, even if he limits himself to only the description of individuals (e.g. membership in groups or professions, opinionmaking power, expertise, etc.); thus, toward properties which are specific for certain situations but are carried by concrete individuals. He selects 'important' persons and neglects, thereby, in certain cases, other important things, e.g. material-medial properties. According to the authors' previous experiences in their empirical studies, this sociological behaviour, which certainly is appropriate at least in the first phase in the field, runs into the following methodological difficulty. In their assumption of everyday behaviour, the observers tend to pay attention to persons, to increase communication with them and to look upon affective integration in the field as proof of their increased 'understanding' and the validity of their observations. Empathy and validity are believed to be equivalent.

However, the observer actually finds himself in the same conflict again and again, wanting to give up either the actor's or the observer's categories (i.e. of the schedule). Only an intensive training programme can enable him to maintain both positions: the actor's categories, in order to be able to better interact, the observer's categories, in order to do justice to his research tasks.

The intended effects of perception training on the standardisation of methods are twofold: it minimises the *'natural' selection* of perception, on the one hand, and on the other, methodically *controls selection* by the observation categories. One approach is to have the observers first write a report during the training course on recent events, i.e. what happened yesterday, their arrival or what they found when they entered the course. A few of these reports might then be read in the plenary session. The assembled observers would then be asked to examine the descriptive nature of these reports in terms of the following aspects: Are actions illustrated? Are adjectives or verbs frequently or infrequently used? Do the descriptions include judgements as to value which cannot be substantiated? The participants might then try to broaden the contents of observations and facts by further inquiry.

Furthermore, training allows larger groups of observers (more than 10) to scrutinise the course of instruction for themselves. In this way, we were able to observe, by sub-groups, three times each, the plenary session and the course directors at one of the courses for the youth centre study. After completion of each of the observation phases, a report appeared before the full assembly, which was unaware of the observers' actual tasks. The participants, all of whom had experienced the observed situations, then discussed the presentation. The effectiveness of this learning process was distinctly noticeable after the third time: the observations contained fewer judgements as to value and interpretations; they were increasingly accepted as better illustrations of what took place in the estimation of those remaining participants. As a result, the observers became more sensitised to those observed to the extent that they confronted the plenary session and individual participants (e.g. withdrawn persons or participants who often sheltered others) with their own behaviour.

Another strategy was chosen for the parallel course, which was directed more toward function (b).

Some of the participants in this second course prepared a fictitious series of events which presumably occurred in a youth centre and, like a play, acted out parts in front of the full assembly. It dealt with the activities of one group, which was interrupted by the centre director's intervention leading to conflict and a group discussion about necessary reactions to the director's behaviour in which conformist, deviant and neutral attitudes of the members were represented. The audience was divided into different groups and asked to observe the plots according to the different dimensions of the schedule allotted them and to make notes of their observations (on the centre director's style of interaction, the group's structure, etc.). Afterwards, these protocols were read to the full assembly and discussed. Above all, this method taught observers to distinguish between complete and incomplete observations, specific or rather discriminating and overlapping dimensions in the schedule and how to apply the proper categories.

Another way to broaden the perception capability of the observers is by means of an experiment suggested by McGaugh (1958, p. 135, f). A number of participants leave the room; those remaining are given the following story to read (McGaugh, slightly rephrased):

A tall, lanky professor almost ran into difficulties as he went to the city last Tuesday. In his briefcase were his lecture notes and on the way home from the college, he was stopped by a small, dark, intelligent Irish policeman.

'Somebody has stolen important government papers,' the policeman said. 'Unfortunately, I have to search your briefcase.' The professor thought that the man might be an Icelandic spy, but because he had nothing to hide, he let the man search the briefcase.

A very friendly, dark-haired, well-dressed man with only a badly hidden safety-razor in his pocket said: 'He's not the one, you can let him go. I can assure you that he wouldn't be capable of doing such a thing.'

The policeman answered: 'I'm not so sure of that, these people are often wolves in sheep's clothing; but I'll let him go.'

The professor hurried home trying to recover a bit of the lost time. He turned into 23rd Street and entered his own house in the middle of the block.

After everyone has read the story, one of those waiting outside is called in and told the story by one of those left in the room. The listener then calls in the next person, relates the story to him and this second person then calls in a third and tells him the story, etc. The audience looks for changes in the story, e.g. in the plot, its completeness, eventually also additional information, changes in the characterisation of the persons (stronger stereotyping). Especially if the stories are taped or the initial story given mimeographed to the audience, do the errors in reception and distortion become clear. If several stories of comparable length and similar contents are presented, then the learning effect in the group can even be tested. After each repetition of the story, the changes are analysed by the observers. The process is repeated as many times as necessary with different stories until the group has obtained a minimum level of omission and distortion.

The fact that errors of observation and reproduction not only occur at the beginning of the period of observation in the field should already be considered in the observation training. During longer periods of time in the field, a familiarity phase often follows the beginning orientation phase. The participant observer feels that he knows the field and can adequately observe it in various situations. Frequently, the selectivity of perceptions also increases with growing familiarity, which, the longer it lasts, can paradoxically lead to a decline in exactness (see section 4.3.3).

This dilemma can be remedied by the following strategy: Before the investigation begins, the observers should conduct one after the other, short *trial observations* of several objects in the field (e.g. various hospitals, different youth centres, different prisons), and under conditions as different as possible and in various situations. Before certain behaviour expectations can be consolidated in one object, they are invalidated in the next. As a result, the observer learns to know successively different dimensions of the field; he becomes sensitive to the field's whole breadth of variations. *Inertia of perception, on account of a growing redundancy of the situations over a period of time, can be weakened as a result.*

This learning process must be intensified in the training (a) by transmission of an 'analytical moral' (methodological misgivings as to one's own protocols and decisions as to categories and the like), (b) by intensive reciprocated criticism of the trial protocols in the team, (c) by repeated tests, e.g.: (i) observation of a sociodrama, (ii) taking protocol afterwards, (iii) oral reproduction after a longer period of time, (iv) critical comparison of both statements, (v) repetition of the sociodrama (change of names, motives etc., but plot more or less the same), (vi) oral reproduction afterwards, (vii) taking protocol after a longer period of time, (viii) critical comparison of both statements, (ix) critical comparison of all four statements, (x) critical comparison of the reproductions by different observers.

Undoubtedly, the psychological prerequisites for optimal observer behaviour can be developed in systematic perception training, as well as for the appropriate role behaviour and the correct application of the observation categories. As previously mentioned, the goal of this training is to sensitise the observers with regard to the dimensions of new situations and to minimise omissions, on the one hand, as well as to enable the observers to differentiate better between empirical descriptions and biased interpretations, on the other. The techniques described above can have several possible applications and, in fact, include group dynamic learning effects.

Kentler, Leithäuser & Lessing (1969, p. 111) likewise stress the listed functions of perception training as a matter of principle. They limit their observers' training, however, to the transmission of simple 'rules of basic behaviour', which as they confess, were not adequate aids. The authors expound the errors of selective perception with the aid of the figure–ground–problem taken from gestalt psychology and write (p. 111):

> We avail ourselves of àn example from the observation practices of Helmut Kentler: 'When I carried out my first participant observation in youth tourism, it was as if I were bewitched by the set task of registering the behaviour of the young vacationers as precisely as possible. Thus, I paid a great deal of attention to what the young people did in the evening and how they did it, but completely failed to see why and how they came to do just that, so that today I don't even know how it really happened that on one evening everyone was on the dance floor, on the next at the go-carts, on the day after window-shopping in the city.' Alone the youths' modes of behaviour had become a fixed figure. The observer's glance was fixated, so that the question as to why, the reason for this mode of behaviour, did not even penetrate his consciousness. Thus, he consequently failed to see signals and symptoms, information about motives, news transmission and techniques of behaviour control which could have been obtained from the young people. They, in turn, remained subjected to the clearly conceptualised figure as an unstructured ground. A simple example from perception psychology makes this relationship obvious. If a finger is held in front of the face, it can either be focused upon and clearly recognised, while the background is blurred, or the background can be clearly distinguished, while the finger remains unclear.

Although the analogy taken from gestalt psychology might seem very attractive, we would like to register a fundamental criticism at this point: according to our concept of standardised participant observation, it would be asking too much of the observers, despite intensive perception training, to autonomously observe the 'origins' of observed behaviour and to reproduce them in relation to this behaviour. This would be an analytical and synthetic achievement, which of course is meaningful for the explorative observation by single researchers, but takes place outside the field in standardised observation. In this case, the motive for actions should arise from the theory – and enter into the observation categories of the schedule,[1] or rather be derived from the correlation of data, while the observer describes properties and events in the situational context, without having to explain motivations as well. Of course, he is also supposed to describe the rationalisations which are linked with the behaviour, if necessary, and observable motives for the behaviour; however, these should not be based on a demand for individual perceptive interpretations.

This viewpoint might be regarded as extremely behaviouristic. We repeat, however, once again that operational perceptive interpretations (a) should be an element of an action theory, upon which the observations are based, and (b) are, in any event, very probable if the observer successfully participates, so that the correct categories are applied anyway.

If this controllable linkage of the action theory (including a theory of motivation), the observation schedule and straightforward note-taking be disregarded, then that figure–ground–problem can very easily reverse itself: the observer is fixated on the search for hidden motives and still selectively observes only the 'suitable' behaviour (figure).

If the facts obtained from participant observation are to be at all comparable, then the observer, as illustrated, is sufficiently made aware of his tasks in the perception training.

One extremely voluntaristic rationale, completely contrary to the logic of participant observation, has been recently advanced by Lessing (1969). In connection with the complex of problems involved in the study of youth tourism, he calls for the 'interested observer' with emancipatory intentions to change his field consciously, to move the actors to act, in order to overcome the restrictions and repressions of the field, which the observer recognises and the actors accomplish: all of which lead to 'better practices' (p. 203).

This strategy has, of course, nothing to do with comparative and controlled observation and, as a result, contains nothing of the 'criticism of the positivistic theory of observation' either. Apart from the fact that the positivistic theory of observation hardly exists (only as an approach), Lessing's considerations deal with a naïve attempt to politicise academic methods. In his emphatic and dialectic criticisms, he fails even to recognise the possibilities for scientifically controlling this doubtlessly interesting form of action research on two levels by means of a rational set of instruments of observation: (a) explorative participant observation by A; (b) systematic change of the field by A stemming from the data obtained from (a); (c) standardised participant observation of (b) by an observer B.

190

In this form, a methodologically sound combination of field experimentation and participant observation can be attained.

Certainly if to (a) and (b) also a scientific or – like Lessing – a 'theoretical' effect should be linked, then (c) must of necessity be subjected to the illustrated rules of the perception training and the 'positivistic theory of observation' (see section 5.3 as well).

11.2   Pretest in the field

We already indicated that the participant observers' chances of attaining sensitivity of perception are of late given only in a pretest with trial observations in the field. The pretest generally brings many observers into contact with the field for the first time, i.e. with a complex of persons and patterns of action, which are uncommon to them, which were unknown to them up to then. This became quite clear in the discussions with observers at the evaluation courses of the youth centre study: some of them complained that they had not seen a youth centre during or before the introductory course; much of what had been told to them about the centres had remained abstract and only after experiences in the centre could they have raised objections and made additions to the observation schedule. *Training without experiences in the subsequent field is accordingly only of limited success.*

Besides the possibility of acquiring experiences in the field, the pretest also offers itself as a test of the instruments to be used. The observers can investigate whether they can handle the given units and, above all, the categories. Is one capable of observing that demanded by the schedule? Is one able to see and describe the field in terms of the schedule's categories? Are the situations (units) sufficiently accessible to the participant observer? In this way, the criticism of the observers corrects the distortions in the observation schedule and, thereby, the inadequate perception of the researcher.

The tasks just named (introduction, testing of the field) can be satisfied by the pretest (Pretest 2) only when the instruments to be used have themselves been developed on the basis of a precise pretest (Pretest 1). Such a Pretest 1 is of central importance for participant observation. Thus, additional information about it is called for at this point.

The researcher(s) first test(s) which possibilities for standardisation exist in the given field of observation. In this context, three of the most important questions are those as to the observer's role, the units of observation and the categories of observation. At the same time, each of these three questions should be viewed in terms of the relevant ways to interpret them, as illustrated in section 4.5.

If a relatively closed field, such as an institution with a high degree of organisation, is in question, then time process can be rather helpful in defining and selecting the units. What happens in the course of a day, when and where? In this manner time periods with spatial limits can be established, which then develop into the units of observation. At the same time, the share which the time span of a single unit has of the total time budget in the organisation's daily plan is, under circumstances, an indicator for the actual relevance of the unit in the field.

Thus, it can be asked about the youth centre: How much time is allotted the 'situation' (unit), 'dance', 'interest group', or 'entrance hall'? In a completely closed organisation (e.g. total institutions), such as a prison, the units 'workroom', 'dining hall', 'prison yard' might be used in the research.

In closed fields with a low degree of organisation (e.g. children's playground) or in relatively open fields (e.g. community, settlement), it is often impossible to use situations as units. In such cases, attempts have to be made to define persons or groups as units of the observation. Of course, it is still scarcely possible (a) first to define all categories of observation (tentatively) and then to standardise as well as (b) to make participant observations on the basis of random samples of the time and room allotments. In the youth centre study, exactly these difficulties arose when the leadership behaviour of the centre's director was supposed to be observed. The unit of observation was not a situation, but persons and groups; thus, the observation categories necessarily remained too abstract, because it turned out that the centre's director showed different leadership behaviour in different situations (depending upon his partners of interaction). An observation on the basis of situations would have been more exact. If a definition of units and categories in the schedule is possible which relates to limited situations, then the possibilities presented in sections 4.5 and 7.1 of ex post standardisation of the observation material remain valid.

Both of the succeeding forms of the pretest offer sufficient opportunity to track down suitable observer's roles in the field. A general strategy for this can, of course, not be given, because the appropriate role depends upon very different factors of the field (see sections 3.2 and 9).

In general, one can perhaps say that in Pretest 1 the possibilities and restrictions for general roles are observed, while in Pretest 2 they are systematically checked as to the appropriate role, the given factors of the observer's integration and the level of intensity offered by participation. A training course at the end of Pretest 2 would then have the function of accumulating the experiences of different observers and upon that basis, of developing a general role strategy as well as of considering the social features of individual objects of observation.

192

11.3 Role finding and training

The special task of providing the determinants of the observer's behaviour cognitively and socially, as analysed in section 9.1.1, belongs to that area of the training related to defining the appropriate observer's roles. The 'social transmission', the role training in a narrower sense, is thereby especially problematic, because a *simulation of the roles to be dynamically assumed in the field can naturally only be attained to a very limited degree during the training course.*

The term 'role training' should characterise that part of the research planning and the observer training, which deals with the anticipation of the possible position, as well as with those expectations and opportunities for action which are supposedly related to the participant observer's role in the field. At the same time, one can only work with certain probabilities derived from the literature available, primary experiences or a pretest. The more exact prior knowledge is, the sooner can later role conflicts be attenuated (see section 12.2). To what extent first experiences in the field can change initial role definitions, even hypotheses and research problems, is shown in the report by Geer (1969, p. 160, f), who observed a camp in preparation for an investigation of the attitudes, behaviour and problems of future students.

The first problem is to find an adequate position for the participant observer. The second problem then consists in having the observer 'learn' and practice the conditions and possibilities for behaviour, which are very probably linked with this position. Except for ethnological studies, it can be assumed that the role of the 'stranger', i.e. a position at first not present in the field, is unsuitable. The most appropriate positions seem to be those for which a change of persons is allowed by the structure of the field: student of youth work programmes in a youth centre, employee in a business, social worker (or even inhabitant) in a prison, nurse or patient in a hospital, etc. If this is impossible for reasons of organisation or the observer's lack of corresponding (technical) qualifications, then the general role of the guest, visitor or trainee must be drawn upon in many fields (see section 9.1.1).

Participant observation of complex organisations encounters special difficulties. Organisations often develop defence mechanisms against any type of investigation; by either simply refusing to grant researchers permission to receive any inside information at all or by means of individual departments (or groups) who obstruct a study (e.g. because they regard the researcher as a spy sent by the upper echelons of the organisation). Argyris (1952, p. 34) very precisely stated these problems and drew the following conclusion from them:

The researcher's task, it seems to us, is to learn to understand the defences in the same manner a clinician understands the feelings of his patient. Viewing defence mechanisms in this light helps the researcher learn to use them in a constructive manner. It seems to us that defence mechanisms are important indicators of the psychological world of the subject, the 'social climate' of the organisation, the quality and strength of the relationship between the researcher and his subject.

In order to encounter just that difficulty of winning over the different hierarchical levels of an organisation for a research project (i.e. for the cooperation, frankness needed for such an observation), Kahn & Mann (1952) suggest the following four ways:

1 'Dual or multiple entry': The researcher is almost simultaneously introduced to key persons of the respective fractions (levels). He stresses the fact that he will also speak with the other fractions and openly presents his project to them.

2 'Contingent acceptance': The researcher seeks to gain approval in a step-by-step decision-making process. He begins with the top management of the organisation, asks for their approval for his project and permission to put questions to persons of the next level. If he gains the approval of those at the top, then he attempts to gain that of the people of the next level of management and at the same time asks them for their permission to pursue his request with their nearest subordinates, etc. This process, if successful, offers an optimal chance for cooperation at all levels of organisation, thereby making sure that decisions of the different levels are not predetermined by the top.

3 'Double liaison': In addition, the research group and members of the organisation who are interested in the project and in a position to make the research project plausible to other members of the organisation, join efforts in an attempt to gain the cooperation of others as well.

4 'Double access': The researcher tries not only to reach the organisation's top management externally (researcher–top), but also internally by indirect communication with the top through important persons at the middle and lower levels of the organisation, who themselves have access to the top of the organisation. Thus, the researcher has a double possibility of communicating with the organisation's top men.

The observer should be equally accessible to all members of the organisation, he should remain neutral and not present himself as an expert, because precisely this lack of knowledge proves to its members that he is not a spy sent by their superiors (Blau & Scott, 1963, p. 22, f).

Especially the top management of organisations or institutions with a high degree of organisation can be expected to object to an investigation.

Their objections include: (a) the objection that the study is too theoretical and whatever they want to research is known anyway; (b) the objection that the study's goal and practical results, for which they would have to answer, are too unclear; (c) the fear of uncontrollable side effects (changes) for the field, as well as very often, (d) a general mistrust of science on the part of 'men in practice'.

In order to counter these and other objections, the researchers should as a matter of principle check to see if they could not give members of the organisation the opportunity to include some questions in the study, in order to reflect problems of the institutions on the one hand, and the needs of the actors in the field on the other (e.g. in the adaptation of the research plan). As a result, the actors would not be degraded to objects of the researcher's interests and his academic career. Finally, attempts should also be made to find assistants in the institution, who themselves have scholarly ambitions and consequently are most likely to assist cooperation with other relevant persons of the institution or organisation.

We have spent much time with the position of the observer in organisations because we assume that the majority of research projects will deal with such fields.

In contrast, open and commercial fields, which are generally more accessible and in which the observer assumes the role of the public, of the normal consumer or interested spectator, make it, of course, much easier for the observer to 'climb aboard': He simply has to participate in the given activities, obtain a membership card, buy a ticket and off he goes, etc.

In this way, he demonstrates the same interest in participation as the other actors, i.e. his special scientific role remains, in principle, anonymous.

The preceding explanations were related to the strategy for assuming a *general* observer's role as far as it arises from conditions in the field which can be anticipated. The conditions for assuming *specific* observer's roles are, however, much more varied and result in part by chance at the start of the role-finding process. The most rational strategy must be developed entirely from the results of the pretest, which are then refined by role training which is related to the concrete situation, i.e. by means of socially sensitising the observer.

We suggest the following single steps as methods for finding and training roles:

1   In *Pretest 1* given field conditions (age, sex, status, qualification, pattern of dominating activities, structure of authority) and the observer's participation (intensity of interaction, overt versus covert observation, integral versus peripheral roles) are studied in order to arrive at a definition of general roles. This can take place by means of evaluating available literature and

documents and/or explorative observation by specially trained observers.
2 The results of this pretest, i.e. empirically ascertained possibilities for
general roles and participation, are presented to the observers-to-be in a
first phase of training. At this point, the observers must inform themselves
of the relevant institutional prerequisites of the field (e.g. legal-political
regulations, practices and customs, etc.) as well as, under certain circumstances, learn the necessary specialised skills.

Beyond this, the future observers are prepared for Pretest 2 by: (a) an
introduction to selected dimensions and units of the already existing observation schedule according to which observations should be made (as far as
this requires revision after Pretest 1); (b) information and cognitive trial
discussions with regard to the given norms of behaviour of the general role;
(c) group analysis of expected covert affective or physical resistance against
the actors and situations; (d) observation and trial training of the skills,
conditions, motives and possibilities requisite for assuming specific roles.
3 *Pretest 2* ensues: trial observation on the basis of (2) and the testing of
the set of instruments (schedule, note-taking) which do not depend on the
roles assumed.
4 On the basis of the results from Pretest 2, the *second training phase*
follows, featuring systematic role training: (a) final agreement on general
roles, or rather on the margin of play available to the assumptions of general
roles after consideration of the experiences made; (b) analysis of the experienced inter- and intra-role conflicts as well as the individual assumption
of specific roles; (c) elaboration of a general orientation scheme as a support
for specific role behaviour: positions, expectations, sanctions, goals, probable
partners of interaction. These analyses optimally lead to assertions of the
following form: 'if situation *B* with the actors *n, m, o* is given, then one
chooses behaviour *s, t* or *x, y, z*'; (d) simulation of social situations and
sequences of action, which includes the observer in group discussions and/
or experimental role-playing (sociodramas), which are systematically evaluated by the courses participants.'

Many different possibilities are conceivable for task (d), which can be
taken from related literature on experiments with group dynamics and work
with training groups (see Spangenberg, 1969). In this regard, it is important
that the training director takes into consideration all of the role determinants which did and did not appear in the pretest and establishes the actual
or rather possible reactions of the observers to them. Thus, the training
director, for example in a group discussion, has a list of these determinants
at his disposal and at the proper time can question the observers purposely
about their reactions. If the observers' information provides cues as to actual
or probable erroneous behaviour in the field, then the group discussion deals

196

with this topic until a consensus on the adequate behaviour has been attained. In similar fashion, the director of the training course proceeds with a socio-drama. When role discrepancies arise, he varies the participants' rules of behaviour until they have been sensitised to their own reactions to the extent that their behaviour in the simulated situation reflects that of observers in the real field situation, i.e. the methodically desired behaviour.

Moreover, it is recommended to supply the observers with a catalogue of general rules of behaviour which serve as a routine prop in the field. One such catalogue with the following contents was used in the youth centre study:

1 Get to know everyone and explain clearly and concisely the reason for your presence to everyone. Give detailed information to anyone interested in it. The explanations should be general so that your later activities make sense to the people and need no further explanation.

2 Greet everyone.

3 Ask for information and cooperation of those with whom you have developed personal contact. First turn to recognised key persons; you will experience the most from them and they are followed by many others. Look for the cooperation of participants, who themselves are good observers and in strategic positions of the observation. Try to interest them in your work and ask them to criticise your results.

4 Avoid discussions on controversial questions.

5 Promise not to spread gossip or confidential communication

6 Interact daily in the same way with many visitors and the staff.

7 Definitely avoid falling into the role of a group's or a person's pet. Bring no uncontrollable tensions into the goings-on of the centre.

8 Clearly establish your own role as their equal by cooperating in the groups. In many situations participants do not wish conformity to any great extent. The role of the student trainee is, thus, especially well suited.

9 Participate as much as possible in the activities of the centre without forgetting your interest in observation.

10 Neither rumours nor secrets should develop about the observer.

11 Withdraw from situations in which you would personally like to engage (avoid the effects of aggressions, frustrations and influence).

12 Be as impartial and neutral as possible, even when you feel closer to certain groups than others.

13 Avoid intimate contact outside the centre.

14 Take your time and do not be too eager to get to know the whole operation right away.

15 Let it be known in your protocols and note-taking whether you are

familiar with the observed situation to the extent that in describing it you can draw on your own life experiences or if, in contrast, it is all very strange to you.

16 In taking protocol of talks, statements, answers, reactions and other understandable behaviour, place yourself in the role of an *average member of the group or* in that of the *acting party* himself. Note in the description which role you have selected.

11.4 Informants and experts

Whereas role training enables the observer to be accepted as a participant in the field, he should also go beyond this and be put in the position to use other actors, who could be helpful as suitable informants or experts on certain areas, for his purposes, i.e. to apply their knowledge of the field as observation information. The observer's recourse to informants and experts represents both an economical necessity and a methodological corrective, even if the first aspect is given priority: The demand that data should depend entirely upon the observation of behaviour is unrealistic, because it assumes ideal comprehension of the field and ideal attention and participation (e.g. continuous presence) on the part of the observer. For that reason, the information from informants and experts, or rather, indirect observations, become necessary additions to the pure observation data, most of which consists of the actors' verbal statements anyway.

The information from informants and experts functions, at the same time, as methodical correctives by forcing the observer to review some of his own generalisations of events, origins of events or motives of the actors, or rather to observe more exactly if contradictions in observations arise.

We have already mentioned the problem of finding appropriate informants in section 3.2. At that time, however, the subject was discussed primarily from the perspective of key persons and their significance for the observer's social integration in and access to the field. The three concepts can be differentiated from one another in the following way:

Key persons are in general persons in strategically well-situated positions around which the happenings in the field crystallise on account of the persons' instrumental or expressive importance (authorities, opinion-leaders, influential, popular, informal or qualified persons).

Those actors are characterised as *informants* who dispose of an especially good (above average) knowledge of the parts of the field (persons, hierarchies, rules of behaviour, accommodations, etc.) important for the observation's aims. *Experts* compose that subgroup of informants, which dispose of this knowledge on account of their formal position or rather instrumental role.

The knowledge obtained from the informants through systematic interviewing is of threefold relevance for participant observation: (a) It intensifies the observer's access to single persons or groups in the field, if only indirectly, by giving him the specific rules of behaviour (see section 3.2). (b) It explains certain field relationships to the observer, which he could not have known from the pretests, refers him to specific conflicts or can give reports about the behaviour and structure of the field in the past, which might be relevant for the interpretation of the field at the present time. (c) Like informant opinions, expert opinions can be drawn on for testing the validity of the observer's judgements about objects accessible to either, e.g. by means of attitude scales. The available results show a rather high amount of agreement (e.g. Campbell, 1955).

Considerable deviations resulted in the youth centre study, however, which are to be attributed to the social-desirability-effect of the attitude scales used and speak in favour of the observers' adequate observation. As a result, great importance is rendered the correct estimation of informant statements, i.e. those controlled by observations.

According to Paul (1953, p. 443, f), most informants are themselves amateur social scientists, equipped with the necessary curiosity about social processes, as well as the ability to verbalise their observations. If the participant observer's tasks allow for it, the observer should seek out informants and utilise their assistance.

Nevertheless, informant opinions are, as mentioned, subject to examination as a matter of principle. 'The informant's statement represents merely the perception of the informant, filtered and modified by his cognitive and emotional reactions and reported through his personal usage' (Dean & Whyte, 1958, p. 34). Dean & Whyte point out – and, in fact, with regard to interviews, which however are relevant to participant observation, too – among other things two sources of error in informants' reports: the informants' statements are very specific as to certain situations, they vary, e.g. with the composition of the circle of listeners to which the observer also belongs. And: the informant's observations depend on his perception, his 'construction of reality'. Applied to the observation, that means that informants are subjected to just that selective perception, which the observers' training attempts to diminish and for whose correction in the observer's field exactly these informants' opinions among others are called upon. At this point, the observer might run the risk of arriving at a circulus vitiosus by naïvely trusting in the truth of those.

Thus, only Dean & Whyte's solution suggesting that several informants' opinions be tested against one another to see whether the informants are telling the truth has yet to be applied to participant observation. This can be done in the following way. 'What do the informant's statements reveal about his feelings and perceptions and what inferences can be made from them about the actual environments or events he has experienced' (p. 38).

The systematic inclusion of informants' opinions in the participant observation demands three skills of the observer: (a) he must find out who the right informant is for a certain sector, (b) he must check the information obtained from the informant for its reliability, (c) he must control the representativeness or rather one-sidedness of the identified informant.

The skills or rather problems (a) and '(c) are very closely related. The training of these skills, in turn, depends very much on the specific structure of the field. In most cases, informants offer their services to the observer in the course of the observer's interactions. As a consequence, the observer must know how to differentiate between those informants who are indeed familiar with the problems and those who are only well-meaning and to weigh their information accordingly, more or less according to Dean's classification (see section 3.2).

The selection becomes much more difficult if the observer must search for informants for all of those dimensions of the field which cannot be directly observed, which, however, are included in the tasks set by the schedule. Criteria for the selection should already be identified in the pretest and passed on to the observers at the training course.

Example:
In a study of a business organisation or administrative authority, the career behaviour of employees or rather officials is supposed to be observed: Who is officially or unofficially considered to be an aspirant for a certain position? Who alone feels he is? According to which criteria are careers formally and informally planned and carried out? How do preferences and disadvantages arise? etc. It is clear that the observation data which are directly accessible (working hours, application forms, pension programme, evidence of performance, personnel policy, advancement proposals, etc.) are not sufficient to explain the interlacing of formal and informal, planned and accidental criteria for advancement. The observer must also obtain information about biographical, informal and private aspects of the potential and actual aspirants' association with the system. The following method is of assistance:
1   Promotion type X is very probably under consideration for positions R, S, T, U. Find out which persons are at these position levels (given exact classification properties).
2   Find out which of these persons theoretically come in question (a) officially, (b) unofficially for promotion X at that time.
3   Question covertly n individuals per group (informants A) about the chances, motives, etc., their own advancement and the alleged chances, motives, etc. of their competitors.

200

4   Ask for the same information from each m superior and subordinate (informants B).

5   Compile various pieces of information according to groups and persons (for a later content analysis) and characterise the sociopsychological type of the informant in terms of each item.

Especially difficult is the representative selection of informants in broad research projects in (a) very open and dynamic fields (e.g. holiday beach, dance hall, conference centre) and (b) relatively balanced, very complex and differentiated fields (organisations).

In the case of (a) the observer is for the most part dependent on random samples, which he, however, – depending on the situation – can more or less control reliably by varying or keeping the number of informants per unit constant.

In the case of (b) the researcher develops a structural-functional model of the informants based on the theoretical frame of reference and from there deduces a classification according to which observers can learn the choice of m persons holding n positions ($m \cdot n$ functional informants).

Example:

The relationship between social integration and pupil performance in comprehensive schools is under investigation (participant observation combined with achievement tests and statistical analysis of the final exam scores). It follows from the pretest and the theoretical frame of reference that the essential mechanisms of formal achievement operate at six functional levels with regard to which the schools can be compared:

1   Formal control of group performance.
2   Individual control and motivation.
3   Informal social control of the pupils.
4   Academic and individual control.
5   Allotment of instruction material.
6   Familial socialisation.

From the schools' structural model, the following agents or rather positions in the system play a decisive role in the working of these mechanisms:

1   Teachers of different levels and courses.
2   School guidance counsellor.
3   Teachers for extra-curricular activities (in all-day schools) and educational tutors.
4   Test psychologists.
5   The pupils' parents.

If, besides the formal and planned social determinants of the individual pupils and groups of pupils' achievement, the observer should discover informal and accidental social determinants, then he must correspondingly question a considerable number of informants from these six groups. When an appropriate processing method and other exactly gathered facts are available, the findings can be dealt with as independent or intervening variables of the pupils' performance as controlled by direct observation.

The tasks of testing the reliability of informants' information has already been expounded in reference to Dean & Whyte (1958). In order to do this, the observer must be trained to do three things: (a) to differentiate between affectively neutral, instrumental and affectively oriented (e.g. frustrated) informants, whereby the former are usually more reliable; (b) to alternately compare information of several informants of the same category: $I_1, I_2, \ldots I_n$, and (c) if informant A's behaviour itself is being investigated, to control information from A (A about A) by information from other informants (B about A, C about A, etc.) by means of content analysis.

In general, it can be said that the more homogeneous the statements of the informants from different positions and backgrounds are with regard to a situation, the more reliably they have described them.

Note

1   See note 11 to section 4.

12 Supervision

Supervision is a word used in participant observation to denote that part of method dealing with the functions of the research leader (or any persons who are specially assigned) concerning the observers. Functions required are:

1 Control of the observation according to the research plan with the goal of countering immediately deviations or disturbances which might arise.

2 Advisory functions in practical situations (see 1 above) and controlling the observer in the field.

3 Necessary expansion or modification of the research design which may arise under certain circumstances as a result of the experiences of the observers in the field.

In view of the enormous amount of independence and isolation of the observer from the research leader, his long-term participation (it usually lasts several weeks), as well as the strain put upon him by divergent expectations and challenges (see section 10), the tasks of advising and controlling are of particular importance. In no way, however, is the observer just a passive object of the researcher in this task. Because of the great amount of time invested, the numerous methodological components and basically limited predictability and assurance of smooth going work in the field, an open, intensive communication between observer and researcher is a necessity. Every bit of information received from the observer during the field work contains a potential feedback for the conception of the research. As a result of this, the researcher is at an advantage (or disadvantage!), because he has a better general view of the similarities and differentiations of the whole field and must make responsible decisions concerning the retainment or modification of the ongoing observation. The observers alone, give him the data upon which he may make such decisions.

In serious consideration of supervision as an aid in minimising errors, the following general rules ought to prove helpful:

1 It is wise for the observers to make written reports about their work in the field (weekly). This allows for a routine check on the field work. They should be general and done in a form which is easy to handle. For example, the observers receive a check-list in which they are asked questions about the observer's role, the schedule, the aids and outlines as well as the inquiry's timetable. These are filled out and sent in weekly.

2 The supervisor evaluates the check-lists immediately and works on any deviations or problems which have arisen. In simple cases he may give the

observers tips either over the telephone or in written form. In difficult cases, it is better to have a personal discussion.

3   In addition to this, several intensive consultations prove helpful, especially in the following inquiry phases: some time after the beginning of the field work, still during the phase of role identification, at about the middle of the observation time, a time when extensive modification is still possible, and just before the end, a time when certain additional observations are possible.

4   Finally, the entire group of observers should be included in the supervision, either by organising meetings between several neighbouring observers in order to exchange experiences (with or without the supervisor), or by planning a general mid-way meeting for all of the observers, similar to the training period before the start of field work.

In the following, the two main areas of supervision should be taken into serious consideration: (a) the instrumental (observation) problems and (b) the problems of participation (role conflicts).

12.1   Problems in participant observation

As we have pointed out several times before, the observation schedule is the most important basis (a) for the standardisation of observation and (b) for the concentration of the observer on the relevant dimensions of the field in terms of the hypotheses of the study. The pretest and training will often not be sufficient to prepare the observer for the correct and complete application of the schedule to the field. This is because on the one hand, the pretest can never extend over the whole field and on the other hand, even in the best analytical and perceptive training, the real situation is impossible to simulate completely. For this reason, one of the jobs of the supervisor is to help the observer solve those problems which result from the insufficiencies of the schedule in the field or from deviations or changes in the field which are not taken enough consideration of the schedule.

The supervisor is there to compensate for the lack of standardisation of the instruments of observation necessary for its application. He analyses the methodological and empirical consequences of the practical problems of observation and arranges the rest of the observation according to them. This can happen in two respects:

1   If misunderstandings exist, individual deviations or errors of the observer, the supervisor must try to modify the observer's way of working by giving him instructions.

2   More problematic is the above-mentioned case where there is an insufficiency in the schedule or deviation in the field which may threaten the operationalisation of the dimensions of the study.

204

In such a case, especially if the field has changed, the supervisor must see in what way the observer must and can use new units or categories of observation to secure the reliability and validity of the observations.

It is very difficult to give exact advice as to the solving of such problems at this point, because this can only really be done in respect of the hypotheses and the research design. We can only list a number of observation problems which the supervisor should be prepared for. Given also are respective questions that should make it easier to find solutions.

1   Insufficient discrimination of the units in perception: The field is different from the assumptions the schedule rests upon. It is more open, fluctuating, and more dynamic. Is a standardised participant observation possible under such conditions? Can one define other units, e.g. instead of situations only spatial units, persons or groups, or units with a broader range of space and time? Can one increase the number of observers and in this way divide the assignments?

2   The perceived units are broader than the units given in the schedule: The observer is overtaxed. Is this due to the lack of analytical selection by the observer? Can the assignments be reduced? Can any of the observation categories be combined? Is it possible to change the time random sample? Is the observer observing from an inconvenient spatial position?

3   Given units and/or categories of observation cannot be perceived or applied (the empirical dimensions of the schedule are wrong): the danger exists that the observer will voluntarily try to find units and/or categories given in the schedule which do not exist in the field. He looks for data or interprets observations to fill in empty spaces in the schedule. The supervisor must recheck the schedule and the field; until this is done, the dimensions in question should remain empty. Is the structure of the object to be observed reduced and is it possible to disregard certain assignments or is one dealing with problems 1 or 2? Is it possible that the pretest was not representative and if this is true, should the contents of the schedule be revised?

4   Units and/or categories are missing in the schedule: Some of the data observed do not fit into the dimensions of the schedule. Can this information be ignored or is it redundant or relevant for the hypotheses? Can one substitute this information for other units and/or categories of less empirical relevance? Do these data also appear in other observations of the same field?

5   Technical problems: Some of the aids of the observation and/or the protocols cannot be used. Or: certain spatial and temporal difficulties arise so that the observer will only be able to take part in some of the situations planned. Can the aids be substituted (film substituted by tape recorder, expert's judgement by observer's judgement; other scale types)? Which units are very relevant? Which units and/or aids can be left out?

6   Sudden changes in the field: Structural changes take place in the field, caused by e.g. reorganisation [roles, objects, sequences are modified and with them, number and kind of units (situations)], departure of some of the participants (thinning out of interactions), changes in the boundaries of the system (new situations are added) conflicts arise (e.g. strikes) etc. Can the participant observation be extended (methodically, temporally, in terms of personnel, financially)? Can missing data be at least partly replaced by informants? Are the given categories still useful for describing the changed units? Can the conceptualisation of the research problem be changed? Are the observers prepared for a possible necessary change in the research design (in perception, role and aids)?

This catalogue is definitely incomplete and really more of an abstract anticipation of the possible difficulties in the field research. In spite of that, however, it gives the researcher important hints about problems which the supervisor might have to solve together with the observer. With these hints, he can plan a rational strategy of consultation and modification of method at the right time.

12.2   Role conflicts

Role conflicts are almost unavoidable for the observer (see sections 3.2 and 9.2.5). They result from the 'schizophrenia' experienced by a subject who is participant and observer at the same time. For this reason, it cannot be one of the jobs of the supervisor basically to ignore these conflicts, or to try and reduce the probability of their occurrence, but rather to minimise the undesirable psychological effects on the observer and the methodological consequences for the validity of the research.

The special problem involved in role conflicts in participant observations becomes clear when one systematically differentiates between intra- and inter-role-conflicts. Claessens (1968, p. 70) differentiates between them in a way, suggested by Gross:

Intra-role-conflict: '. . . here problems arise in taking and playing a role to which differing single expectations are directed – as there is always more than one expectation involved with a role.'

Inter-role-conflict: 'This is caused by taking on two (or more) roles at which, according to definition, different expectation "clusters" are directed which cannot be ignored.'

The complexity of the observer roles results from at least three levels of reference at which the observer acts; this is not including any specific individual problems the observer might have: (a) different reference systems of the method (observation versus participation), (b) different reference groups in the field (subject A versus subject B), (c) different roles in the field (function x versus function y).

From this we can set up the following classification of possible role-conflicts of the participant observer:

Table 12.1

Classification of role-conflicts of the participant observer

Level of conflict	Level of role	Contradictory expectations and reference systems
Intra-role-conflicts	1.1 Role of the researcher	Observation versus participation
	1.2 General role in the field	Subject A versus subject B
Inter-role-conflicts	2.1 Participant observer	Subjects versus research leader
	2.2 Field roles	General versus specific roles
	2.3 Field roles	Specific role a versus specific role b

One can see that the conflict groups 1.1 and 2.1 overlap: 1.1 refers to the standpoint of the observer as a scientist, 2.1 refers to an external standpoint. *The situation of the participant observer becomes even more difficult, because he must orientate himself to so many different expectation and reference systems, and depending on the system, an intra-role-conflict can at the same time become an inter-role-conflict.*

It is clear, then, that a conflict solution favouring participation and at the same time neglecting the observation (type 1.1) is not necessarily a realisation of the expectations of the subjects to the disadvantage of the research leader (type 2.1); the integration of general and specific roles (type 2.2) does not necessarily mean the congruity of different specific roles (type 2.3).

The methodological problem of these diverging possibilities can be found in the fact that one cannot principally predict whether and when different types of conflicts accumulate as sources of error or if they compensate each other. This depends on the numerous structural and individual characteristics of the observation situation. Important for supervision is: consultation and aid should be given to the observer to solve his role-conflicts as soon as these conflicts arise in the field. This will hinder the appearance of further conflicts (further conflict types).

On the other hand, the problem of role-conflicts should not be over-emphasised, as long as the research plan and observer training have been carried through efficiently. Pretests and role training can outline at least the strategical framework within which the probability of role-conflicts 1.1 to 2.1 appearing is pretty small. If they do unexpectedly occur, then it is probably because of either an unexpected change in the field, an individual crisis of the observer or because the questionable object of research strongly deviates from the average of the whole field. If the second case is true, one may have to change the observer. If the first or third case occurs, especially in comparative studies, the observation will have to be stopped. In the case of a high, analytical investment in the preparation for the research (pretests, development of instruments, perception and role training), something which is necessary for a methodologically reliable and accurate research, it will be expected that role-conflicts appear principally as conflicts between roles in the field (type 2.2 and 2.3), i.e. at a more informal level of participation involving specific roles.

When such role-conflicts arise, the supervisor has first to check which solutions seem to be optimal in the given situation. This depends basically on the phase the observation is in: e.g. in the first phase it will be possible to vary the field roles themselves or to take over new ones. In such a case the supervisor would have to provide the observer with new ways of behaving. In a later phase, it may prove better to limit the participation respectively by taking the observer out of certain situations, or by stopping interaction between him and certain persons in the field.

It is only possible to give the following general tips for supervision in the different conflict types:

For types 1.1, 2.1: Here it is the job of the supervisor to strengthen the observer's ability to maintain cognitive distance and to differentiate. This can be done through (consultative) conversations with the observer (see section 3.2). If necessary, a timetable, as exact as possible, must be set up with the observer, determining the phases in which the observer alternatively completely takes part or devotes himself completely to the job of observing. Especially active and sensitive observers should be advised to keep the intensity of their participation at a minimum. Here it might be generally suggested to proceed with the participant observation in the form of time intervals (random samples) and not to do it continually. Friedland (1969, p. 107) reports a similar solution. He did research with students as participant observers in camps of migrant workers: '. . . it was necessary for students to have a "break" out of the camps from time to time to maintain balance and perspective.'

208

Here one must mention aids that might allow the observer to find a spatially convenient position for observation which is not too terribly burdened with intensive communication demands or aids which may help him remember important events in case his chances for recordings are delayed for any reason (events which last over a longer period of time) (see Lindgren, 1935; Jahoda, Deutsch & Cook, 1967, p. 86, f).

For type 1.2: It often happens that in highly organised fields, the planned role of the observer is defined one way by one subject and another way by another subject. If this happens, the supervisor and observer must discover in a (consultative) discussion if it is wise to limit the participation to the less common behavioural expectations of different subjects, or to fit it more to the expectations of one subject (see sections 9.1.1 and 11.3). The choice should be made according to the goal of the research which the supervisor must recognise as valid, while the observer offers his better knowledge of the roles possible in the field. It is important to consider this fact because the supervisor often has the function of reaching a compromise between the goals of the research and the legitimate individual interests of the observer (e.g. his psychic hygiene) which may result from his participation in the field.

For type 2.2: This conflict results as a rule from an incompatibility between the official observer's role and the behavioural expectations of individual subjects resulting from informal contact. It is typical in fields with strong group heterogeneity and little formation of social relationships. Here one must check during a (consultative) discussion if one of the following principle possibilities for solving the conflict can be applied: (a) the observer reduces his interactions with certain subjects down to that behaviour bound to his general role, i.e. he withdraws from informal relationships; (b) the observer tries more than ever to react to one subject or situation in his general role, depending on the rise of conflict, of course, and to the other subject or situation more in his specific role. I.e. he suppresses in a conflict situation that role which represents a disturbing factor to the dominant subject in that situation. The supervisor must support this 'shifting of role expectations' by giving helpful tips.

For type 2.3: Enduring and solving these conflicts between the specific expectations of different persons belong to the trials and tribulations of everyone's individual life. The supervisor must make the observer aware of this fact, if the observer sees this as a burden to his job. The observer must clearly understand that his attempts at solving these conflicts must not imply a field changing partiality to one subject, to the disadvantage of the other. The supervisor can offer him a number of strategic alternatives. In addition to those related to type 2.2 he may lean back on key persons (the observer rationalises his behaviour which has not been accepted in respect of a subject in that he relates it to the opinion of a key person knowing that the subject will agree with this person); careful attempts at appeasing and explaining slow changes of orientation to one subject.

The supervisor has the additional possibilities: (a) as a quasi neutral party, to talk with the subjects of the field (e.g. the staff of an organisation) in order to define the position of the observer and what is expected of him more exactly; (b) to allow the observer to observe only at certain times or in certain situations; or (c) to replace or support the observer by another one.

In certain cases, he can interrupt the observations, add a further training phase and then let the observations continue. In the field, one can justify this break as vacation or sickness.

The most important jobs of the supervisor when such problems arise will be (a) to relieve the observer and (b) to test the possible changes of the field as well as the conceptualisation and the research design. It is hardly possible to imagine participant observation without conflict, without partiality for one group or without intervention in the structure of the interactions in the field; these kinds of actions, however, must be talked over with the supervisor if they lead to grave changes, in some conditions even to modifications of the schedule of observation.

Appendices

Criteria for Planning a Study by Participant Observation

1 Method and sample

1.1 Will problem and hypotheses be best studied by using participant observation?
    1.1.1 In total or only parts?
1.2 Which additional methods can be applied
    a – to gain access to data not directly observable,
    b – to have external validity criteria?
1.3 How can the field under study be defined as a class of comparable observation objects?
    1.3.1 Should observation be done in one or in several objects (or has it to be done)?
    1.3.2 Which object/objects are to be included?
1.4 How long is the observation to last?
    1.4.1 Is this a time and period representative for the action in the field (e.g. no holidays, no seasonal bias)?
1.5 Should there be one or several observers for each observation object?
    1.5.1 Should observers work simultaneously or on a division of labour basis?

2 Units and instruments

2.1 Which relevant dimensions of observation follow from the hypotheses and variables of the research problem?
2.2 Into what observation units and categories can they be transformed?
    2.2.1 Do these units discriminate according to the existing body of research and to results of pretests?
    2.2.2 Is it possible and/or necessary to draw a sample of situations?
    2.2.3 Does the observation schedule have precise, simple, discriminating, consistent and complete observation categories?

2.3 Which directions of interpretation are to be used?

2.4 Are indices, check-lists, rating scales, matrices, etc. to be used?

2.5 What sort of aids in observation and protocolling can be used?

2.6 Which is the optimal order of observation units for the observation?

2.7 Can particularly favourable sites in the territory for the observer be defined?

2.8 Will the observer be able to protocol in short intervals without being noticed and disturbed?

3 Access to field, participation and role

3.1 How can access and introduction ('entry') of the observer be managed best in an organisational and psychological respect?

3.2 Is there a ('vacant') position in the field for the observer?

    3.2.1 Which expectations will he have to meet, can he take the role?

    3.2.2 Are problems in the area of general versus specific roles to be faced?

    3.2.3 How intensive shall his participation be?

    3.2.4 Which actions/behaviour should be avoided by the observer?

    3.2.5 By which key persons can he optimise his participation?

3.3 Which informants and experts will he have to see?

3.4 Shall the observation be overt or covert?

3.5 In which situations at the periphery or outside the field shall he participate?

4 Pretest, training and supervision

4.1 Design of the pretest?

4.2 Which problems have to be taken into account in Pretest 2 on the basis of results of Pretest 1?

4.3 Which problems are of particular importance when training observers?

4.4 Are observers well prepared for their field job by successes during training and by field knowledge?

4.5 Reliability of observers on single observation categories?

4.6 Are observers sufficiently prepared for special situations and events in the field?

4.7 Can checks of observation be systematically done by super-vision?

4.8 What aids for decisions in case of observation problems can be deduced from the research design by the supervisor?

4.9 What are the functions of discussion and/or data-analysis meetings with the observers during field work and/or at the end of field work?

Factors relevant to costs of a participant observation study

Number of observation objects
Size of observation staff
Number of supervisors and hired hands
Length of field period
Number, complexity and duration of pretest(s)
Number and duration of training sessions and meetings
Regional distribution of observation objects
Frequency of contacts with observers
Type of observation aids
Financial contributions of field agents to costs of research (e.g. in case observers are employees)
Number of dimensions and variables
Complexity of research design (and data analysis)

Aids for Observation Strategy in Various Fields

The following classification was prepared to help the researcher in deciding which strategy of participant observation is to be used in his field of observation under study. For given determinants of the fields the classification indicates the most probable situations, informants, aids, role expectations. Fields are classified by their general type of social organisation:

A Social-ecological systems, e.g. communities, neighbourhood-units, holiday resorts, ecological systems like recreation or business centres
B Complex utilitarian organisations, e.g. firms, factories
C Complex service organisations, e.g. hospitals, youth centres, schools, civil administration, prisons
D Organisations based on voluntary association, e.g. youth organisations, associations, clubs, social movements, churches
E Goal-directed communication systems with limited participation e.g. seminars, discussion groups, party and club meetings
F Accidental, heterogeneous groups or unions with limited participation, e.g. holiday camps, travel groups
G Homogeneous marginal groups or subcultures, e.g. gangs, asylums

As can be easily seen, the above list is rather a typology than a classification, the single types are still insufficiently isolated and therefore overlap. Irrespective of a future refinement and explication the list might already in its present status prove helpful to choose a more adequate observation strategy.

In the following matrix the marks (x) refer to those research problems that cover the entire observation field, not to special problems or dimensions of fields. Variations within fields, subgroups or extreme cases (objects) are not taken into account. The classification is intended to give some overall help and is due to revision after a pretest.

Field structure, situations, informants, aids		Field types						
		A	B	C	D	E	F	G
Openness of field borders, interaction with environment	High				x		x	x
	Medium			x	x	x		
	Low	x	x			x		
Dominant modes of situations	Simplicity: few diffuse and isolated situations					x		x
	Complexity: many specific and less isolated situations	x	x	x	x		x	
Openness of situations	Relatively limited and closed situations	x	x	x	x	x		
	Relatively open and floating situations	x					x	x
Necessity of situation-sampling	Yes	x	x	x	x		x	
	No					x		
Possibility of time-sampling	High			x	x			
	Medium	x				x	x	
	Low					x	x	x
Relevant informants	Key persons	x	x	x	x		x	x
	Experts	x	x	x		x		
Aids	Film	x			x		x	
	Tape				x	x	x	

Role structure: probable expectations towards the observer		Field types						
		A	B	C	D	E	F	G
Achievement, instrumental qualifications			x	x		x		
Formal authority			x	x		x		
Informal authority		x			x			
Ascriptions due to age, sex and physical appearance		x				x	x	x
Solidarity, expressive qualities				x	x	x		x
Role: 'guest', 'visitor', 'stranger'		x			x			x
Role: 'trainee' or equivalent			x	x				
General role is inconsistent, specific to single situations or irrelevant		x			x		x	
Level of definitions of general roles (subsystems)	Several	x		x	x		x	
	Few		x	x		x		x
Stability of the system of general roles	High		x	x	x	x		
	Medium	x				x	x	x
	Low	x					x	x
Probable role-conflicts	General roles: A versus B	x	x	x			x	
	General versus specific roles			x	x		x	
	Specific roles: a versus b	x		x	x		x	x

Examples of Observation Schedules

1 Hospital (Lüdtke *et al.*, unpublished study, research conducted as a part of a course at the University of Hamburg, summer 1970)
2 Non-Custodial Prison (Friedrichs, Dehm, Giegler, Schäfer & Wurm, 1973)
3 Police (Reiss, 1971)
4 Shoplifting (Blankenburg, 1973)
5 Children's playground (Friedrichs *et al.*, unpublished study, research conducted as part of a course at the University of Hamburg, summer 1970)
(See section 4.3 for a detailed discussion.)

Observation schedule 'Hospital' instructions

Technique of applying the schedule

Seven form sheets were developed, or rather instructions for form sheets were given, which were to be drawn up by the observers.

The following observation instructions as to the single parts of the observation schedule were formulated:

The observers identify the head of each single protocol sheet by noting (a) their name, (b) the ward, (c) the date, (d) the number of the form sheet.

Form 1: Matrix of the situations. In every protocol, the situation (i.e. initials-number-combination) should be given to which the observation refers. E.g. $D\ 1 =$ Patients' Lounge 10.00–11.30 o'clock.
Form 2: The observer takes notes of every interaction between the staff and the patients on this protocol sheet, whereby he notes the respective time and situation on top within which the interaction took place. Each observation consists of a statement in each of the three lines. If an activity occurs without interaction, then lines Int. and React. simply contain a stroke.

In this case the following rule is valid: a member of the staff is characterised by a two-number: 1 Position = Number of the profession on the staff sheet, 2 Position = Number per profession.

A patient is characterised by a number (= room number) and a small letter (3*a*, *b*, *c*, etc. clockwise from the door!!). In line 'Int.' the first figure is

221

1 Observation units of the observation schedule 'Hospital' (Lüdtke et al., unpublished)

Situations* / Time \ Rooms	Patients' rooms	Nurses' rooms	Ward room	Patients' lounge	Hallway	Bath	Tea-kitchen	Wash-room	Outside ward
7.00 make the beds, breakfast, clean up	A 1							F 1?	
8.00 breakfast staff		B 1					K 1		
8.30 alternating activities	A 2		C 1?		E 1?		K 2		
9.00 visit	A 2				E 2?				G
10.00 diverse nursing activities	A 3?		C 2?	D 1				F 2?	
11.30 lunch, alternating activities	A 4				E 3?			F 3?	
13.00 lunch staff		B 2					K 3		
14.00 coffee, paper work		B 3	C 3	D 2	E 4?				
15.00 taking temperatures	A 5								
16.30 supper									
18.30 supper staff		B 4					K 4		
19.00 diverse nursing activities, preparation for the night	A 6	B 5	C 4		E 5?			F 4?	

*The symbols in the cells refer to situations of strategic importance for the observation.

that of the person (staff or patient) who started the interaction (e.g. **rang the bell**, called, addressed someone, asked a question). Only in doubtful cases are different related categories used in line 'Int'. Several observations are protocolled for longer interactions relating to different categories, e.g.

Activity	*RO*		
Interaction	Fra 31/3 *b*	Inf 3 *b*/31	Aff 3 *b*/31
Reaction	Neut	Pos	Pos

Form 3: Staff Sheet: it contains a structural classification of the ward personnel according to professional standing (formal status) and 6 other variables. Personal status: single, engaged, married, divorced/separated widowed with number of children. Living conditions: in the Nurses' Centre or outside. Note nationality.

Form 4: According to this sheet the observed conversations are systematically described on extra protocols. In the first two days of systematic observation (as of Monday), the observers depict not only the corresponding categories of conversation (capital letters) but the exact content of the conversation (topic abbreviated) as well.

Form 5: Here the observers briefly protocol the information which they obtain from certain informants (staff, patients), i.e. in talks between observer and informant or in observed talks between different informants. In such a case, the informant (staff or patient number) should be differentiated from the person (staff or patient number) to which the information refers. The information is written in abbreviated form in the related matrix cell. It should include information from informants about themselves which might involve an overlapping of the data registered in Form 4!

Form 6: Patient Sheet: Application is analogous to Form 3. As much as possible of the necessary information must be taken from the medical records. Give exact professional standing. Eventually ask for the German name of a given illness.

Personal status c = constantly confined to bed
                   p = partially confined to bed

In the first two columns the patient's room number at that time and his consecutive letter and room number are recorded for exact identification, e.g. 3 *b*: Patient *b* (clockwise from the door) in room 3.

Form 7: Please take note in diary form of all problems and events which arise in connection with the ward's activities. Here the observer renders an account of his activity and role in relation to the structure of the field. (The observers worked as trainees and were introduced as such.) Please characterise each protocol as 'Form 7'.

Some problems which are relevant here: manner of introduction to the ward, friendliness of the reception (how was it noticeable?); reason for their work; form and process of seeking contact with other actors; how are informants found; how are they questioned or rather spoken to? (Staff + Patients!) manner of their official operation; difficulties of participating in certain situations; difficulties in note-taking; devices used (cards, lists, loose sheets, etc.); how were the observation random samplings made? (e.g. in time sequences of the relevant situations, by chance, according to activity to be exercised or otherwise?). Technique of note-taking, at which point? Conflicts, tensions, sympathy, antipathy with regard to certain members of the staff, motivations for them, form of solution; to what extent and through which means was the field changed as a result of an observer's activities? Please give the most important empirical criteria for these and other problems!

Observation schedule 'Hospital' sheet 1

Observation criteria for the activities of the staff

Code	Categories	Indicators
Med	Medical treatment of patient	Needles, bandaging, taking temperatures, giving medicine, giving drops, oxygen treatment, taking blood, etc.
Nurs	Other nursing of the sick	Cleaning, bathing, rubbing in, enemas, feeding, nail care, making beds, arranging beds, etc.
Din	Mealtime service	Bringing the food, setting it up, cleaning up, etc.
Tra	Transporting patients	
Ca	Cleaning and arranging of rooms and equipment	Dusting, polishing, removing the garbage, cleaning instruments and furniture, arranging flowers, bringing towels, rearranging chairs, kitchen duties, etc.

Code	Categories	Indicators
Prep	Preparation and transport of equipment and medicines	Prepare injections, wrap bandages, lay out swabs, sort medicines, set up medical equipment, prepare operations, etc.
Doc	Writing, reading, looking at documents	Functions with written matter, photos, files, forms, lists
Com	Functional communication	Questions, instructions, talks, consultations about treatment and organisation with other staff members
Free	Free time	Eat, rest, individual reading, informal social conversations, aimless walking
Ot	Other activities	

Observation schedule 'Hospital', sheet 2

Observation categories for the communication of staff members with patients

1   Interactions of the personnel

Code	Categories	Indicators
Imp	Imperative rules of behaviour	Clear, definite regulations, 'orders', instructions, warnings, guideline in relation to a desired behaviour or rather the patient's adaptation *without* foundation and discussion
Beh	Rules of behaviour with factual foundation or corresponding requests or suggestions	Rules, requests or suggestions with regard to desired behaviour or rather the patient's adaptation *with* explanation and foundation or discussion

Code	Categories	Indicators
Ques	Questions to the patients	Interested, attentive questioning of the patients as to how they feel, their wishes and problems
Inf	Patient's information	Factual information given to the patient about diagnoses, treatment, doctors, conditions, dates, etc.
Conv	Informal conversation	Conversation with patient about subjects independent of the treatment, e.g. family, profession, children, weather, politics, private affairs, work, vacation, etc.
Aff	Affective gratification (short behaviour)	Smiles, statements, gestures, mimicking, physical contact, questions which imply emotionally coloured confirmations, attempts to cheer up, offer support and show solidarity
Reb	Rebuttals (short behaviour)	Analogous to the above, however, with implications of rejection, dismissal, emotional refusal, gruffness *et al.* (e.g. No time! Not on your life! No! Not responsible! You'll have to wait! Don't get so excited!, etc.)

2   Reactions of the patients

Code	Categories	Indicators
Pos	Positive reaction	Agreement, satisfaction, delight, consent, understanding, thanks, insight, affective gratification, smile, analogous to Aff

Code	Categories	Indicators
Neut	Neutral reaction	No noticeable emotions, factual statements, direct conformity
Neg	Negative reactions	Rejection, anger, protest, irony, contradiction, aggression, devaluation of the others *et al.*

Observation schedule 'Hospital', sheet 3

Communication among staff members

Here protocol is taken of each conversation between different members of the staff, whereby the observer should especially concentrate on the situations *B, C, E, K* (kitchen).

Each observed conversation should be described according to the following dimensions:

Persons: Which persons participated? State the staff members' numbers! Who *introduced* the conversation: *underline* the number of the respective staff member!

Context of the situation: Room (situation according to matrix)
Dominant activity of the participants (according to activity categories)
Other persons present who did not participate or remained silent
Length of conversation in minutes

Topic/contents of the conversation:

A Topical matters, problems, working conditions:
   e.g. visits, treatment, organisation, orders of superiors or doctors, behaviour of the patients in connection with the treatment, routine, etc.
B Everyday topics not related to work:
   e.g. weather, politics, sports, fashion, bringing up children, leisure time, family, etc.
C Private affairs:
   personal problems and conflicts which go beyond B and touch especially private matters, e.g. sex, family, superiors, colleagues, money problems etc., which one would rather discuss with personal friends than others.
D Shared interactions:
   dates, joint plans, shared experiences, etc.

E   Gossip about third persons:
     e.g. colleagues, superiors, doctors, subordinates, patients with negative tendencies (disparagement, sensation, discrimination, denunciation, self-righteousness, etc.).
F   Aggressions and conflicts:
     disputes, conflicts, aggressive rebuttals, threats, 'complaining', etc.
G   Expressive statements:
     emotionally confirming short interactions such as jokes, nonsense, gags, curses, etc.
H   Others:
     Please indicate the subject matter concerned!

Observation schedule 'Non-custodial Prison', sheet 1

Observer: Date:

Persons *W*:

     S: Situation No:

1 Topics of conversation	I. – I.		I. – W.		W. – W.	
	Topic		Topic		Topic	
	occurred (no. of cases)	did not occur	occurred (no. of cases)	did not occur	occurred (no. of cases)	did not occu
Topical questions						
Everyday topics						
Private sphere						
Collective interactions						
Gossip about 3rd persons						
Talking about 3rd persons						
Conflicts						
Expressive statements						
Offence, sentence, guilt						
Date of discharge						
Plans after discharge						
Visits of relations						
Vocation plans						
Other (specify)						

2 Observation units of the observation schedule 'Non-custodial Prison' (Friedrichs et al., 1973, p. 219)

Room		6.00–6.29	6.30–6.59	7.00–11.29	11.30–11.59	12.00–12.29	12.30–12.59	13.00–16.29	16.30–16.59	17.00–17.29	17.30–20.15	20.15–ca.22.00
Cell			7	14	26	39	50	61	73	85	97	108
Workroom I				15	27			62	74	86		
Workroom II				16	28			63	75	87		
Casino (staff)					29	40	51					
Hall		1	8	17	30	41	52	64	76	88	98	109
Central office		2	9	18	31	42	53	65	77	89	99	110
Floors	A	3	10	19	32	43	54	66	78	90	100	
Floors	B	4	11	20	33	44	55	67	79	91	101	
Floors	C	5	12	21	34	45	56	68	80	92	102	
Yards	Garden			22	35	46	57	69	81	93	103	
Yards	Sport			23	36	47	58	70	82	94	104	
Kitchen		6	13	24	37	48	59	71	83	95	105	
Table-tennis-room				25	38	49	60	72	84	96	106	
Lounge											107	

7 = very important.

Topics/contents of conversation:

A **Topical questions, problems, working conditions:**
e.g. treatment, organisation, jobs given by supervisors, behaviour of inmates, topics related to the prison; inmates, warders, staff; routines

B **Non-work related every-day topics:**
e.g. weather, politics, sport, leisure, family

C **Private sphere:**
personal problems and conflicts that touch the private sphere more deeply than B, e.g. sex, family, warders, lack of money – topics discussed preferably with friends

D **Collective interactions:**
dates, collective plans, collective experiences

E_1 **Gossip about 3rd persons:**
e.g. inmates, warders, staff, disparaging remarks, discrimination, sensation, denouncing, self-righteousness, etc.

E_2 **Talking about 3rd persons:**
talking about 3rd persons without disparaging remarks

F **Aggressions and conflicts:**
bickering, conflicts, aggressive rebuttals, threats, 'grumbling', etc.

G **Expressive statements:**
short emotionally corroborating interactions such as jokes, nonsense, wisecracks, curses or other external inducements

Observation schedule 'Non-custodial Prison', sheet 2

Observer: Date   Situation No.

---

2 Evaluation of sentence
   (No. of I.)
   .... none
   .... just
   .... unjust

3 Self-legitimisation (No. of I.)
   .... none
   .... society, state, law
   .... conditions, family, socialisation, distress, alcohol
   .... instinct

4 Walk in cell of other I.
   .... n.o.
   .... observed .... no. of I.

5 Passing each other, I.–I.
   .... n.o.
   .... dropping a few words
   .... no verbal interaction

6 Alone in TV-room (evening)
   .... n.o.
   .... no. of I.

230

7 Spatial distance of standing/sitting groups

.... no such groups observed

.... did not occur

o	o	o
o	o	o
o	o	o

X = Observer
direction of
contact

8 Leaving the group as first

.... n.o.

.... others follow .... no. of cases

.... nobody follows .... no. of cases

9 Did A. or S. have eye-contact with I. in situation?

.... n.o.

.... no. (= .... min.)

.... yes, half the time

(= .... min.)

.... yes, almost total/total time

(= .... min.)

10 Cells

.... n.o.

.... observed cells (no.)

.... more than one I. in cell

11 Conflicts I.–I.

.... n.o.

.... no. of conflicts

.... intervention by W.

(after .... min.)

.... intervention by S.

(after .... min.)

.... intervention of present I.

.... intervention of sent for I.

.... conflict resolution by group

12 Structure of group of I.

.... n.o.

.... only sexual offenders

.... only other offenders

.... mixed

13 Passing member of S.

.... n.o.

.... not addressed by I.

.... addressed by I.

14 Conversation I.–W.

.... n.o.

.... no. of observations initiated (e.g. by walking up to some-one) by

.... I

.... W

.... Observer

15 Group of I.:	n.o.	Name of I.:
most eye-contacts		
non-interruption		
special skills		
middle position in room		
member of TV/radio committee		
floor speaker		
caretaker		

16 Interaction I.–W.

.... n.o.

.... no. of observed instructions by W.

    .... without giving reasons by W.

    .... reasons given by W.

    .... instrumental reasons

.... cigarettes offered (no. of cases)

    .... I. to W.   .... by W. to I.

.... W. joins group/dyad of I.
(no. of cases)

    .... conversation stops

    .... conversation does not stop

---

17 Sejourn of W.

.... n.o.

.... min. observed, thereof

    .... min. in control glass box

I = Inmate
W = Warder
S = Member of staff

3 Observation schedule 'Police Raids', excerpt (Reiss, 1971, p. 11 f)

32   Was a personal and/or property *search* attempted or conducted by the police?
(1) yes (go to 32a); (2) no (go to 33).

32a   What kind of search was attempted or conducted? (1) personal ('frisk') (go to 32b); (2) property (e.g., auto or house) (go to 32c); (3) both personal and property (continue with 32b *and* 32c).

32b   If 'personal':

32b–1   Would observer say this 'frisk' was necessary for the protection of the officer(s)? (1) yes; (2) no; (9) don't know.

32b–2   Did the police ask the possible offender's permission before this 'frisk' was conducted? (1) yes; (2) no; (9) don't know.

32b–3   Did the possible offender(s) *object* to being 'frisked'? (1) yes (go to 32b–3a); (2) no (go to 32b–4).
    32b–3a   What was said by each of the offender(s)?
    32b–3b   What was said by each of the officers?
    32b–3c   Was the 'frisk' conducted after objection? (1) yes; (2) no.

32b–4   Was a weapon or other possible evidence found? (Check all that apply.) (1) gun; (2) knife; (3) other weapon (Specify); (4) narcotics evidence (Specify); (5) stolen property (Specify); (6) other evidence (Specify); (7) none found; (9) don't know.

32c   If property:

32c–1   Was this search attempted or made prior to an arrest? (1) yes; (2) no; (9) don't know.

32c–2   How did the police attempt or manage to gain entrance? (1) simply entered without asking permission; (2) asked and were granted permission; (3) asked permission and were refused, did not enter; (4) asked permission and were refused, entered anyway; (5) gained entrance with search warrant; (6) other (Specify); (9) don't know.

32c–3 Were there any objections to the attempt to gain entry? (1) yes; (2) no; (9) don't know.

    32c–3a What was said by the parties objecting? (Specify for each party.)

    32c–3b What was said by each officer?

32c–4 Were there any objections to the search? (1) yes; (2) no; (9) don't know.

32c–5 Was a weapon or other possible evidence found? (1) gun; (2) knife; (3) other weapon (Specify); (4) narcotics evidence (Specify); (5) stolen property (Specify); (6) other evidence (Specify); (7) none found; (9) don't know.

32c–6 Was a property search of a *vehicle* attempted or conducted? (1) yes (go to 32c–6a); (2) no; (9) don't know.

    32c–6a Was the vehicle search attempted or conducted at or near the scene of a possible crime? (1) yes; (2) no; (9) don't know.

        32c–6al Where was it conducted? (1) street or alley away from traffic or public view; (2) moved to parking area or yard away from public view; (3) moved to police station; (4) other moved (Specify).

    32c–6b Did the police look closely at the vehicle's interior without actually reaching or climbing into it? (1) yes; (2) no; (9) don't know.

    32c–6c Did the police enter the vehicle and search it at any time? (1) yes; (2) no; (9) don't know.

    32c–6d Was any weapon or other possible evidence found in the search? (1) gun; (2) knife; (3) other weapon (Specify); (4) narcotics evidence (Specify); (5) stolen property (Specify); (6) other evidence (Specify); (7) none found; (9) don't know.

4 Observation schedule 'Shoplifting', (Blankenburg, 1973, p. 128, f).

Observer

Address:	Process of theft:
Size of shop:	Thief stood where?:
Day, Time:	Thief observable?:
	Someone near?:
Employees:	
How many?:	Employees
Where:	Customers
	Has someone observed the act of stealing?
Present activity of employees:	
Talk to shop service test:	yes
How long?:	no
	undecided
Customers:	Employees
Number buying:	Customers
Number at the cash-desk:	

Nr of shopliftings:

Time thief spent in shop:

Setting:

Number of cash-desks?:

Fresh meat service?:

Mirrors?

Special observation facilities?

General impression:

Repacking of goods – where?

Observable?

    yes

    no

Someone near?

    Employees

    Customers

Has someone watched the repacking?

    yes

    no

    undecided

    Employees

    Customers

(Observer: Supply drawing of shop, setting and location of activities.)

5　Observation schedule 'Children's Playground' (Friedrichs *et al.*, unpublished), sheet 1

(Check every 2 hours)　　　　　　　　　　　Form R

Observer:　　　　　　　　　　　Playground: Karolinenstrasse
Date:　　　　　　　　　　　　　　　　　　Schulterblatt 61
Time: from............ to...............　　　　Mittelweg
　　　　　　　　　　　　　　　　　　　　Sülld. Kirchenweg

1　Weather

    Sky: —— clear

    —— cloudy

    —— rainy

    Temperature:

    —— up to 20°

    —— more than 20°

2　Equipment of playground:

    —— climbing arch　　—— horizontal bars

    —— wading pool

    —— merry-go-round　　—— seesaw

    —— swing

    —— sand box　　—— wooden house

    —— tree stump

    —— square climbing frame

    —— rocking horse

3 Size of equipment:
— only for up to 6 years old
— also for older children

4 Age of children: (number)
— up to 6 years old
— 7 years and older
— not classifiable

5 Toys brought along: (number)
— ball
— car chain
— tricycle
— bicycle
— pistols, rifles
— playing cards
— shovel
— pail
— doll
— scooter
— bow and arrow
— marbles
— special dresses (Cowboy, Batman)
  Which?:..

6 Clothing (all children present)		white-light	medium	dark
trousers/skirt/dress	Jeans, leather, plastic			
	other materials			
shirt/blouse	without			
	with			
stockings	without			
	with			
shoes	without			
	with			
sports dress,	without			
swimsuits	with			
creases	without			
	with			

235

Observation schedule 'Children's Playground', sheet 2

(Check every 15 minutes)   Form SG 1

Observer: Playground..........Karolinenstrasse

Date: ....Schulterblatt 61

Time (Quarter commencing):   ....Mittelweg

                                  ....Sülld. Kirchenweg

SETTING

1 —— children, including —— girls
   —— adults, including —— parents
   —— children with parents

2 —— groups (10 min. interaction)
   —— play groups (5 min. interaction)
   —— dyads (child-child)
   —— isolated

SINGLE PLAYGROUP

3 —— boys —— girls
   —— respective parents

4 Equipment used in play
   (see list in Form R)

5 Toys brought along:
   —— ball
   —— car chain
   —— tricycle
   —— bicycle
   —— pistols, rifles
   —— playing cards
   —— shovel
   —— pail
   —— doll
   —— scooter
   —— bow and arrow
   —— marbles
   —— special dresses (Cowboy,
      Batman)
      Which?:...

7 Conflict:
   —— not observed
   —— want the same thing simul-
      taneously (toys, equipment)
   —— throwing sand
   —— destruction
   —— disregard of rules of game

8 Interference by adults:
   —— not observed
   —— by parents
   —— by other adults
   —— no interference

9 Mode of interference by adults:
   —— not observed/no interference
   —— to go to
   —— to call
      .... 'dirt'
   —— to be called

10 Mode of conflict resolution by
    children:
    —— not observed/no incidence
    —— verbal
    —— physical

11 Solidarity:
    —— not observed/no incidence
    —— helpful
    —— let others have toys
    —— acceptance of newcomers

12 Type of game played:
    ....

13 Duration of play
    —— min.

236

Observation schedule 'Children's Playground', sheet 3

Form SG 2

Observer:

Date:

Time (Quarter commencing):

Playground............Karolinenstrasse

............Schulterblatt 61

............Mittelweg

............Sülld. Kirchenweg

6 Status

Criteria \ not observed	observed		
	running letter of child	sex	applies to child .... also
other children flock to child			
adds conditions to playing with him			
defines rules of the game			
others stop play because of child			
physical strength			
older than the rest			
possesses toys			
other criteria			

Observation schedule 'Children's Playground', sheet 4

(Check every 15 minutes)   Form KE

Observer: Playground............Karolinenstrasse
Date: ....Schulterblatt 61
Time (Quarter commencing):   ....Mittelweg
                                                            ....Sülld. Kirchenweg

---

SETTING

1 —— children, including —— girls
   —— adults, including —— parents
   —— children with parents

2 —— groups (10 min. interaction)
   —— play groups (5 min. interaction)
   —— dyads (child–child)
   —— isolated

SINGLE K.–E. RELATION:

3 —— child(ren), incl. —— girls
   —— parents
        —— mother
        —— father
        —— other

4 Child(ren) play(s):
   —— alone
   —— with other children
   —— with parent(s)

5 Initiation of game:
   —— not able to be decided
   —— parent(s)
   —— child

6 Social control by parent(s):
   —— metres distance to child
   —— can see child
   —— cannot see child
   —— looks on continually/most of time
   —— looks seldom/never
   —— reads or does something similar
   —— talks to other parent/adult

7 Sanctions:
   —— none observed
   —— intervention in play after ...... min.
      reason:...

8 Dirt:
   —— no corresponding occasion
   —— occasion and no reference by
      parent(s)
   —— occasion and reference by
      parent(s)

9 Children with parents in play-group:
(a) —— not observed
   —— no intervention in play
   —— intervention in play after ...... min.
      reason:...
        —— parent(s) were called
        —— parent(s) came without call
        —— conflict solved by children
           themselves

(b) status of child in group
   —— not able to be decided
   —— higher than other children
   —— same as other children
   —— lower than other children

10 Duration of play:
   —— min.

11 Type of game:
   ....

K = children
E = parents

238

Bibliography

Abbreviations:

AJS = American Journal of Sociology
ASR = American Sociological Review
HO   = Human Organisation
JASP = Journal of Abnormal and Social Psychology
KZfS = Kölner Zeitschrift für Soziologie und Sozialpsychologie
PB   = Psychological Bulletin
PR   = Psychologische Rundschau
SF   = Social Forces
ZeaP = Zeitschrift für experimentelle und angewandte Psychologie

Albert, H., *Probleme der Wissenschaftslehre*, in: König 1967b.
Anderson, N., *The Hobo: The Sociology of the Homeless Man*, Chicago 1923.
Arensberg, C. M., 'The Community-Study Method', *AJS*, 60, 1954, pp. 109–24.
Argyle, M., *Social Interaction*, London 1969.
Argyris, C., 'Diagnosing Defenses Against the Outsiders', *Journal of Social Issues*, 8, 1952, pp. 24–34.
Argyris, C., *Intervention Theory and Method*, Reading, Mass. 1970.
Arrington, R. E., 'Some Technical Aspects of Observer Reliability as Indicated in Studies of the "Talkies" ', *AJS*, 38, 1932, pp. 409–17.
Arrington, R. E., 'An Important Implication of Time Sampling in Observational Studies of Behavior', *AJS*, 43, 1937, pp. 284–95.
Atteslander, P., 'The Interactiogram', *HO*, 13, 1954.
Atteslander, P., et al., *Konflikt und Kooperation im Industriebetrieb*, Köln/Opladen 1959.
Atteslander, P., *Methoden der empirischen Sozialforschung*, Berlin 1969.
Back, K. W., *The Well-Informed Informant*, in Adams, R. N. & Preiss, J. J. (eds), *Human Organization Research*, Homewood. Ill. 1960.
Bain, R. K., *Die Rolle des Forschers: Eine Einzelfallstudie*, in König 1967a.
Bales, R. F. & Gerbrands, H., 'The "Interaction Recorder". An Apparatus and Check List for Sequential Content Analysis of Human Interaction', *Human Relations*, 1, 1948, pp. 456–63.
Bales, R. F., *Interaction Process Analysis*, Cambridge, Mass., 1950.
Bales, R. F., *Die Interaktionsanalyse: Ein Beobachtungsverfahren zur Untersuchung kleiner Gruppen*, in König 1967a.
Bals, C., *Halbstarke unter sich*, Köln/Berlin 1962.

Bandemer, K.–F., *Das Verhältnis von Lehrer– und Schülertätigkeit im Englisch-Unterricht*, Manuskript, Marburg 1962.

Becker, H. S., 'Problems of Inference and Proof in Participant Observation', *ASR*, 23, 1958, pp. 652–60.

Becker, H. S., *et al.*, *Boys in White*, Chicago 1961.

Becker, H. S., & Geer, B., 'Participant Observation and Interviewing: A Comparison', *HO*, 16, 1957, pp. 28–32.

Becker, H. S., *Participant Observation: The Analysis of Qualitative Field Data*, in Adams, R. & Preiss, J. J. (eds), *Human Organization Research* Homewood, I11. 1960.

Bender, I. E. & Hastorf, A. H., 'The Perception of Persons: Forecasting Another Person's Responses on Three Personality Scales', *JASP*, 45, 1950, pp. 556–61.

Berger, B. M., *Working Class Suburb*, Berkeley 1960.

Bernard, H., 'Observation and Generalization in Cultural Anthropology', *AJS*, 50, 1945, pp. 284–91.

Birdwhistell, R. L., *Kinesics and Communication*, in Carpenter, E., & McLuhan, M. (eds), *Explorations in Communication*, New York 1960.

Birdwhistell, R. J., *Kinesics*, in Sills, D. L. (ed.), *International Encyclopedia of the Social Sciences*, vol. 8, New York, 1968.

Bittner, E., 'The Police on Skid-Row: A Study of Peace-Keeping', *ASR*, 32, 1967, pp. 699–715.

Black, D. J., 'Production of Crime Rates', *ASR*, 35, 1970, pp. 733–48.

Blankenburg, E., *Die Selektivität rechtlicher Sanktionen. Eine empirische Untersuchung von Ladendiebstählen*, in Friedrichs 1973a.

Borgatta, E. F., 'A New Systematic Interaction Observation System: Behaviour Scores System (BS-System)', *Journal of Psychological Studies*, 14, 1963.

Borgatta, E. F., & Crowther B., *A Workbook for the Study of Social Interaction*, Chicago 1965.

Bruner, J. S. & Postman, L., *An Approach to Social Perception*, in Dennis, W. (ed.), *Current Trends in Social Psychology*, Pittsburgh 1951.

Bruyn, S. T., 'The Methodology of Participant Observation', *HO*, 22, 1963.

Bruyn, S. T., *The Human Perspective in Sociology: The Methodology of Participant Observation*, Englewood Cliffs, N. J. 1966.

Burgess, R. L. & Bushell, D. jr (eds), *Behavioral Sociology*, New York 1969.

Buzby, D. E., 'The Interpretation of Facial Expression', *American Journal of Psychology*, 35, 1924, pp. 602–04.

Campbell, D. T., 'Systematic Error on the Part of Human Links in Communication Systems', *Information and Control*, 1, 1958, pp. 334–69.

Campbell, D. T., The Informant in Quantitative Research, *AJS*, 60, 1955, pp. 339–342.

Campbell, D. T. & Stanley, J. C., *Experimental and Quasi-Experimental Designs for Research in Teaching*, in N. L. Gage (ed.), *Handbook of Research in Teaching*, Chicago 1963.

Catton, W. R. jr, *From Animistic to Naturalistic Sociology*, New York 1966.

Champney, H., 'The Measurement of Parent Behavior', *Child Development*, 12, 1941, pp. 131–66.

Cicourel, A. V., *Method and Measurement in Sociology*, Glencoe, Ill. 1964.

Claessens, D., *Rolle und Macht*, München 1968.

Claster, D. S. & Schwartz, H., 'Strategies of Participation in Participant Observation', *Sociological Methods & Research*, 1, 1972, pp. 65–96.

Cressey, P. G., *The Taxi Dance Hall*, Chicago 1932.

von Cranach, M. & Frenz, H.–G., *Systematische Beobachtung*, in Graumann, C. F. (Hrsg.), *Sozialpsychologie. Handbuch der Psychologie Band 7/1*, Göttingen 1969.

Cronbach, L. J. & Meehl, P. E., 'Construct Validity in Psychological Tests', *PB*, 52, 1955, pp. 281–302.

Dahrendorf, R., *Homo Sociologicus*, Köln/Opladen 1964[4].

Dalton, M., *Men Who Manage*, New York 1959.

Dalton, M., *Preconceptions and Methods in 'Men Who Manage'*, in Hammond P. E. (ed.), *Sociologists at Work*, New York 1964.

Dean, J. P., *Participant Observation and Interviewing*, in Doby, J. T. (ed.), *Introduction to Social Research*, Harrisburg, Penn. 1954.

Dean, J. P. & Whyte, W. F., 'How Do You Know if the Informant is Telling the Truth?' *HO*, 17, 1958, pp. 34–8.

Denzin, N. K., *The Research Act of Sociology*, London 1970.

Devereux, E. C., *Functions, Advantages, and Limitations of Semi-Controlled Observation*, Ithaca, N.Y. 1953.

Dore, R. P., *City Life in Japan. A Study of a Tokyo Ward*, Berkeley 1967.

Duncan, S. D. jr, 'Nonverbal Communication', *PB*, 72, 1969, pp. 118–37.

Douglas, J. P. (ed.), *Observing Deviance*, New York 1970.

Edwards, A. L., *The Social Desirability Variable in Personality Assessment and Research*, New York 1957.

Ekman, P., Friesen, W. V. & Taussig, T. G., *VID-R and SCAN: Tools and Methods for the Automated Analysis of Visual Records*, in Gerbner, G. (ed.), *Content Analysis*, New York 1969.

Enoch, R., *The Role of the Participant Observer in Social Research*, in *Proceedings of the Southwestern Sociological Association*, 1963.

Erikson, K. T., 'A Comment on Disguised Observation in Sociology', *Social Problems*, 14, 1967, pp. 366–73.

Estes, S. G., 'Judging Personality from Expressive Behavior', *JASP*, 33, 1938, pp. 217–36.

Eyferth, K., *Methoden zur Erfassung von Erziehungsstilen*, in Hermann, T. (Hrsg.), *Psychologie der Erziehungsstile*, Göttingen 1966.

Feest, J., *Die Situation des Verdachts*, in Friedrichs 1973a.

Ferraby, J. G., 'Planning a Mass-Observation Investigation', *AJS*, 51, 1945, pp. 1–6.

Feshbach, S. & Feshbach, N., 'Influence of the Stimulus Object Upon the Complementary and Supplementary Projection of Fear', *JASP*, 66, 1963, pp. 498–502.

Festinger, L., Riecken, H. W. & Schachter, S., *When Prophecy Fails*, Minneapolis, 1956.

Feuchtwang, S., 'Field Report', Vervielf, *Man. of the School of Oriental and African Studies*, London 1968.

Finckh, H., *Das Verhältnis zwischen Lehrer- und Schüleräußerungen*, Manuskript, Marburg 1962.

Fink, R., 'Techniques of Observation and their Social and Cultural Limitations', *Mankind*, 5, 1955, pp. 60–8.

Firth, R., *We, the Tikopia*, London 1936.

Fischer, E. & Zanolli, N., 'Das Problem der Kulturdarstellung. Vorschläge zur Methode der Ethnographie', *Sociologus*, 18, 1968, pp. 1–19.

French, J. R. P. jr, *Experiments in Field Settings*, in Festinger, L. & Katz, D. (eds), *Research Methods in the Behavioral Sciences*, New York 1972.

Friedland, W. H., 'Making Sociology Relevant: A Teaching Research Program for Undergraduates, *The American Sociologist*, 4, 1969, pp. 104–11.

Friedrichs, J., *Werte und soziales Handeln*, Tübingen 1968.

Friedrichs, J. (Hrsg.), *Teilnehmende Beobachtung abweichenden Verhaltens*, Stuttgart 1973 (1973a).

Friedrichs, J., *Methoden der empirischen Sozialforschung*, Reinbek 1973 (1973b).

Friedrichs, J., Dehm, G., Giegler, H., Schäfer, K. & Wurm, W., *Resozialisierungsziele und Organisationsstruktur. Teilnehmende Beobachtung in einer Strafanstalt*, in Friedrichs 1973a.

Friedrichs, J., Pongratz, L., *et al.* 'Soziale Erwartungen. Voruntersuchung an einer Stichprobe von Arbeitern', *Kriminologisches Journal*, 2, 1970, Heft 4.

Gage, N. L., 'Judging Interests from Expressive Behavior', *Psychological Monographs*, 66, 1952, no. 18, Whole No. 350.

Galtung, J., 'The Social Functions of a Prison', *Social Problems*, 6, 1958, pp. 127–40.

Galtung, J., *Theory and Methods of Social Research*, (3rd ed.), London 1970.

Gans, J. J., *Die Levittowner*, Gütersloh-Berlin 1969.

Geer, B., *First Days in the Field: A Chronical of Research in Progress*, in McCall, G. J. & Simmons, J. L. (eds), *Issues in Participant Observation*, Reading, Mass. 1969.

Gesell, A., *Körperseelische Entwicklung in der frühen Kindheit*, Halle 1931.

Gluckman, M., *Custom and Conflict in Africa*, Oxford 1963.

Goffman, E., *The Presentation of Self in Everyday Life*, Garden City, N.Y. 1959.

Goffman, E., *Verhalten in sozialen Situationen*, Gütersloh 1971 (1971a).

Goffman, E., *The Presentation of Self in Everyday Life*, London 1971 (1971b).

Goffman, E., *Interaction Ritual*, London 1972.

Gold, R. L., 'Roles in Sociological Field Observations', *SF*, 36, 1958.

Goldstein, R. L., 'The Participant as Observer', *Phylon*, 25, 1964.

Grauer, G., *Jugendfreizeitheime in der Krise*, Weinhaim/Basel 1973.

Graumann, C. F., *Grundzüge der Verhaltensbeobachtung*, in Meyer, E. (Hrsg.), *Fernsehen in der Lehrerbildung*, München 1966.

Guilford, J. P., *Psychometric Methods*, New York 1954[2].

Gussuw, Z., 'The Observer – Observed Relationship as Information about Structure in Small Group Research', *Psychiatry*, 27, 1964.

Haag, F., Krüger, H., Schwärzel, W., Wildt, J. (Hrsg.), *Aktionsforschung*, München 1972.

Haferkamp, H., *Theorie und Praxis kriminalsoziologischer Forschung*, in Friedrichs 1973a.

Hall, E. T., 'A System for the Notation of Proxemic Behavior', *American Anthropologist*, 65, 1963, pp. 1003–26.

Hall, E. T., 'Proxemics', *Current Anthropology*, 9, 1968, pp. 83–108.

Hall, E. T., *The Hidden Dimensions*, New York 1969.

Hallwachs, H., *Beobachtungsverfahren in der Tourismusforschung*, in *Studienkreis für Tourismus e.V. (Hrsg.), Motive – Meinungen – Verhaltensweisen. Einige Ergebnisse und Probleme der psychologischen Tourismusforschung*, Hektograf. Man., Starnberg 1969.

Hannan, M. T., *Problems of Aggregation and Disaggregation in Sociological Research*, Chapel Hill 1970.

Harbordt, S., *Die Subkultur des Gefängnisses*, Stuttgart 1967.

Harder, J. J. & Lindemann, E. C., *Dynamic Social Research*, London 1933.

Hasemann, K., *Verhaltensbeobachtung*, in *Handbuch der Psychologie, Bd. 6: Psychologische Diagnostik*, hrsg. v. Heiss, R., Göttingen 1964.

Hastorf, A. H. & Bender, I. E., 'A Caution Respecting the Measurement of Empathic Ability, *JASP*, 47, 1952, pp. 574–76.

Heimstra, N. W. & Davis, R. T., 'A Simple Recording System for the Direct Observation Technique', *Animal Behaviour*, 10, 1962.

Heyns, R. W., *Functional Analysis of Group Problem Solving Behavior*, (mimeographed), Ann Arbor 1948.

Heyns, R. W. & Zander, A., *Observation of Group Behavior*, in Festinger, L. & Katz, D.(eds), *Research Methods in the Behavioral Sciences*, New York 1953.

Heyns, R. W. & Lippitt, R., *Systematic Observational Techniques*, in Lindzey,

G. (ed.), *Handbook of Social Psychology*, vol. I, Cambridge, Mass. 1954.

Hofstätter, P. R., 'Uber Ahnlichkeit', *Psyche*, 9, 1955, pp. 54–80.

Hofstätter, P. R., *Einführung in die Sozialpsychologie*, Stuttgart 1966[4].

Hofstätter, P. R., *Psychologie*, Frankfurt 1957.

den Hollander, A. N. J., 'Soziale Beschreibung als Problem', *KZfS*, 17, 1965, pp. 201–31.

Homans, G. C., *Theorie der sozialen Gruppe*, Köln/Opladen 1960.

Homans, G. C., *Social Behaviour*, London 1961.

Hooker, E., *The Homosexual Community*, in Simon, W. & Gagnon J. H. (eds), *Sexual Deviance*, New York 1967.

Hoppensack, H.–C., *Über die Strafanstalt und ihre Wirkungen auf Einstellungen und Verhalten von Gefangenen*, Göttingen 1969.

Hummell, H. J., *Psychologische Ansätze zu einer Theorie des sozialen Verhaltens*, in König 1969.

Hummell, H. J., *Probleme der Mehrebenenanalyse*, Stuttgart 1972.

Humphreys, L., *Tearoom Trade*, Chicago 1970.

Humphreys, L., *Toiletten-Geschäfte. Teilnehmende Beobachtung homosexueller Akte*, in Friedrichs 1973a.

Hymann, H. H., *Survey Design and Analysis*, Glencoe, Ill. 1954.

Hymann, H. H. & Sheatsley, P. B., *The Authoritarian Personality: A Methodological Critique*, in Christie, R. & Jahoda, M. (eds), *Studies in the Scope and Method of the Authoritarian Personality*, Glencoe, Ill. 1954.

Hymann, H. H., et. al., *Interviewing in Social Research*, Chicago 1954.

Jahoda, M., Deutsch, M. & Cook, S. W., *Beobachtungsverfahren*, in König 1967a.

Janes, R. W., 'A Note on Phases of the Community Role of the Participant Observer', *ASR*, 26, 1961, pp. 446–50.

Jansyn, L. R. jr, 'Solidarity and Delinquency in a Street Corner Group', *ASR*, 31, 1966, pp. 600–14.

Jantke, C. (Bearb.), *Bergmann und Zeche*, Tübingen 1953.

Jensen, H. E., 'Social Methodology and the Teaching of Sociology', *AJS*, 42, 1937, pp. 543–50.

Kahn, R. & Mann, F., 'Developing Research Partnerships', *Journal of Social Issues*, 8, 1952, pp. 4–10.

Kantowsky, D., 'Möglichkeiten und Grenzen der teilnehmenden Beobachtung als Methode der empirischen Sozialforschung', *Soziale Welt*, 20, 1969, pp. 428–34.

Kaplan, A., *The Conduct of Inquiry*, San Francisco 1964.

Katz, D., *Field Studies*, in Festinger, L. & Katz, D. (eds), *Research Methods in the Behavioral Sciences*, New York 1953.

Kentler, H., Leithäuser, T. & Lessing, H., *Jugend im Urlaub*, 2 Bde. Weinheim/Berlin/Basel 1969.

Kerlinger, F. N., *Foundations of Behavioral Research*, New York 1964.

Kirkpatrick, E. L., 'Can Standards of Living Be Rated from Observation?' *AJS*, 39, 1933, pp. 360–7.

Kluckhohn, C., *The Place of Theory in Anthropological Studies*, in Hoebel & Jennings (eds), *Readings in Anthropology*, 1955.

Kluckhohn, F., 'The Participant-Observer Technique in Small Communities', *AJS*, 46, 1940, pp. 331–43.

Kluckhohn, F., *Die Methode der teilnehmenden Beobachtung*, in König 1967a.

Kluth, H., Lohmar, U., Pongratz, L. *et al.*, *Das Heim der offenen Tür, hrsg. von der Arbeitsgemeinschaft für Jugendpflege und Jugendfürsorge*, München 1955.

Knauft, E. B., 'Construction and Use of Weighted Check List Rating Scales for Two Industrial Situations', *Journal of Applied Psychology*, 32, 1948, pp. 63–70.

König, R., *Die Beobachtung*, in König 1967b.

König, R., *Beobachtung und Experiment*, in König 1967a.

König, R. (Hrsg.), *Das Interview*, Köln/Berlin 1962[3].

König, R. (Hgb.), *Beobachtung und Experiment in der Sozialforschung*, Köln 1956, 1967, (1967a).

König, R. (Hgb.), *Handbach der empirischen Sozialforschung*, vol. I, Stuttgart 1962, 1967[2] (1967b); vol. II, Stuttgart 1969.

Kutner, B., Wilkins, C. & Yarrow, P. R., 'Verbal Attitudes and Overt Behavior Involving Racial Prejudice', *JASP*, 47, 1952, pp. 649–52.

La Barre, W., *Paralinguistics, Kinesics and Cultural Anthropology*, in Seboek, T. A., Hayes, A. S. & Bateson, M. C. (eds), *Approaches to Semiotics*, Den Haag 1964.

de Laguna, F., 'Some Problems of Objectivity in Ethnology,' *Man*, 57, 1957, pp. 179–82.

de Landsheere, G., *Einführung in die pädagogische Forschung*, Weinheim/Berlin/Basel 1969.

La Piere, R. T., 'Attitudes vs. Actions', *SF*, 13, 1934, pp. 230–7.

Lautmann, R., *Teilnehmende Beobachtungen in der Strafjustiz*, in Friedrichs 1973a.

Lautmann, R., *Justiz – die stille Gewalt*, Frankfurt 1972.

Lazarsfeld, P. F. & Rosenberg, M. (eds), *The Language of Social Research*, New York 1955.

Lessing, H., *Integrationstendenzen im Jugendurlaub. Diplomarbeit (Man.)*, Frankfurt 1967.

Lessing, H., *Von der teilnehmenden zur beteiligten Beobachtung: Zur Kritik der positivistischen Beobachtungslehre*, in *Studienkreis für Tourismus e.V.* (Hrsg.), *Motive – Meinungen – Verhaltensweisen. Einige Ergebnisse und*

Probleme der psychologischen Tourismusforschung, Hektograf. Man., Starnberg 1969.

Leventhal, H. & Sharp, E., *Facial Expression as Indicators of Distress*, in Tomkins, S. S. & Izard, C. E. (eds), *Affect, Cognition, and Personality*, New York 1965.

Lévi-Strauss, C., *Das Ende des Totemismus*, Frankfurt 1965.

Lévi-Strauss, C., *Strukturale Anthropologie*, Frankfurt 1967.

Lewin, K., *Group Decision and Social Change*, in Maccoby, E., Newcomb, T. & Hartley, E. L. (eds), *Readings in Social Psychology*, New York 1958.

Lewin, K., *Feldtheorie in den Sozialwissenschaften*, Bern/Stuttgart 1963.

Lewis, O., *Life in a Mexican Village: Tepoztlán Restudied*, Urbana 1951, ppb. ed. 1963.

Lewis, O., *Controls and Experiences in Field Work*, in Kroeber, A. L., *et al.* (eds), *Anthropology Today*, Chicago 1953.

Liebow, E., *Tally's Corner*, Boston 1966.

Lindemann, E. C., *Social Discovery*, New York 1924.

Lindgren, E. J., 'Field Work in Social Psychology', *British Journal of Psychology*, 26, 1935.

Linn, L. S., 'Verbal Attitudes and Overt Behaviour: A Study of Racial Discrimination', *SF*, 43, 1965, p. 353–64.

Linton, R., *The Cultural Background of Personality*, London 1957.

Lippitt, R., 'Field Theory and Experiment in Social Psychology: Autocratic and Democratic Group Atmospheres, *AJS*, 45, 1939, pp. 26–49.

Lohmann, J. D., 'The Participant Observer in Community Studies', *ASR*, 2, 1937, pp. 890–7.

Lüdtke, H., *Jugendliche in organisierter Freizeit*, Weinheim/Basel 1972.

Lüdtke, H. & Grauer, G., *Jugend-Freizeit-'Offene Tür'. Methoden und Daten der empirischen Erhebung in Jugendfreizeitheimen*, Weinheim/Basel 1973.

Lynd, R. S. & Lynd, H. M., *Middletown*, New York 1939.

Lynd, R. S. & Lynd, H. M., *Middletown in Transition*, New York 1937.

Madge, J., *The Tools of Social Science*, London 1953, 1967[5].

Madge, J., *The Origins of Scientific Sociology*, London 1963.

Madge, J. & Harrison, T. (eds), *First Years Work by Mass Observation*, London 1938.

Malinowski, B., *Argonauts of the Western Pacific*, London 1922.

Mass-Observation, *War Begins at Home*, London 1940.

Mass-Observation, *War Factory*, London 1943.

Matarazzo, J., Holman, D. C. & Wiens, A. N., 'A Simple Measure of Interviewer and Interviewee Speech Durations', *Journal of Psychology*, 66, 1967, pp. 7–14.

Mayntz, R., Holm, K. & Hübner, P., *Einführung in die Methoden der empirischen Soziologie*, Köln/Opladen 1969.

McCall, G. J., *Data Quality Control in Participant Observation*, in McCall, G. J. & Simmons, J. L. (eds), *Issues in Participant Observation*, Reading, Mass. 1969 (1969a).

McCall, G. J., *The Problems of Indicators in Participant Observation Research*, in McCall, G. J. & Simmons, J. L. (eds), *Issues in Participant Observation*, Reading, Mass. 1969, (1969b).

McCall, G. J. & Simmons, J. L. (eds): *Issues in Participant Observation*, Reading, Mass. 1969.

McGaugh, J. L., *Student Workbook for D. Krech & R. S. Crutchfield, 'Elements of Psychology'*, New York 1958.

Mehrabian, A., 'Some Referents and Measures of Non-Verbal Behaviour', *Behav. Res. Math. and Instrumentation*, 1, 1969, pp. 203–7.

Meili, R., *Lehrbuch der psychologischen Diagnostik*, Bern/Stuttgart 1961[4].

Melton, A. W., 'Some Behavior Characteristics of Museum Visitors', *PB*, 30, 1933, pp. 720–1.

Melton, A. W., *Problems of Installation in Museums of Art*, in *Studies in Museum Education*, Washington, *DC*, 1935.

Milewski, M., 'Courtroom Encounters', *Law and Society Review*, 5, 1971, p. 473.

Miller, S. M., 'The Participant Observer and "Over-Rapport" ', *ASR*, 17, 1952, pp. 97–9.

Muchow, M., *Der Beobachtungsbogen*, in Peter, R. & Stern, W., *Die Auslese befähigter Volksschüler in Hamburg. Beih. z. angew. Psychol.*, 18, 1922, pp. 23–48.

Müller-Petersen, E., *Kleine Anleitung zur pädagogischen Tatsachenforschung und ihre Verwendung*, Marburg 1951.

Nadel, S. F., *The Foundations of Social Anthropology*, Glencoe, Ill. 1951.

Nadel, S. F., *The Theory of Social Structure*, London 1957.

Noelle, E., *Umfragen in der Massengesellschaft*, Reinbek 1963.

Naroll, R., *Data Quality Control*, New York, 1962.

Notcutt, B. & Silva, A. L. M., 'Knowledge of other People', *JASP*, 46, 1951, pp. 30–7.

Opp, K.-D., *Methodologie der Sozialwissenschaften*, Reinbek 1970 (1970a).

Opp, K.-D., 'Zur Anwendbarkeit der Soziologie im Strafprozeß', *Kritische Justiz*, 1970, pp. 383–98 (1970b).

Osgood, C. E., Suci, G. J. & Tannenbaum, P. H., *The Measurement of Meaning*, Urbana 1957.

Parsons, T. & Shils, E. A. (eds), *Toward a General Theory of Action*, New York/Evanston 1962.

Paul, B. D., *Interview Techniques and Field Relationships*, in Kroeber, A. L. et al. (eds), *Anthropology Today*, Chicago 1953.

Peak, H., *Problems of Objective Observation*, in Festinger, L. & Katz, D. (eds), *Research Methods in the Behavioural Sciences*, New York 1953.

Pearse, F. H. & Crocker, L. H., *The Peckham Experiment*, London 1943.

Peters, D., 'Die Genese richterlicher Urteilsbildung und die Schichtverteilung der Kriminalität', *Krim. Journ.*, 2, 1970, pp. 210–32.

Piliavin, J. A. & Piliavin, I. M., 'Effect of Blood and Reactions to a Victim', *Journal Pers. Soc. Psychology*, 23, 1972, pp. 353–61.

Pinther, A., *Grundprobleme der Beobachtungsmethode*, in Friedrich, W. (Hrsg.), *Methoden der marxistisch-leninistischen Sozialforschung*, Berlin (Ost) 1971.

Pocock, D., *Social Anthropology*, London 1959.

Polsky, N., *Hustlers, Beats, and Others*, New York 1969.

Polsky, N., *Forschungsmethode, Moral und Kriminologie*, in Friedrichs 1973a.

Polsky, H. W. & Kohn, M., 'Participant Observation and Delinquent Subculture', *Am. J. Orthopsychiatry*, 24, 1959, pp. 737–51.

Popper, K. R., *Die offene Gesellschaft und ihre Feinde. Bd. 2: Falsche Propheten*, Berlin 1958.

Popper, K. R., *Logik der Forschung*, Tübingen 1969[3].

Powdermaker, H., *Stranger and Friend*, London 1967.

Radcliffe-Brown, A. R., *The Andaman Islanders*, London 1922.

Reiss, A. J. jr: 'Studies in Crime and Law Inforcement in Major Metropolitan Areas', *Field Studies* II, vol. II, section I, Washington 1967.

Reiss, A. J. jr, *Stuff and Nonsense About Social Surveys and Observation*, in Becker, H. *et al.* (eds), *Institutions and the Person*, Chicago 1968 (1968a).

Reiss, A. J. jr, 'Police Brutality – Answer to Key Questions', *Trans-action*, 5, 1968, pp. 10–9 (1968b).

Reiss, A. J. jr, *Systematic Observation of Natural Social Phenomena*, in Costner, H. L. (ed.): *Sociological Methodology* 1971, San Francisco 1971.

Robinson, W. S., 'Ecological Correlations and the Behavior of Individuals', *ASR* 15 1950, pp. 351–7.

Roeder, P.-M., 'Versuche einer kontrollierten Unterrichtsbeobachtung', *Psychologische Beiträge*, 8, 1965, pp. 408–23 (1965a).

Roeder, P.-M., *Sprache, Sozialstatus und Bildungschancen*, in Roeder, P.-M., Pasdzierny, A. & Wolf, W., *Sozialstatus und Schulerfolg*, Heidelberg 1965 (1965b).

Roethlisberger, F. J. & Dickson, W. J., *Management and the Worker*, Cambridge, Mass. 1956.

Roghmann, K., *Dogmatismus und Autoritarismus*, Meisenheim am Glan 1966.

Roy, D., 'Quota Restriction and Goldbricking in an Machine Shop', *AJS*, 57, 1952, pp. 427–42.

Sader, M., *Möglichkeiten und Grenzen psychologischer Testverfahren*, Bern 1961.

Scheflen, A. E., 'Human Communication: Behavioral Programs and their Integration in Interaction', *Behav. Science*, 13, 1968, pp. 44–55.

Scherer, K. R., *Non-verbale Kommunikation*, Hamburg 1970.

Scheuch, E. K., *Artikel 'Methoden'* in König (Hrsg.), *Soziologie. Das Fischer-Lexikon*, Frankfurt 1958, Neuausgabe 1967.

Scheuch, E. K., Das *Interview in der Sozialforschung*, in König 1967b.

Schneider, E. V., 'Limitations on Observation in Industrial Sociology', *SF*, 28, 1950, pp. 279–84.

Schoggen, P., 'Mechanical Aids for Making Specimen Records of Behaviour', *Child Development*, 35, 1964, pp. 985–8.

Schütz, A., 'Common-Sense and Scientific Interpretation of Human Action', *Phil. and Phenomenol Research*, 14, 1953, pp. 1–38.

Schumann, K. F. & Winter, G., *Zur Analyse der Hauptverhandlung im Strafprozeß*, in Friedrichs 1973a.

Schwartz, M. S., *The Mental Hospital: The Research Person in the Disturbed Ward*, in Vidich, A. J., Bensman, J. & Stein, M. R. (eds), *Reflections on Community Studies*, New York 1964.

Schwartz, M. S. & Schwartz, C. G., 'Problems in Participant Observation', *AJS*, 60, 1955, pp. 343–53.

Scott, M. B., *The Racing Game*, Chicago 1968.

Selltiz, C., Jahoda, M., Deutsch, M. & Cook, S. W., *Research Methods in Social Relations*, New York, rev. ed., 1962[3].

Sherif, M., *A Preliminary Experimental Study of Intergroup Relations*, in Rohrer, J. H. & Sherif, M. (eds), *Social Psychology at the Crossroads*, New York 1951.

Short, J. F. & Strodtbeck, F. L., *Group Process and Gang Delinquency*, Chicago/London 1965.

Siegrist, J., 'Erfahrungsstruktur und Konflikt bei stationären Patienten', *Z. f. Soziologie*, 1, 1972, pp. 271–80.

Siersted, E. & Hansen, H. L., 'Réactions des petits enfants au cinema: résumé d'une serie d'observation faites au Danemark', *Revue Internationale de Filmologie*, 2, 1951, pp. 241–5.

Sixtl, F., *Meßmethoden der Psychologie*, Weinheim 1967.

Slotta, G., *Die pädagogische Tatsachenforschung Peter und Else Petersens*, Weinheim 1962.

Sommer, R., 'Some Costs and Pitfalls in Field Research', *Social Problems*, 19, 1971, pp. 162–6.

Sommer, W., *Empirische Aufnahme des Unterrichts. Das Verhalten der Schüler einer Sexta*, Manuskript, Marburg 1963.

Spangenberg, K., *Chancen der Gruppenpädagogik*, Weinheim/Berlin/Basel 1969.

Spergel, I., *Racketville Slumtown, Haulburg*, Chicago/London 1964.

Stouffer, S. A., *et al.*, *Measurement and Prediction*, Princeton, N. J. 1950.

Strecker, I., *Methodische Probleme der ethno-soziologischen Beobachtung und Beschreibung: Versuch einer Vorbereitung zur Feldforschung*, Diss. Göttingen 1969.

Sullivan,. M. A. jr, Queen, S. A. & Patrick, R. C. jr, 'Participant Observation as Employed in the Study of a Military Training Program', *ASR*, 23, 1958, pp. 660–7.

Suttles, G. D., *The Social Order of the Slum*, Chicago 1968.

Swingle, P. G. (ed.), *Social Psychology in Natural Settings*, Chicago 1973.

Taft, R., 'The Ability to Judge People', *PB*, 52, 1955, pp. 1–23.

Taguiri, R., *Person Perception*, in Lindzey, G. & Aronson, E. (eds), *Handbook of Social Psychology*, Cambridge, Mass. 1969, p. 2. A.

Tausch, A., 'Die Auswirkungen der Art sprachlicher Verbote erziehender Erwachsener auf das Verhalten von Schulkindern', *Z. f. Psychologie*, 1960, 164, pp. 215–54.

Tausch, A. & Tausch, R., 'Reversibilität/Irreversibilität des Sprachverhaltens in der sozialen Interaktion', *PR*, 16, 1965, pp. 28–42.

Tausch, A., Barthel, A., Fittkau, B. & Hübsch, H., 'Variablen und Zusammenhänge der sozialen Interaktion in Kindergärten', *PR*, 19, 1968, pp. 267–79.

Tausch, R., 'Merkmalsbeziehungen und psychologische Vorgänge in der Sprachkommunikation des Unterrichts', *ZeaP*, 9, 1962, pp. 474–508.

Tausch, R., Köhler, H. & Fittkau, B., 'Variablen und Zusammenhänge der sozialen Interaktion in der Unterrichtung', *ZeaP*, 13, 1966, pp. 345–65.

Tausch, R. & Tausch, A., *Erziehungspsychologie*, Göttingen 1965[2].

Tausky, C. & Piedmont, E. B., 'The Sampling of Behavior', *The American Sociologist*, 3, 1968, pp. 49–51.

Teuscher, W., 'Die Einführung des Forschers in die Untersuchungsgruppe durch Status- und Rollenzuweisung als Problem der empirischen Forschung', *KZfS*, 11, 1959, pp. 250–6.

Thomae, H., *Beobachtung und Beurteilung von Kindern und Jugendlichen*, Basel 1954.

Thomas, D. S., *et al.*, *Observational Studies of Social Behavior*, New Haven 1933.

Trasher, F. M., *The Gang. A Study of 1,313 Gangs in Chicago*, Chicago 1927.

Treiber, H., *Wie man Soldaten macht*, Düsseldorf 1973.

Trow, M., 'Comment on Participant Observation and Interviewing: A Comparison', *HO*, 16, 1957, pp. 33–5.

Turner, V. W., *Schism and Continuity in an African Society*, Manchester 1957.

Turner, W. J. & Mass-Observation, *Exmoor Village*, London 1947.

Vidich, A. J., 'Participant Observation and the Collection and Interpretation of Data', *AJS*, 60, 1955, pp. 354–60.

Vidich, A. J. & Shapiro, G., 'A Comparison of Participant Observation and Survey Data', *ASR*, 20, 1955, pp. 28–33.

Vidich, A. J. & Bensman, J., *Small Town in Mass Society*, Princeton, N. J. 1958.

Vidulich, R. N. & Bayley, G. A., 'A General Field Experimental Technique for Studying Social Influence', *Journal of Social Experiment*, 69, 1966.

Volkelt, H., 'Einige neue Methoden der Verhaltensbeobachtung und Protokollierung', *Arch. f. d. ges. Psychol.*, 91, 1934, pp. 229–40.

Warner, W. L. & Lunt, P. S., *The Social Life of a Modern Community. Yankee City Series*, vol. I, New Haven 1941.

Warner, W. L. & Lunt, P. S., *The Status System of a Modern Community. Yankee City Series*, vol. II, New Haven 1942.

Warr, P. B. & Knapper, C., *The Perception of People and Events*, New York 1968.

Webb, E. J., Cambpell, D. T., Schwartz, R. D. & Sechrest, L., *Unobtrusive Measures: Nonreactive Research in the Social Sciences*, Chicago 1966.

Weick, K. E., *Systematic Observational Techniques*, in Lindzey, G. & Aronson, E. (eds), *Handbook of Social Psychology*, Cambridge, Mass. 1968.

Weinberg, M. S., *Sexuelle Schamhaftigkeit im F. K. K.-Lager*, in Friedrichs 1973a.

Weinberg, M. S. & Williams, C. J., *Field Work Among Deviants: Social Relations with Subjects and Others*, in J. Douglas (ed.), *Research in Deviance*, New York 1972.

Weinberg, M. S. & Williams, C. J., *Soziale Beziehungen zu devianten Personen bei der Feldforschung*, in Friedrichs 1973 a.

Weiss, C. H., *Evaluation Research*, Englewood Cliffs, N. J. 1972.

Williams, C. J. & Weinberg, M. S., 'Being Discovered: A Study of Homosexuals in the Military', *Social Problems*, 18, 1970, pp. 217–27.

Whiting, B. B. (ed.), *Six Cultures*, New York 1963.

Whorf, B. L., *Sprache, Denken, Wirklichkeit*, Hamburg 1963.

Whyte, W. F., *Street Corner Society*, Chicago 1943, 1955, 1961.

Whyte, W. F., *Human Relations in the Restaurant Industry*, New York 1948.

Whyte, W. F., *Observational Field Work Methods*, in Jahoda, M., Deutsch, M. & Cook, S. W. (eds), *Research Methods in Social Relations*, vol. 2, New York 1951.

Whyte, W. F., *The Organization Man*, Garden City, N.Y. 1956.

Willcock, H. D., 'Mass-Observation', *AJS*, 48, 1943, pp. 445–56.

Winnefeld, F., *Pädagogischer Kontakt und pädagogisches Feld*, München/ Basel 1957.

Wood, M. M., *The Stranger*, New York 1934.

Wylie, L., *Dorf in der Vaucluse*, Frankfurt 1969.

Yablonsky, L., *The Violent Gang*, New York 1962.

Zander, A., *Systematische Beobachtung kleiner Gruppen*, in König 1967a.

Zelditch, M. jr, 'Some Methodological Problems of Field Studies', *AJS*, 67, 1962, pp. 566–76.

Zetterberg, H. L., *Theorie, Forschung und Praxis in der Soziologie*, in König 1967b.

Zimmermann, E., *Das Experiment in den Sozialwissenschaften*, Stuttgart 1972.

Zimmermann, G. E., 'Observation of Adolescent Behaviour', *Child Study Centre Bulletin*, 2, 1966.

Index

Indexer's note: The reader is invited to study the two headings, OBSERVATION and OBSERVERS, from which he should discover any section of the text required.